THEATR

By the same author

Theatre

THEATRE 1954-5
SHAKESPEARE
FIRST PLAYER
PARTIES OF THE PLAY
MASQUES AND PHASES

Autobiography

THE WAY OF MY WORLD

Topography and History

BALMORAL
SUMMER IN SCOTLAND
WINTER IN LONDON

Satire

MASTER SANGUINE

Word Books

CHOSEN WORDS

Novels

YEARS OF PLENTY
LIGHTING-UP TIME
MARINE PARADE

IVOR BROWN

THEATRE

1955-6

MAX REINHARDT · LONDON

First Published 1956

Printed in Great Britain at
THE STELLAR PRESS LTD
UNION STREET, BARNET, HERTS

CONTENTS

v

vi

ILLUSTRATIONS

Report on the Year

Those who are always eager to bury the English Theatre were still crying 'This Way to the Tomb'. But the supposed corpse, as usual, has refused to acknowledge the onset of *rigor mortis* and the average play-goer has not been aware that he is a celebrant of last rites. The abounding appetite for Shakespeare has, as in previous years, been as much a handicap to the casting of modern work as it has been creditable to public taste. Critics in full practice can now reasonably shudder at the very mention of Shakespeare. They have, during the past year, been confronted with no less than three Othellos, without having recourse to University stages in search of more. (B.B.C. Television offered another production and those who were also film-goers had two further portraits of the Moor, one provided by Orson Welles, the other by Soviet Russia.) The 'Old Vic', because of its American tour in the autumn, added three more Shakespearean productions to its usual winter's ration while Stratford continues to lay on its annual five. This year we had, for full measure, the Peter Brook production of HAMLET that was taken to Moscow. The number of Shakespearean addenda which could have been 'covered' in academic quarters or at 'reps' suggests that a record-hunter might now pile up in any one year a colossal score of Bardic attendances.

Our directors were certainly in form, for Tyrone Guthrie's TROILUS AND CRESSIDA at the 'Old Vic' was a masterly handling of a 'problem play', while Brook's work on the revival of T. S. Eliot's THE FAMILY REUNION brought out its inherent dramatic values and concealed (or at least minimised) its affectations. It is noticeable that our best producers seem happier in their results the more difficult is the play they have to tackle. HAMLET can hardly go wrong, yet Brook's HAMLET managed to displease many judges. But set him to TITUS ANDRONICUS and he triumphs. Set him to THE FAMILY REUNION and again he triumphs, despite the fact that he has to deal with bloody nonsense (in the literal sense) in the former and with a baffling mixture of Greek choruses, Christian ethics, and the curious palaver of landed gentry sipping sherry and talking

A

poetry in the latter. Give Peter Brook the impossible and he will solve your problem. But it would be unwise, I fancy, to trust him with safe jobs. Only with the unfailing can he fail. Guthrie, in the same way, can make something tremendous out of TAMBURLAINE and something most pertinent and witty out of TROILUS AND CRESSIDA. But he again is likely to become bored and so run to over-cleverness if he is presented with an obvious favourite. It is a rich theatre that has these two in reserve for coping with the odd and the intractable.

Visitation was rich and London owes a great debt to Peter Daubeny for his work as impresario at The Palace Theatre and for his unquenchable willingness to be host to all good guests. London had the opportunity of studying the various arts of the theatre, if not from China to Peru, at least from China to the African jungle. France was represented first by Edwige Feuillère, whose visit suggested that she had been over-praised in advance, and afterwards by Jean Vilar's troupe, playing, in their simple, economic style, Molière, Hugo, and Marivaux. Later came Roland Petit's Ballets de Paris, while, as I write, Jean-Louis Barrault is on the expected list. Spanish Ballet, Austrian Opera, and Hungarian Song and Dance have been seen to advantage. The Chinese players were an immediate 'sell-out' and thousands more would have gone to see them could they have hoped to get in. In this extremely International Year, in which even the Circus had its Moscow interlude, it was a proper coincidence that Sir John Gielgud should have toured and visited London in a production of KING LEAR whose decoration owed more to Asia than to Europe.

We are sadly handicapped in making the return gesture. Foreign Governments endow the export of their artists – with the conviction that here are assets to be shown. Whitehall responds only in a negligible way. The British Council's budget for drama with which we should be able to make a counter-display on European stages is so small that only very few demonstrations of our acting and productive talent can be shown, unless this can be undertaken by private enterprise. Fortunately, both Stratford and the 'Old Vic' have been able to tour during the year covered by this volume, the former in Europe and the latter in Australia; the 'Old Vic', as I write, is preparing to send a company across the Atlantic and to create a new one of no less strength for the benefit of the Waterloo

2

Road. But visits to the Continental capitals are not as common as they should be and many invitations to European Festivals have to be rejected altogether or accepted with a minimum response for financial reasons.

From this it may be derived that those play-goers here who have a taste for foreign acting are getting more than they give, but this applies only to London and the Edinburgh Festival. The capital has had much to appreciate and, inevitably, some items of which to complain. But those who groan with horror after a futile and embarrassing 'first night' must realise that the theatre is always a roulette board on which it is easier to make a wrong bet than to win even humbly on 'the band'. It is the country as a whole which goes in danger of becoming as theatreless as America outside New York. The better repertories survive and do distinguished work – but mostly with endowment. The Number One theatres of the big cities can only stand up to television's competition with really attractive 'attractions' and these are by no means easy to find. The Number Twos dwindle: many of them have proved too small to take sufficient money in a good week to counter the losses on a bad one. Herewith I salute the town of Cheltenham whose Municipal Council recently took over the local Opera House to save it for the theatre, and I sincerely hope that it is finding the requisite support to justify this audacious step, taken in a place once thought of as a natural home of sleepy conservatism.

Stratford and the 'Old Vic' have for the time being consolidated their strong positions built up in recent years and have loyal publics unlikely to desert these theatres unless there is some deplorable betrayal of standards inside them. The Burial Party, so vociferous about our drama's demise, should remember that we have other institutions and individuals sustaining ambitious and creditable theatres. I would mention John Clements' work in management at the Saville as well as Peter Daubeny's at the Palace. The firm of H. M. Tennent has got back into its normal stride, the Haymarket is itself again, and the Phoenix Theatre has been working on a valuable series of Peter Brook's productions. Henry Sherek has given the Scots good reason to feel ashamed if they do not support their own players and playwrights when a London manager has given them every chance to do so. Peter Ustinov was at his best, as actor and author, in the political-satirical piece called ROMANOFF AND JULIET.

The English Stage Company has been established at the Court, a proper address since that house has such a fine tradition of theatrical innovation. (I am not thinking only of the Vedrenne-Barker seasons: Sir Barry Jackson did much there, including the presentation as juveniles of most of those who are now our theatrical knights. It was there that I saw a young man called Laurence Olivier play his first lead in London, the King in Tennyson's HAROLD.) The E.S.C. is not another of those Classical Revival Societies; its assignment is the discovery and production of new plays, of which it staged five within its first three months, four of them English. One, LOOK BACK IN ANGER by John Osborne, became a talking-point, with violently contrasted opinions about its merits: nothing could be happier for a new venture than having found a play which makes conversation quarrelsome and is a necessity for party prattle. The Arts Theatre Club, which will, it is hoped, be able to extend its activities, has again been a nursery-garden for plays which were successfully transplanted, like Anouilh's WALTZ OF THE TOREADORS, and for the private display of others which our avuncular and vigilant Lord Chamberlain regards as unhealthy blossoms liable to poison the public air. It is one of the curious aspects of the British Government's protection of our lives and our innocence that, while safety from fire and from mental contamination is rigorously insisted on if you buy a seat at the door, you can suffocate or burn to death and die of all manner of intellectual infection provided you join a club to do so. In that case both the L.C.C. and St James's Palace are prepared to smile benignly over the smouldering bodies or polluted minds of the audacious citizens who have paid subscriptions to this end.

When things go wrong in the theatre it is customary to blame everybody but the public, whose choice of good or bad is, after all, the determining factor. Since I have sometimes been play-going quite late in the run of a piece I have been able to hear the muttered opinions of those who are more representative of public opinion than are the attenders of first nights. There is resentment of the outward structure of our theatres. That, since these are mostly old or irremediable, is to grumble in vain. There is also much, and easily remedied, complaint about the quantity as well as the quality of the entertainment provided.

How often, for example, do the critics comment on the length of a play? Yet that is an important point with the public. Daily paper critics like short plays for the obvious reason that they can get away early and are not so rushed in their job. Do they ever complain that a certain piece does not offer value for money because it is over too soon? But people seeking entertainment, who in London may have paid over fifteen shillings for a seat and then get only a tiny little comedy, do complain – and rightly.

Recently I attended a piece of this kind which was excellently acted and had a most amusing second act with a most effective 'curtain'. The start was five minutes late. (There was no great harm in that, since late-comers will be late-comers.) But there were two intervals of twelve minutes and the whole thing was over in just a few minutes more than two hours. That is to say the audience were paying for little over an hour and a half of actual performance.

Theatre attendants hear the comments made in the intervals and at the close, and so may be shrewd assessors of the saleable qualities of a play. One of them, whom I happen to know, said to me on this occasion, 'Of course it is an amusing play and it's very well done. But people want a bit more. I hear them grumbling at the size of it. They don't want to be in at 7.30 and out even before 9.40. After all, they know what they get at the local cinema for a quarter of the money.' In Scotland I heard this comment, after the failure to attract of a trifling piece destined for London, 'It was too short for Glasgow.'

Such pieces could easily have been built up to make better-sized shows. I cannot understand why managers and 'backers' do not insist on a certain quantity of playing time. (But too long is as bad as too short; fears for the last bus or train can be fatal.) If a play is universally praised and discussed, people will go to it whatever the length. But, where the play is struggling along, 'a near miss' as they say, I am sure that the excessive brevity can be irritating and so a serious handicap to good business.

In our stage history quantity has nearly always gone with quality. Shakespeare's plays, which seem very long to us, were followed, even when they were tragedies, by 'a jig', *i.e.* a dance with some clowning. The Georgian and Victorian play-bills were immense. A fair-sized farce would be introduced at the end of the main item. In the cheap seats there were even cheaper prices for those who came in at half-time; they still could get substantial entertainment.

5

When I was a boy short comedies in the West End were preceded by a 'curtain-raiser', usually a one-act play in which the understudies got a chance to appear; this was useful and encouraging for them; sometimes a solo entertainer held the stage with songs at the piano or some similar turn. So the advertisements announced, according to the time-scheme of the period, a main play at 8.45 or 9 and a short piece at 8.15. A few people, especially those who wanted to sit over their dinner and not be rushed could, and did, arrive for the main item only; but the bulk of the audience wanted value for their money and were entertained accordingly from 8.15 till 11. This practice, moreover, gave a chance not only to the understudies, whose life is a dreary and frustrating one, but to the emerging playwrights who were only too glad to get a 'one-acter' professionally accepted and produced. But nobody thinks of reviving the habit.

Fifty years ago plays were much more substantial than they are now. Pinero's usually ran to four acts and often had a sub-plot as well as a main plot. They were genuine pieces of architecture. Many of Shaw's plays were of a full, three-hour length: if they happened to be shorter a one-act piece of his, such as THE MAN OF DESTINY or HOW HE LIED TO HER HUSBAND might be included. I began my play-going as a 'pittite' and we did not expect to queue for a seat and then be fobbed off with only ninety minutes of acting. One rarely meets full-size, four-act plays today; compared with Pinero, Noel Coward, who set the fashion in brevity, looks like a sketch-writer, a very clever one, no doubt, but using a revue technique in the wrong place.

That brings me to another point. Many of the short three-act plays that I see contain only one effective situation: that constitutes the second act. The first act is a light piece of preparation and the third provides a cursory solution of the characters' dilemma which has been amusingly established in the middle of the evening. In essence, the affair is a one-act play, perhaps a very neat one-act play, elongated at both ends. There is an economic explanation of that. Nobody seems to like one-act plays in the professional theatre: they are left to the amateurs. (I am not dismissing the amateurs lightly; I know how well they may write and act their 'one-acters', as the British Drama League's Festival shows each year.) The author who seeks to write for the larger, professional and far more remunerative market must, therefore, provide

6

three acts in order to put forward a saleable article. If his play's idea is not sufficient for more than one strong or amusing situation, he inevitably starts to pad.

The belief that the public must have three-act plays has, however, been most effectively contradicted by Terence Rattigan. His policy has been to write two-act plays, or plays of two-act length, if his theme will not support three, and to put two of these into one programme, thus re-establishing the substantial quantity of the old four-act drama. The fear that the public would be deterred by this has been shown to be groundless. With THE BROWNING VERSION and HARLEQUINADE, and even more successfully, with SEPARATE TABLES he proved that there could be a very wide welcome for this provision of quantity as well as quality. I am surprised that he has not had imitators. Perhaps it is thought that this two-course (but substantial) meal would still be unpalatable unless the chef had the skill of Mr Rattigan. But some author of considerable, if not equal, accomplishment might 'have a go'. He would certainly have me on his side, for I am very weary of the little 'three-acters', which contain the essential matter of only one and are inflated accordingly.

If managers might, to their own advantage, give more in quantity, there seems to be no need for them to lay on the colour and lure the public with spectacle. The theatre, indeed, has become increasingly unspectacular. This is partly to be explained by the high cost of staging and partly, I think, by a genuine appetite for the seamy and the shabby sides of life. Glamour is 'out' and grubbiness is 'in'!

The well-dressed play is as dead as the well-made play. There was a time when part of the news of a First Night in the West End was the lead it gave to the costumiers. What were the gowns – one, of course, for each act – worn by Stella Starlight? And what guidance as to the correct thing in *couture* did these afford to an eager feminine public? It is not an aspect of the drama's attractions whose absence serious play-goers will regret. Those three-act comedies with one act in Mayfair, one in Surrey, and one in his lordship's villa near Cannes have vanished with all their lawns and seascapes, their elegance and their epigrams. I am not mourning their departure. Nor is the manager. In 1956 he does not want, with his new play, to be loaded with expensive dress bills and with the provision of three sets including a section of the Mediterranean sea. They were mostly immemorable plays. Only the most loyal devotees of delights that have passed can think them worth remembering.

But are we not going to the other extreme? If we cannot pay for, or if we actively dislike, good clothes in good places, must we make a deliberate cult of squalor? The year of 1955–6 in the London theatres was remarkable not only for the absence of the well-dressed play but for the presence of the ill-dressed drama that is so down-at-heel and out-at-elbows that the actors might make their theme song begin with the one-time cry of the Peronist Argentines, 'We, the shirtless!'

Since the apparel oft proclaims the man and since man, in the opinion of the younger writers and younger public, is capable only of a life that is nasty, brutish and short, it is now widely held that the scene of a play should be as nasty as can be found, the behaviour of the characters appropriately brutish, and the apparel a bundle of rags.

A friend of mine, a senior play-goer, revisiting the London theatres after a longish interval, observed that the present taste in *milieu* and setting suggested chiefly a public appetite for seeing one bit of dirt-track after another. For the devotees of slumming there was WAITING FOR GODOT, hailed as a revelation of twenty contradictory kinds of profundity by a score of judges all of whom declared it to mean something profoundly different. The expectant parties, it will be remembered, were tramps with sore feet, physically incontinent, and with no obvious addiction to washing, if the chance had been offered. Their road-side conversation was conducted in surroundings as sordid as possible. If, having had enough of Godot, the play-goer voted for a musical, he might find himself in the world of industrial relations in the textile trade or watching the Germany of the 1920s putting the England of the 1720s in its place. This place was, for Herr Brecht, the author of THE THREEPENNY OPERA, the mud. Gay could bring grace to robbery under arms, but neither Gay nor grace were admitted to the production of the German version of THE BEGGAR'S OPERA. There could be no colour, no style. These things are not wanted. They do not accord with the kind of décor dear to those who consider a bombed site to be the most desirable model for a fashionable 'set'.

It was significant that, when the new English Stage Company went into business in Sloane Square, it had to drop very quickly

8

Ronald Duncan's play about Don Juan, who, in poetry, loved women among the blaze and blossom of sunny Spain, and bank upon the snarling prose of Mr John Osborne's LOOK BACK IN ANGER, in which a youngster of today hated all men and all things among the débris of as squalid a one-roomed flat as ever mouldered among dingy and deplorable 'digs'. Among the E.S.C's public there seemed to be little appetite for Mr Duncan's new views of old Spain, and little for Angus Wilson's moonlit Oxford lawns which provided one scene of THE MULBERRY BUSH, a play of merit also quickly dropped. Mr Osborne had the right idea, misanthropy among the garbage cans. Out of Mr Osborne's attic window one must have seen, if it was not so dirty as to prevent one seeing anything, a bombed site with lidless, overflowing dustbins.

I am not for a moment saying that bombed-site scenery is inexcusable. If the test of dramatic values be relevance to the life and labour of the great majority, then obviously realism (assuming it still to have dramatic value) demands more spectacle of the sombre mills and factories, dustbins included, than it does of the Home County greens and the Mediterranean blues. That is self-evident and agreed. All that I suggest is a little balance in these matters and a reluctance to accept railing against life in a rag-and-bone setting as essentially and mentally more truthful and more illuminating than the tolerance, even – dare we say it? – the cheerfulness, of civilised people not deeming personal cleanliness to be reactionary and undemocratic.

Yet in all directions the lure of the shabby was dominant. Prison-life with an execution pending was added to the slum-life and tramp-life plays in THE QUARE FELLOW by Brendan Brehan, a play of rich dialogue brought in by Theatre Workshop. When we met America in London it was among the tattered and depressed relics of a middle-class family who were declining into the early stages of dementia in one of the more genteel sections of Poverty Square. I enjoyed MORNING'S AT SEVEN. It was well written, justly praised, and held on for longer than I expected. It had the requisite appeal to the taste of the time, since most of the characters had a good grumble and none of them had a good tailor. When Graham Greene's THE POWER AND THE GLORY took us further south to see the sufferings of the Church in Mexico, how spectacular the poverty, how debased and debauched the possessing class, how abundant the sweat as

9

well as the tears, how gorgeously squalid the dentist's surgery, and how grubbily alcoholic the priestly hero of the tale!

Just north of Mexico, but no less steamy and sweaty, and far more whisky-sodden, sex-ridden, and foul-spoken, dwell the kind of folk whose passions are so frankly and fiercely proclaimed by Tennessee Williams. His play called CAT ON A HOT TIN ROOF has, at the time of writing, been kept by the Censor from our public stages; a review of the text appears elsewhere in this book. It is sufficient to say here that, whatever its merits of power and veracity in portraying the domestic brawls of a rough planter's family, the piece has a further claim to favour by being right in line with the demand for a generous deposit of squalor. The parties concerned are not poor, but they live without any visitation of grace or decorum and bawl each other out with the ugliest kind of domestic 'creating'.

It is customary to praise the 'dynamic' qualities to be found in the Squalor Belt of the theatrical continent. It is one of the habits of our time to assume that, if you use the word 'dynamic' in any critical discussion of the arts, you have settled the case in your favour and that there is no more to be said against anything described as being galvanic or, more crudely, full of guts. When I have been arguing about the preference for grotesque distortion in graphic or sculptural art, I have repeatedly been informed that the curious monsters or patterns before me are dynamic, and I am to understand that this assumption is also their justification. In vain do I protest that to call a thing dynamic carries the argument no further. A Dynamo may be a footballer in Moscow; in Manchester, as well as in Moscow, it is a machine and a source of power. Machinery and power-sources are material objects which may or may not look well. Their appearances are unimportant matched with their utility. A Dynamo is not intended or valued as an aesthetic achievement; it is a work of use.

Nor is an explosion a work of art although some art critics, in approving certain aspects of modern painting, appear to think it is. A work of art, to be properly praised, needs more than jubilant whoops about its dynamic, galvanic, and explosive powers. Form, proportion, and sustained purpose are important in the arts. This is a belief certainly not held by the more active and vociferous natives of the Squalor Belt or by impassioned immigrants thereto.

10

To write of sordid people sordidly has become recognised as evidence not only of progressive politics and freedom from 'reaction' but also of unquestionable ability. Yet, curiously enough, in our recent history the best dramatists of the Left in politics were averse to squalor and managed to put forward Radical or Socialist opinions without filling the stage with the kind of scenery and types that ought, from their appearances, to be smelling of bed-bugs or at least of stale perspiration. Granville-Barker, for example, wrote of swindling solicitors and the economics of the drapery trade and thus conveyed at least a few of his Socialist notions of Edwardian society within the framework of middle-class domesticity.

Shaw was challenged by some of his Socialist supporters to write more about 'the workers' by which was meant the workers by hand and the minders of machines. To this Shaw replied that in order to write plays that would be effective the dramatist must concern himself in the main with characters who are not tied to factory hours, have some freedom to move about, and are capable of framing their opinions in sufficiently lucid conversation. Shaw practised on these lines with the result that CANDIDA, his play set in the poorer reaches of the East End, is housed in a vicarage, not a slum tenement, introduces a poet as well as a parson, and puts on view a scandalous employer instead of the poor wretches he employs. When he turned to the Salvation Army he did show us one or two of the private soldiers, but he is much more concerned with Major Barbara, Undershaft the monarch of the Munitions Industry, and a professor of Greek. He wrote, in brilliant epigrams, the Revolutionist's Handbook and made the supposed author a Member of the Idle Rich Class with freedom to travel. He wrote several times of the millionaire or millionairess and not of the 'wage-slaves' who created (or helped to create) their millions.

This may have been sly conduct on the part of Shaw the Dramatist, who was evading the propagandist obligations of Shaw the Socialist. But there was sound sense in it for several reasons. The Socialist authors of fifty years ago were middle-class people who knew very little about the workers whom they championed and championed justly, for the contrasts in wealth of the Edwardian community were shocking and the amount of over-paid idleness and under-paid labour appalling. But it was not the habit of Fabian Socialists to seek close contact with the

11

down-and-outs. They dealt in figures, reports, Blue Books and the paper-chase of anti-capitalist propaganda. It was not the custom or the pleasure of Mr and Mrs Sidney Webb to seek first-hand evidence of working-class opinion in public houses: did Shaw commune frequently with football-crowds or spend his leisure fact-finding in Blackburn or Blackpool? It was left to George Orwell to take the road to Wigan Pier. Shaw's occasional 'workers' or 'work-shies' were not drawn from life as the Socialist vicar in CANDIDA was so cleverly and accurately drawn from the clerical Left Wing. They are comic relief, like the Dustman in PYGMALION, Drinkwater in CAPTAIN BRASSBOUND'S CONVERSION, and Gunner in MISALLIANCE. Excellent comic relief it usually was. Shaw was a dramatist in the theatre and kept his sociology for elsewhere until his latest years.

The last case is particularly interesting, because Gunner, as the illegitimate son of the wealthy, philandering Tarleton, is Shaw's idea of the embittered proletarian, a sweated clerk and a spouter of propaganda in public places. Shaw, though naturally ready to be sympathetic to the under-paid quill-drivers of Edwardian commerce, turns Gunner into a comic and sympathetic character, a fact which Donald Pleasence demonstrated in the spring of 1956 with his unforgettable performance of the part in the revival at Hammersmith. Needless to say, Shaw dodged the shabby side of business life by staging his play amid the Surrey Highlands and bringing the pathetic rebel to the heather of Hindhead, which Shaw knew well, instead of following him to his home or digs in Mean Street. But when Mr John Osborne in LOOK BACK IN ANGER showed us his Jimmy Porter as the embittered proletarian of 1956, a non-stop spouter of class-hatred, a youth with a Redbrick University education, a habit of reading *The New Statesman*, but unable to find, in a world of full employment, any better occupation than running a sweet-stall, he did not lure this fellow into prosperous society as Shaw would have done. Osborne could easily have managed this, showing Jimmy wooing his middle-class wife in the home of a Colonel: instead he puts his play in a singularly squalid one-room flat and brings the Colonel to it in order to rub his nose, as well as the noses of his audience, in the squalor not only of Jimmy's deplorable character, a compound of callousness, self-pity and misanthropy, but of Jimmy's deplorable notion of a home.

12

No doubt Mr Osborne has based on a real person or persons his type of cavilling chatterbox, lazy, selfish and ready to blame anybody but himself for the squalor of his living. It can fairly be said in this case that the dramatist is playing fair and not taking the evasive action practised by Shaw when he set up business as a Socialist playwright and used the old personnel and scenery of the bourgeois drama. But it may, I think, be said of Mr Osborne that he gave the appearance of cultivating squalor for squalor's sake.

Sean O'Casey has never spared us the slum-tenement: and quite rightly. He knew his Dublin in blood and sweat and tears and he writes of it magnificently. Yet there is a remarkable difference between the physical squalor of an O'Casey tenement and the general moral squalor of Jimmy Porter's lodging in John Osborne's play. O'Casey's frauds and scamps, his loafers and tipplers, are given a lift and exhilarated with the author's wine of laughter as well as being washed with the waters of his pity. His poor are poor in cash, but not in character; they have their own kind of largeness as well as the essential lustre of the author's use of language. But Jimmy Porter and his kind have nothing whatever to their credit: they will not work to better themselves while screaming at the poverty of their state. They are small, lack-lustre folk. They have neither manners nor common decency. Being bored as well as brash himself, Jimmy Porter became, with his repetition of rancour, a considerable source of boredom to me. His kind of squalor, utterly different from the squalor of Juno and his Paycock and of the soaks and pretenders in THE PLOUGH AND THE STARS, has nothing to mitigate the monotony of its world-scolding and world-cursing.

Shaw was crafty in his way because he realised that if you want to entice 'the workers', if only the clerical and intellectual workers, into the theatre (the horny-handed are unlikely to be lured in by any means), the last thing these workers want is to see themselves. During Miss Horniman's famous repertory seasons at Manchester, developing the 'social realism' which Shaw had diversified with his own brand of wit and fancy, praiseworthy efforts were made to make 'the people' enter the auditorium to face 'the people' on the stage. It was an experience more fruitful in renown than in results. The workers, if they went to the theatre at all, much preferred to see plays about the well-dressed idlers put on glamorous view in some neighbouring house. They shrank from plays concerned with anything so shabby as the truth. What Shaw knew then is still true now.

If WAITING FOR GODOT had been thrown open free to the general public and the fact widely publicised, how many tramps would have visited the Criterion Theatre, even with the promise of somewhere to sit in the warmth during a cold evening or a wet afternoon? O'Casey knew perfectly well that, if some wealthy patron had hired a hall and run O'Casey seasons free in the poorer parts of Dublin or any other large city, the penurious locals would much rather have gone to the races or stayed in pubs than come in to be confronted with O'Casey's picture of themselves pub-crawling. Shaw and Granville-Barker and Galsworthy were right. We shall never create effective theoretical propaganda against the misuse of wealth by revealing poverty in the theatre. The persuasion must come by implication.

The theatrical squalor of our time, so conspicuous in the past year, is not propagandist in any direct form. WAITING FOR GODOT, if it meant anything, meant what the audience cared to make it mean. It did not solicit your vote. The young misanthrope in LOOK BACK IN ANGER called himself a Liberal and did not advocate 'the nationalisation of the means of production, distribution and exchange', to quote the now rather faded formula which was put forward on a myriad platforms to lift the hearts of the workers. Tennessee Williams is not, as far as I know, an active politician. As a Southerner he is presumably a Democrat; but I cannot imagine that the old Southern gentlefolk greatly approve of his plays. In any case he is not telling us to do anything about the bad habits and bad language of his Southern types, except to enjoy them as raw material for the drama that is called 'Dynamic'.

So it may be claimed on behalf of dramatic squalor in our time that it is more honest than Shaw's evasion of it and more frank than the old preference for conveying radical opinion through portraits of conservative society. But it has its own weariness. The squalor that many people find oppressive is not that of slum-scenery: it is the ethical squalor caused by complete lack of moral standards and by the continual staging of characters who recognise no code of conduct, especially in matters of sex. I do not mention this as a lecturer on morals. I am not complaining about the endless flow of sexually promiscuous characters with their sleazy kind of dialogue who are praised as courageous because they offend against Christian or conventional regimen. What bothers me is that life without morals of some kind – I do not postulate any particular creed or code – is life without meaning and therefore life without interest.

Turning to lighter matters there was the usual expectation of life for American Musicals. Whether or not they get good notices these imports rarely fade away in a swift and sad decline. Plain or fancy, be their setting pastoral or industrial, Far Western or Far Eastern, long life is here their portion. But SUMMER SONG, at the Princes, which in spring received a unanimous acclamation for its happy use of the Dvorak story and melodies, together with delightful performances by Sally Ann Howes and Laurence Naismith, could not stay through the summer. Was it too civilised? Or did it just suffer from the usual offence of lacking a Broadway label?

Perhaps the address was a handicap. The same could be said of the A. P. Herbert-Vivian Ellis musical play THE WATER GIPSIES. It lasted on well at the Winter Garden, but it might have lasted better if sited closer to Piccadilly. In this Dora Bryan confirmed her position as a contemporary leader in what used to be called the soubrette class. But soubrettes, like their contrasted types, the ingenues, are ladies of long ago. What is their nomination now? Cuties and Simps? I prefer the French.

Anglo-French relations in the theatre are really most odd. Mr Curtiss, in the chronicle of the Parisian stage during the past year which he has contributed to this volume, points out that the most popular pieces there have been versions of English plays: but here we are repeatedly told that only the French (and Herr Brecht) know how to write plays. Across the Channel M. Anouilh's reputation and box-office returns have their ups and downs: but in London he is regarded as infallible and, since I am regarded as beyond the pale for daring to criticise anything that he writes, I am glad to welcome his WALTZ OF THE TOREADORS. This holds its place at the Criterion Theatre with full justification of much gaiety and some grimness. In the sphere of revue the uninhibited Gallic humours (and graces) of Robert Dhéry's show LA PLUME DE MA TANTE profited both by its own native entertainment value and by the tenancy of the Garrick Theatre, that salesman's paradise with its fine shop-window and huge hoarding-space in the Charing Cross Road. Thus

15

M. Dhéry's team, singing summer as well as winter songs for me and my aunts, stayed much longer than they can have at first expected.

The interest shown in CRANKS by Princess Margaret doubtless assisted this intimate, angular, and rather abstract revue to hold its own at the St Martin's, the Duchess and Hammersmith, without star-names or the usual resources. With a small company it stressed the possibilities of cranking up the human form for mime and the advantages of substituting dumb show for spoken comedy. This practice may save fees to sketch-writers, but it demands considerable mimetic talent and throws a big responsibility on the producer. I was surprised that the witty FRESH AIRS, with Max Adrian and Moyra Fraser, did not hold on longer at the Comedy. At the time of writing it seemed that FOR AMUSEMENT ONLY was well set for a long stay at the Apollo: this brisk affair, or brisk after a sluggish twenty minutes, brought on view some of the players who had been so much liked during a very long run at the Criterion Theatre of INTIMACY AT 8.30. Peter Myers and Ronald Cass were the chief writer and composer and did their work with dexterity. Thelma Ruby, who had been so amusing in THE BUCCANEER, and Dilys Laye led for the ladies, while Jimmy Thompson, Hugh Paddick and Ron Moody proved themselves the right men to carry any satirical fun upon its way.

The Cambridge Footlights went to town once more and their review ANYTHING MAY, at the Lyric Theatre, Hammersmith, though less praised than previous inventions, had quite enough good features to justify the journey: in addition it provided, in the person of Daniel Massey, another proof of that family's capacity for taking the stage. If not a Daniel come to judgment, he was certainly a Daniel come to give most acceptable evidence on his own behalf.

To add to the year's pleasures there arrived in London, just at the end of my time limit, an American actress of most charming accomplishment, Geraldine Page. She played the part of a gawky, shy, unwanted young woman in a rather sentimental American piece called THE RAINMAKER, which followed the aforementioned CRANKS at the St Martin's Theatre. Richard Nash, the author of this folk-story accompanied with folk-songs, had put together the kind of play which one would not greatly care to read but which actors really enjoy acting and we,

16

Ronald Lewis and Vivien Leigh in SOUTH SEA BUBBLE
at the Lyric (*Angus McBean*)

Brenda Bruce and Hugh Griffith in THE WALTZ OF THE TOREADORS
at the Arts and the Criterion (*Houston Rogers*)

thanks to that, can really enjoy seeing and hearing. The scene is the Far West and the time is that of intense drought. A family of ranchers watch their herds wilting and perishing for lack of water: a wandering (and good-looking) stranger walks in and proclaims himself a water-bringer. He can, with a certain magic of his own, summon rain from the sky – for a hundred dollars. Of course he is a fraud, and wanted by the Sheriff's men, but he is given a chance. And that chance is also the opportunity of plain Liz, the daughter of the house, downcast and mocked because she is still unmarried in a world where women are meant for men only and careers are out of the question. The rainmaker can make love if he cannot make a downpour. In a way he earns his money by healing a heart.

Obviously this picture of Tramp Charming and the farmhouse Cinderella might be only a trite little 'tear-jerker'. But it was given such quality by Sam Wanamaker and Geraldine Page that it delighted those least likely to be 'pixilated' by such a fairy-tale. Miss Page, with her nervous flutterings between grief and joy, fear of the man and acceptance of him, gave a performance of superb technical achievement; we must keep her with us and see her in more and larger plays than THE RAINMAKER.

All in all, it has been as good a year as most for the London theatre and better than the last. It was not a year, as I have noted, to please the editor, writers, and readers of "The Tailor and Cutter" or the merchants and students of feminine *couture*. The advertisements that confront viewers of Commercial Television give such incessant advice on how to keep ourselves and our underwear and napery spotless that a visit to many of the plays had the merits of a complete change with their panorama of foul linen and of broken boots.

17   B

Waiting for Codot

WAITING FOR GODOT

by Samuel Beckett   *Arts and Criterion Theatres*

Some told me it was a wonderful piece of fancy, some, more numerous, that it was a wilderness of words. Some said it was prose-poetry of the finest, others that it was pretentious piffle. It was intimated that you were not fit to dine in elevated company or to join in the consumption of cocktails laced with culture unless you had seen, heard, digested – or failed to digest – Godot. I waited for Godot, secretly fearing that I was going to be found wanting and yawning, a boorish objector to the alleged masterpiece. At last I nerved myself for the occasion, went in leisure, and repented in haste.

It must, I decided, be a joke of a too familiar kind, another venture in the salesmanship of 'Cod'. That jest has been played in the other arts: it consists of concocting a bit of fake nonsense for the Egg Heads and watching the Egg Heads' enraptured receipt of it. The prose of an instructional text-book was chopped up and served with appropriate typography as a fine specimen of Modern Verse. Some Egg Heads were found to pronounce with grave enthusiasm on its poetic quality. I have not the words of their pronouncement, but I can easily imagine them. 'Striking integration of fourth-dimensional vision with bold existentialist imagery combined with a striking use of sprung rhythm, almost sur-rhythmic in its audacity.'

The trick has also been played with painting and the Avant-Garde judges duly gave their acclaim to some jocosity vamped up, mock specimens of Art in the Abstract. I could only assume, after my brush with the much-expected and never-appearing Godot, that Mr Beckett was leg-pulling in the same manner. If so, he won. There were the appropriate raptures. Of course, if Mr Beckett was taking himself seriously, then – well, you could knock me down with an Egg Head's egg-shell.

On the stage were a couple of tramps resting amid the débris of a dirt-track with a background supposed to be sky, and looking like Lincrusta. There was a withered tree which was discussed as a possible gallows for suicidal uses, but was never,

18

alas, so employed. The two 'bums', Estragon and Vladimir, in the intervals of discussing body odour and sore feet and slouching off to relieve themselves, remarked with devastating iteration that they were 'Waiting for Godot'. Godot. Godot. Godot. He never came and nothing happened. Patience was never more in demand.

Godot, I had been warned by those who understood these things, is God. Had Mr Beckett any theology to communicate? Had he anything at all to communicate? If he had, it did not reach me. The symbolically dead tree sprouted some symbolically live foliage during the talkative exercise and this may have signified much. But it did not strike me as a fresh or fruitful essay in the imagery of rejuvenescence or resurrection. In any case, none of the characters rejuvenesced.

Instead of Godot there joined the tramps one Pozzo, a massive creature vastly prognathous, who suggested Mussolini dressed as John Bull. He carried with him a whip and dragged with him on a halter a forlorn, half-witted and debilitated serf called Lucky whom he addressed, or roared at, as Pig or Hog. If Pozzo was a symbol of wicked Capitalism, he was an even cruder cartoon of Dives than was Will Dyson's Fat Man of the 1910 epoch. Dyson was a brilliant draughtsman and had witty ideas which gave some subtle invention to his castigation of Fat. I could discover nothing subtle or new in the bellowings of Pozzo.

Mr Beckett, I gather, is an Irishman who lives in France, writes in French, and translates himself. He is evidently not a student of sociology. The striking feature of Capitalism today is not that it bullies, but that it surrenders: at least it surrenders on the surface, welcoming the Welfare State, shortening hours, piling up wages, looking sweetly reasonable and also piling up prices and profits. Most of the profits, it is true, go in taxation, but one can distribute bonus shares and make capital gains. The wages are inflated, the capital is watered, the consumer is fleeced, and Private Enterprise is, at the end of it all, sufficiently popular to keep the Conservatives in power. Since the alternative offered by Labour is only further doses of collectivism, which is sufficiently damned by the dismal record of the nationalised services, it should not be difficult for Big Business to go on triumphantly masquerading as a Big Brother, especially if it makes a good show of profit-sharing schemes.

19

The man with a fixed pension or the man who struggled to save can see his hopes of a decent old age dwindle as the value of his money vanishes. But who cares? He is helpless and alone. On with inflated capital, inflated wages, inflated illusions of a good time for all. A swindle you may call it, but it has nothing to do with Mr Beckett's Pozzo the Slave-driver, who is many years out of date. Pozzo of today knows better than to crack the whip and roar. He speaks smooth things while he bumps up his prices. The Trade Unions put up a routine snarl from time to time: but they know that, on the whole, they can play ball with Pozzo. So the supposed satire on Pozzo in Mr Beckett's play is merely childish to anyone who ever reads the City column and the reports of a Trade Union Congress.

I have no objection to plays in which nothing happens. Discussion drama is old and familiar and acceptable if the discussion is good. Shaw provided plenty of it and, whether you agreed with him or not, he had ideas, he voiced ideas, he put his ideas into clear and cogent English. So, more recently, did J. B. Priestley and Jacquetta Hawkes, in DRAGON'S MOUTH. Their four characters talked to a theme – or themes. But not one of the rapturous appraisals of WAITING FOR GODOT have mentioned any proof of a definite opinion about anything. They say we must not look for anything so crude as intellectual content. We are insensitive to fine shades of feeling if we do not respond to the evacuations, material and emotional, of the tramps who merely wonder what it's all about and where it's all going and get no sort of answer. I can find no satisfaction in the moanings of the mentally deficient.

It rambled on. A few members of the audience left after Act I. They had the freedom of departure, having, presumably, paid for their seats. But a critic must earn his complimentary allotment and do his Casabianca act even if the others have left the burning deck of the sinking ship. So there I was, waiting, piously, grimly, despairingly, for Godot – and a grain of sense. The rest of the audience, as I surmised from their pious demeanour and puzzled whisperings during the interval, felt that they were doing a cultural drill and earning good marks in some register of artistic endeavour. 'I don't see the point'. 'Where does it all get to?' If these doubts and questions had been put to me, I could have offered no enlightenment. The tramps continued to grunt and twitter their respective brands of misery and hopelessness. Pozzo barked away and bullied Lucky. Lucky, long dumb, broke into a mixture of speech and eructation. My sympathy for the actors was profuse. Under Peter Hall's direction they strove nobly to put variety into monotony, something into nothing, and a good face on the devil of a job.

Hugh Burden dithered amiably as Vladimir. That clever young actor from Cambridge, Peter Woodthorpe, as Estragon, transmitted a mixture of the saturnine and the plaintive with first-rate competence, continually making play with the donning and doffing of a pair of battered boots – deep symbolism there, no doubt; the aching feet spoke of the constricted life. As Pozzo, Peter Bull displayed a great thrust of chin and even greater power of lungs, while Timothy Bateson was poignantly kicked about and pulled about as the starveling helot, Lucky. The pace was wisely rapid: it is best not to linger over the utterance of nothing.

After writing this I was informed by assorted champions of the play
(1) That two of the characters are facets of the same person.
(2) That all the characters are the same person.
(3) That to be told that we are all waiting for nothing to turn up is a notable piece of wisdom.
(4) That Pozzo, not Godot, is God or that Pozzo is Godot, or that Pozzo is Godot and God too.
(5) That it was a superb tragedy.
(6) That it was a superb comedy.
(7) That it cheerfully lifted the heart and struck resounding notes of hope.
(8) That it was a fine piece of pessimism, proper to the doomed and dismal world we live in.
(9) That the author had told one of the actors that he himself didn't know what it meant. He was just having his bit of fun.

Large numbers of people seem to enjoy play-going in Puzzle Corner. I am apparently a fogey if I assert that the function of art is communication, that is to say, the expression, in whatever medium the artist chooses, of thought or feeling or both. If such expression only creates the turmoil of opinion which the verdicts cited above indicate, the artist has failed. I think myself justified in believing that a competent artist should be reasonably explicit. By this I do not mean that he should write out everything in

21

words of one syllable or paint in a wholly realistic way. What I detest is the mood of those who say, 'I haven't the faintest idea what it is all about, but it is wonderful'.

In re-reading Compton Mackenzie's novel, 'Extraordinary Women' (1928), just after my collision with Godot, I found this passage: 'I'm mad about André Gide. I can't understand a word he says. Oh, I tell you, André Gide's some writer. You just can't understand him, Rosalba.'

The remark is attributed to a character called Zoe Mitchell, a wealthy, beautiful, and moronic American lady. Moronic. But that was in 1928. Now the intellectuals have caught up with Zoe. They are repeating about Mr Beckett her observations about M. Gide . . . and repeating them word for word.

Here's to Progress, S'welp me Godot.

At Edinburgh

THE WORLD'S WONDER
by Alexander Reid   *Palladium Theatre, Edinburgh*

THE HEATHER ON FIRE
by Moray McLaren   *Gateway Theatre, Edinburgh*

OUR MAGGY
by D. Heddle   *Gateway Theatre, Edinburgh*

COME TO THE FAIR
by R. J. B. Sellar   *Gateway Theatre, Edinburgh*

The Scottish Theatre would be very well off if it had a tougher Scottish audience. It is the common experience of those directing the Scottish repertory play-houses that the public has to be coaxed along with lumps of sugar. That, my fellow-Scots might angrily and reasonably reply, is just as true of England. There too you can only stiffen a repertory programme at considerable risk. But the Scots are reported to be serious folk; they are certainly commendable patrons of the authors and publishers. What English town of similar size to Edinburgh could equal the number and the excellence of Edinburgh's book-shops? But the ardent readers of the city are not the ardent play-goers. To collect a repertory audience of sufficiently rewarding size in a large town it is necessary to please the bus-party that comes rolling up from the village or the small town. Bus-parties are not out for brain-work: they want a hearty laugh in between journeys. And Edin-burgh is no exception to this custom of jaunt and jollity.

The bus-parties make a right and proper demand and good luck to those who include a theatre visit in the outings of the Jolly New Coaching Days. The trouble is that those who seek for something larger in the theatre are so few; not enough will undertake a trip from suburb to town-centre to see a big play while so many others will come over miles of bank and brae to see a little one. But this journeying is all in accord with the con-temporary itch for mobility. There is a constant allure in the automobile, whether public or private. There it stands: let us use it. The dominating passion is to be taken for a ride.

The Central London theatres, too, are more and more depen-dent on the coach-party that comes from thirty or even fifty miles away. In their search for pleasure the folk of the Home Counties are certainly not stay-at-homes. Stratford-upon-Avon, which I long ago said would now be better named Stratford-upon-Petrol, knows well that no distance deters and that those who would not stroll down the street to see a Shakespeare play in their own town, however well presented, are avid for the Bard when he is obtainable by hours of transportation. Even the least likeable plays, the box-office bogeys, such as ALL'S WELL THAT ENDS WELL, can be sold as part of an outing. Our world is densely populated with those who travel hopefully; and the theatre would be conducted on imbecile lines if it did not ac-knowledge and profit by the fact. Profit is, perhaps, too optimis-tic a term. 'Avoid loss' would be more accurate.

The personality of the player is naturally one of the magnets. But how many Scottish players are widely magnetic? Duncan Macrae is undoubtedly one of them. During three Edinburgh Festivals he has packed, or been mainly instrumental in packing, the Edinburgh Palladium, at a time when every hall, in a city very rich in halls, as well as its major theatres and concert-halls offering their starry Festival attractions, were not only inviting audiences but obtaining them. (And that does not include the thousands who brave the climate of the Castle Rock to watch the flood-lit Tattoo nightly or twice nightly, all the usual patrons of the numerous cinemas, and a few more thousands who find their heart's desire satisfied by a Musical on Ice.) The Edinburgh Festival has justified itself by quality and that is not

23

surprising since the city has put brains, heart and purse into the business. What is astonishing is the gigantic number of people who are paying to see something somewhere during the Festival weeks. But all this competition has no sort of power to cause empty seats at the Palladium if Macrae is on the job.

I saw him in what can accurately be called a Mediaeval Miracle play by Alexander Reid, a talented Scottish dramatist of our own time. To the Scottish town of Dubbity, seemingly in the period and region of the Border ballads, comes Michael Scott, a warlock or wonder-worker; there also arrives an impostor in the same line of business. They become involved in assorted conflicts: there is a struggle between the two hocus-pocus merchants. There is also the need to outwit a knavish Provost. It is an old story in both senses of old, historical and customary, and what matters is the telling of it, which is charming.

Mr Reid has a nice gift of fancy and of phrase and with Duncan Macrae as Michael Scott, the play provided a delightful two hours of chicanery and stage-managerial fireworks. The magic laid on by the warlock must be good theatrical stuff with flames coming out of the top. But the essence of it was Macrae's command of mischief: his lean, wry-faced, angular figure became an admirable agent of the comically supernatural. Particularly well supported by Roddy McMillan and Laidlaw Darling he captured the Edinburgh laughter to the full in a play which, without Macrae, had not, I believe, won such plaudits in a less responsive Glasgow. With magic his theme, Macrae gave an appropriately wizard performance and, no less appropriately, held his audience spell-bound.

To say that Moray McLaren is an Edinburgh man is to make a mild statement of his knowledge of and devotion to the city in all its mists and moods; he can be lyrical without being sentimental, over its sky-lines and its skies. He knows its history, its architecture, the sinister streets of the Old Town and the spacious splendours of the New, the Old built protectively in fear, the New built confidently in the faith that light and learning, claret and the classic arts had come to stay. THE HEATHER ON FIRE is set in Victorian Edinburgh, Stevenson's Edinburgh in which lively sons slipped out of the solemn New Town houses of their august parents to mingle with drabs and drunks in the tavern-life of the mean streets round the corner; they sought not

24

merely to practice drinking and drabbing but to let blaze the spark of life that could hardly flicker in the cold severity of the lawyers' quarter. In this play a son writes and revels: a sister secretly assists him in the writing. Genius is suspected by a London publisher who comes to find the man and foster his work. But whose is that genius, the son's or the sister's? The story takes us from the solemn home to the Bohemian junketings where all classes are united by song, dance, and 'the social glass'.

It is never easy to make Bohemianism plausible on the stage: in studio-parties the players so often seem to be animate with only a pretended hilarity, but in this case the contrasted decorum of the young writer's home and the song-and-dance of his escapes and escapades were genuinely effective. Miss Lennox Milne, as the sister, carried complete conviction, while Tom Fleming, as the writer, persuaded me to the full that the lad was everything that his father had warned him against. A preposition, I know, is a bad word to end a sentence with, so let me add, and not only for stylistic propriety's sake, that James Gibson played a bibulous piper and gave a very happy picture of one of the ragged rascals who run round the city's rugged rock. The result was more than an agreeable evening: it lit up the gas-lamps of Stevenson's youth and threw illumination on the two Edinburghs, grave and gay, of Stevenson's period.

The other two plays that I saw at the Gateway Theatre were smaller matters usefully coping with the search for laughter without brain-fag. Both happened to deal with actresses of dubious talent. In OUR MAGGY a Miss Margaret Ross from Glasgow amusingly dismayed her gusty teacher at a Dramatic Academy. In COME TO THE FAIR a daughter of the Manse returned, after a not too happy career as 'a theatrical', to assist at a village gala, and was rescued from further internment in parochial life by the arrival of an American film-director in search of a Scottish type.

Both D. Heddle (Mr or Miss?), who wrote OUR MAGGY, and Robert Sellar, who wrote COME TO THE FAIR, shewed the right knowledge of how to make a good second act carry a three-act play and satisfy the normal appetite for easy laughs. There was intimate knowledge of the Dramatic Academy in the first place and of the Manse in the second. Mr Sellar gave us good company in the Minister's wife who would have a fling with stocks and shares, the fling being limited to two or three shares at a time. Nell Ballantyne was her excellent self in both plays. For the actresses who had leading parts in the two stories there were young players of accomplishment in Mary Helen Donald and Jean Martin. I visited COME TO THE FAIR on the kind of January night when 'Come to the Fire' would have been a rival invitation hard to resist. But a bus-party had come from over the snowy hills and far away, and plenty more were booked. They would be well satisfied, for such audiences chiefly, I gather, prefer a home from home on the stage, authentic in its annals of the parish and in its types of the township. They were safe with Mr Sellar who, in this piece, made no effort to swim in deep waters but paddled, a trusty friend, cordially in the burn, content with the gowans and not seeking larger laurels.

The Kettle Boils

MR KETTLE AND MRS MOON
by J. B. Priestley   *Duchess Theatre*

Mr George Kettle is Branch Manager of a bank at Brickmill. Brickmill appears to be one of the dingier environs of Birmingham. On a wet Monday morning it is, to Mr Kettle, as close to hell as it is to Birmingham. Daily he performs Operation Banker and goes, bowler-hatted, properly pin-striped below and black-coated above, to supervise the accounts of his Brickmill clientèle. He is a lonely man (his marriage broke up during the war), and he has a taste for music on the air. None the less, the gramophone, even when it belches the more rousing sections of 'Prince Igor,' is not enough.

So, on a most tenebrous, rain-sodden and soul-afflicting Monday, he decides, in his despair, that Brickmill is 'nowhere to go for a lark'. And lark he will. The daily discipline has become intolerable. No more will he a-banking go. Instead of conforming to Operation Bowler he bashes in his tile of office and substitutes the playful exercise known as 'Bonnet Over the Windmill'. He stays at home, drinks whisky before the Brickmill sun, if any, has even approached the yard-arm, makes music, plays children's games, and later plays a more adult game with Mrs Delia Moon, wife of Henry Moon, estate agent.

She, too, is in the habit of being a good Brickmillian and resenting it. She does business at the Bank on behalf of a charity, going about her civic duties in very sober guise. But she, like George Kettle, has a lark pent up inside and longing to escape. She calls on the now sportive Kettle. But so do several others. Brickmill has banking business to be done. Alderman Hardcastle, of Hardcastle's Stores, wants an Extension loan and comes roaring along in search of his absentee bank-manager. Henry Moon is not in the Hardcastle class of stentorians, but he has a natural interest in the whereabouts and what's a-foot of his wife. So he arrives, peering and grunting, churlish with some reason. The Police Superintendent has heard of strange doings and must, in duty bound, come along to do a bit of superintending. Mr Kettle's 'help', Mrs Twigg, thinks that Mr Kettle has fallen ill. Her daughter, Monica, takes a lively and sympathetic interest in Mr Kettle's case, for she was never one to go willingly to work and hold a job down. A grave senior, Mr Clinton, Birmingham district bank manager with Mr Kettle's branch under his survey, is called in to inquire about Mr Kettle's absenteeism. He brings the bank's psychiatrist with him. They have had these Jekyll and Hyde cases before. Even bank-managers can be schizophrenics, liable to bowler-bashing and windmill-bonneting.

Mr Kettle's second and Dionysiac self, it seems, has asserted itself over his primary and go-to-business self. These problems of double personality can be medically handled nowadays. A little hypnotic treatment, for instance, might smooth out the psychic complications. Having been gently knocked out by the Superintendent, Mr Kettle, prone and unconscious, is a good object for such psychotherapy.

However, Mr Kettle can reassert that second self and Delia Moon is quite ready to play. Finally they elope, without, apparently, money or prospects. I did not feel that, on those terms, life-long happiness was their certain future. But he, Kettle, steaming and bubbling over, and she, glamorously Moonstruck, are going to enjoy love's young dream in early middle-age. So to hell with banking, Brickmill and the Aldermanic, estate-broking lot of them!

Mr Priestley's comedy was such a light one that it could hardly be said to give unethical advice and to counsel all good members of the black-coated salaried to cultivate absenteeism and adultery when it's a wet Monday and life seems to have no meaning. Judged simply as a frolic the piece lumbered somewhat in its first act, and displayed most amusing episodes thereafter. Clive Morton as the rebel banker was far better company when he had got over his children's games and his home-made music. The life and soul of the party, for me, was the stodgy, uncomprehending Mr Moon, delightfully played by Raymond Francis. His efforts to cope with Mr Kettle's second and Dionysiac self and to counter his errant wife's quick-witted retorts to his appeals to play the game plumbed the comic depths of bourgeois bewilderment. The doctor, too, played by John Moffat, was masterly in the self-assurance of scientific youth, and in the pattering of his psycho-therapeutic jargon. Wendy Craig, as Monica Twigg, was every inch a daughter of Brickmillian revolt. She wanted a career and a larger world than that of Olde Oake Cafés and Hardcastle's Stores.

As Delia Moon elevated – or, if you in strictness prefer it, debased – from being a tweedy, spectacled Brickmillian spouse to the status of a Bad Woman, Frances Rowe took her primrose path with great skill. Mr Priestley had not been in his Messenger mood, for which he is apt to be blamed. (But not by me, for I am not so terrified of a play with a purpose and prefer the presence of an idea to absence of mind.) In this case the play-goers, spared his pot of message, could happily consume his mess of hilarious pottage without pangs of conscience. It is more than doubtful whether absenteeism of bank-managers and seduction of their clients' wives has notably increased since Mr Priestley set his Kettle boiling.

Fleet Street Dances

THE BUCCANEER

A Musical Play by Sandy Wilson

Lyric, Hammersmith, and Apollo Theatres

While THE BOY FRIEND continued to retain and extend its innumerable friendships, Sandy Wilson's second venture was not so beloved. THE BUCCANEER had six months at Hammersmith and a brief promotion to Shaftesbury Avenue. So Tennent

Productions had a fair run for their money, but nothing Marathonic in the manner of Mr Wilson's first creation. I was surprised at this, for I found the tunes most agreeable and the story of a boys' magazine in decay and recovery gay and fresh.

The journal in question was 'The Buccaneer': this veteran had been going its old way for too many years and telling the old, old story with too complacent a repetition. Dear little Mr Donkin came in with his weekly slab of the serial and dear, silvery Mrs Barraclough saw the journal tranquilly to press. But the juvenile public was tiring of the routine product issued by this sweetly senile partnership. With circulation growing dangerously feeble, 'The Buccaneer' was likely to fade anaemically out of a Fleet Street where redder blood was in demand and the newer fictions of the Space Ship age were being profusely 'put across'. Putting across novelties was not a technique of authorship understood by Mr Donkin nor was brisk innovation a practice likely to be shrewdly and snappily exercised by Mrs Barraclough. The world had passed them by.

It is a happy merit of Mr Wilson's work that he can laugh at the old folk without slapping them down. In THE BOY FRIEND he had smiled with the nineteen-twenties instead of sneering at them. In THE BUCCANEER he was blithely chivalrous to the innocent old fuddy-duddies who were so complacently unaware of changing methods in 'The Street' and of changing tastes in the young idea.

Change might come by way of America or through the intervention of the pert son of a vastly wealthy and moronic mamma. That lady was a grand creation and, as played by Thelma Ruby, a constant joy. Miss Ruby presented a wondrous image of a beaky, peering, over-dressed, over-sexed, over-rich and under-witted inhabitant of the best hotels. William Chappell in his production made the most of this delicious booby, and Miss Ruby took all her chances. As her son, Montgomery, perky and precocious, Kenneth Williams was admirably the prod-nose, the know-all, and the intellectual 'smarty' whose notions of journalism were as far removed from Mrs Barraclough's as a strong shot of gin from a nice cup of tea. With this casting and with Betty Warren, all dulcet conservatism, as Mrs Barraclough the contrast of age that cared and did not know with youth that knew and did not care was most effective.

29

Here our sadness must break in to mitigate the cheerfulness. Eliot Makeham, who played the frail Mr Donkin with a perfect presentation of the old gentleman foundering in a world of new 'toughs', died during the run. He was an actor with just the right physique and style for the little man of good intentions: he beamed benignity as Donkin, as he had done in many a similar role. He was an admirable Tobit, for example, in Bridie's TOBIAS AND THE ANGEL. With his early training in the best repertories, Miss Horniman's in Manchester and Alfred Wareing's in Glasgow, he had developed a felicitous touch both in comedy and pathos. Though in his seventies, he bravely took to song as Sandy Wilson's Donkin and piped up finely on behalf of Donkin's fictional hero, Captain Fairbrother, and also as a contributor in the play's theme-song, 'Good Clean Fun'. Eliot Makeham's death marred my pleasant memory of THE BUC- CANEER and his absence from such roles will be a permanent loss.

THE BUCCANEER did not survive him long. I could see no reason why a public which demanded THE BOY FRIEND and SALAD DAYS year after year was comparatively shy of this further experience in the native 'musical' with a similar infec- tious simplicity of music and a similar good-tempered kind of fun. Inexplicable occurrences of this kind are part of theatre life. But I shall retain the kindliest thoughts of Mrs Barraclough and Mr Donkin and of their brash successors who knew the meaning of 'pep' and the way to achieve it.

Should Murder Amuse?

THE WHOLE TRUTH
by Philip Mackie   *Aldwych Theatre*

Throughout most of the year two of Agatha Christie's contribu- tions to the drama of detection continued on their long-distance way. One naturally mourned the absence from more ambitious matters of fine actors, such as Mr Felix Aylmer, penned up for years in the compound of lime-lit criminology. However, it is not a critic's business to set up an 'Artists' Advice Bureau' and to instruct distinguished men and women of other professions on the use of their talents and the conduct of their finances.

'The drama's laws the drama's patrons give', and the mass patronage in our time is lavishly bestowed upon the corpse stowed in the cupboard or tossed behind the sofa while the owner of the flat is being grilled at his own fire-side. Yet it seems that merely to be puzzled for a couple of hours is not quite enough. Agatha Christie does not only complicate clues: she creates characters. In the way of detective fiction Ngaio Marsh is my favourite in this kind because her people are so well drawn that they could take their places in fiction of the highest class. I wish she would work specifically for the stage, since she is stage-trained and knows these ropes. One of her best stories, 'Surfeit of Lampreys', was adapted for stage purposes a few years ago, but unfortunately its action was too mobile for adaptation. At any rate, something went wrong. I am sure that, if she would compose a 'Whodunit' solely for the theatre, it could be triumphantly theatrical. One reason for that confident assertion is that Ngaio Marsh would mix genuinely living people, instead of crime-play dummies, with the mysteriously dead whose presence is essential to these affairs.

Furthermore, she might, as Agatha Christie so successfully did, with Margaret Lockwood's able assistance, in THE SPIDER'S WEB, mingle murder with amusement. Laugh while the bell tolls? Why not? The bell tolled grimly enough in MACBETH. Yet there was the Porter. There were corpses galore in HAMLET, but the grave-yard had its genial grave-digger. The hero of a tragedy is none the worse for having a wit as sharp as any dagger, as the Prince of Denmark amply proves. Poison in jest? Why not? No offence in the world, if artistry be sufficiently there in the high tragedy of the old theatre and artifice be present in the popular crime-play of the present time.

Mr Philip Mackie's THE WHOLE TRUTH had the right initial ingenuity. It went off to a cracking start. It was a good idea and a neat beginning to make the characters aghast at the seemingly certain news of a murder that had not happened and then to have it happen half-an-hour later in their own front garden. That the story ended with some very odd behaviour both of the servant of the law and of the killer himself did not greatly matter. But I surmise that what denied Mr Mackie one of those Marathonic runs was surely his omission to make his characters more interesting and to relieve his criminal manœuvres with some tactful invitation to a smile.

31

At the end we could only conclude that his murderer was a candidate for Broadmoor and as mad as they make them. The criminal's early motives had been insufficiently suggested. A man who kills without some believable cause is not of much theatrical value. If he were mad with jealousy, then let it be made plain. The assassin in this case was suitably enigmatic at the start and the ingenious performance of Leslie Phillips in the part was a pleasure to watch. But the dramatist had not explained this sleek, sly creature's reason for his journey up Sinister Street. The fellow had to behave like a homicidal maniac later on and take risks far beyond sanity. Killing that is merely maniacal is, or can be, tedious whatever the expertness of its interpreter.

In THE WHOLE TRUTH the victim of arrest was a film-producer who had neglected a dull wife for a gaudy vixen. Ernest Clark is an actor who can bestow veritable character and abundance of human quality on almost any part if he is given half a chance: in this play he had not even a quarter of an opportunity. The film-producer was a puppet of the plot and his interior was of sawdust only. His poor wife had even more of the marionette in her composition. She had merely to stand about and register consternation, just 'loungen round en suffern', as Uncle Remus said. The vixen of the studios was a much livelier party and Faith Brook came sailing in with great animation. The temperature rose with her performance but she had to sail out again, all too rapidly, being condemned to perish untimely at the end of the first act of three.

Enter the Law. Arnold Bell is usually a master-hand at the familiar Inquiry Scene: but the Detective Inspector handed to him to play had no sort of character beyond an unbelievable capacity for abusing his office and behaving as though he were Cop, Judge and Jury rolled into one. The really skilled exponents of 'Whodunit' drama have taken trouble to prove that the Law is not wholly an ass or inevitably a bore. From gaunt Holmes to the podgy Poirot, from Miss Marsh's brisk Alleyn and phlegmatic Foxy to the serenely sagacious Miss Marple who replaced Miss Christie's Poirot, the story of the hunted has been profitably enlivened by the curiosity-value of the hunter.

Detective fiction, at its best, has been a game of 'cards'. There never was such a 'card' as Holmes; and hence came the immortality of Conan Doyle's stories, many of which seem crude

32

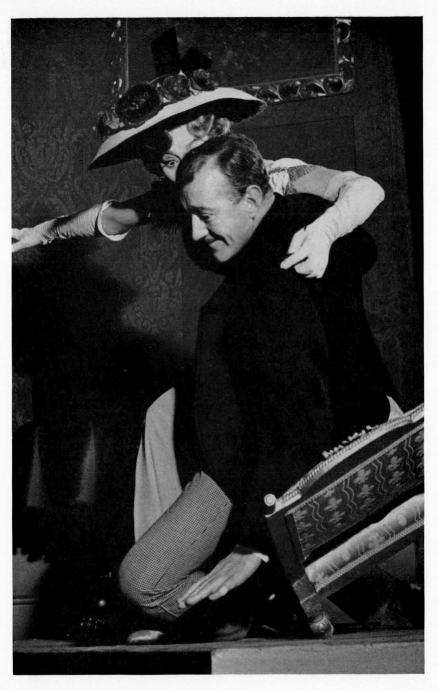

Irene Worth and Alec Guinness in HOTEL PARADISO
at the Winter Garden (*Armstrong Jones*)

Martita Hunt in HOTEL PARADISO at the Winter Garden (*Armstrong Jones*)

and silly on re-reading in these times of much more ingenious and intricate plot-construction; silly they are, especially some of the later ones, but superbly readable. Crudity does not hamper where the 'card' is king. Holmes and Watson are still as grand a pair of comics as literature has produced. Hence all the stolen 'sparklers', which they set out to recover, sparkle still; hence the corpses, which cause their sleuth-work, rise from the dead and live for ever.

But Philip Mackie's Inspector in THE WHOLE TRUTH was even more sawdusty than the film-producer and his wife. Except for a natural capacity to feel sleepy after a long day at the grill, he had nothing of the lively dramatic quality essential to keep us enlivened in a theatre. The strong arm of justice banged the table with a leaden weight. Should murder amuse? Of course it should, if it is to descend from tragedy's high theme to the arena of box-office entertainment. Shakespeare, who knew about these things, took trouble to give good lines to his gaolers and executioners, tiny though their parts may be. What a speech is this to a man about to be hanged! (I quote from CYMBELINE, Act V, Scene IV.)

First Gaoler: A heavy reckoning for you, sir. But the comfort is, you shall be call'd to no more payments, fear no more tavern-bills; which are as often the sadness of parting, as the procuring of mirth; you come in faint for want of meat, depart reeling with too much drink; sorry that you have paid too much, and sorry that you are paid too much; purse and brain both empty, – the brain the heavier for being too light, the purse too light being drawn of heaviness; of this contradiction you shall now be quit. – O, the charity of a penny cord! it sums up thousands in a trice; you have no true debitor and creditor but it; of what's past, is, and to come, the discharge; – your neck, sir, is pen, book, and counters; so the acquittance follows.

One does not expect the modern manufacturers of 'Whodunits' to write like that. If they did, none might mark them. But there is a hint in the logic of it. Great dramatists give character to all their characters. Shakespeare frequently offered to a small part lines as brilliant as any given to the leading man.

'O, the charity of a penny cord!' It takes the breath; and it may have been entrusted to a beginner.

Greek and Italian

A LIFE IN THE SUN
by Thornton Wilder   *Assembly Hall, Edinburgh*

SUMMERTIME
by Ugo Betti, translated by Henry Reed   *Apollo Theatre*

THE QUEEN AND THE REBELS
by Ugo Betti, translated by Henry Reed   *Haymarket Theatre*

At Edinburgh Irene Worth played the part of Alcestis in Thornton Wilder's re-drafting of the old Greek play about the wife who volunteered to die in order that her husband Admetus might live. Having done her unusually good deed Alcestis is then pulled out of Hades by that universal provider of rescues, Heracles. Euripides did not take the matter very seriously: out of it he made one of his 'Satyric dramas', which are near to comedies, and not one of his tragedies. Mr Wilder, adding a third act of the 'twenty years after' kind, took it very seriously indeed and was endeavouring, I vaguely gathered, to link the self-sacrifice of Alcestis with Christian doctrine.

My own idea of the Alcestis story is that it should be treated ironically, with an undertone of bitter laughter. Did Alcestis take her husband's recumbent place at the funeral ordained by the gods because she loved a man so selfish and so brutish as to accept such a sacrifice? The idea is ridiculous. I visualise Admetus as an egotistical bore from whom she was only too glad to escape, even if death was the only way out. Then the blundering but well-intentioned Heracles came along and hauled her out of her happy refuge in the underworld. This, of course, would have made the poor lady hopping mad. Just when she had found some peace, she was planted back in the arms of the pompous, selfish and tedious fool whom she had inadvertently married. To Hades with Heracles! Like Gregers Werle in THE WILD DUCK, he must go round Doing Good. And, like the officious Gregers, what a mess he made of it!

34

Thornton Wilder was not thus sardonic. I gathered from my fellow play-goers that he proclaimed much wisdom, but this I could not gather for myself because, in the Assembly Hall, owing to the shape of its platform, I could only intermittently gather shreds and patches of his text. It would be wrong to criticise a play thus removed from any chance to apprehend it. What I can, and do, criticise is the platform stage in the Assembly Hall at Edinburgh, which may have some advantages for plays of pageantry but is a severe handicap to any piece whose spoken word demands to be followed closely.

There is a Left Wing vogue for 'theatre in the round', 'theatre in the square', and for any kind of theatre in which the actors break loose and caper in the middle of the audience. At Edinburgh a long platform is thrown forward from one wall and the audience sits on three sides of it. I was sitting on the left flank of this dais, directly facing other members of the audience on the right flank. The players accordingly had to propel their lines in three directions, right, left and centre. There may be some players so gifted and so well trained to this form of theatrical architecture that they can be audible everywhere. But the players in this case were not so gifted nor so trained. When Irene Worth spoke the vitally important part of Alcestis she quite properly gave some speeches to the right wing of the audience and some to the left wing, and rather more to the centre. What else could she do? The result was inevitably that I, as a left-winger, missed some seemingly important passages. Moreover, with this kind of staging, visibility becomes as 'chancy' as audibility. There will inevitably be 'masking' of the actors when the platform is at all fully occupied unless the tiers of seats rise up very sharply: but they do not rise up sharply on the floor of the Assembly Hall and I spent much of my time and effort during my observation of the production in trying to see the speaker who was obscured by other characters.

Tyrone Guthrie enjoys this kind of production: he can set his players scampering onto the platform by making them charge down the aisles among the audience; the occupants of gangway seats are thus exposed to very close, and even menacing, contact with the players and their weapons. Mr Guthrie handles this kind of hurly-burly with skill and with delight. But Mr Wilder's play was not designed, I think, for hurly-burly. It was designed to be acted and spoken and the long platform stage defeated this normal purpose of theatrical performance. If we are to have more of the method which leaves the chief players only seen and heard at intervals, I suggest that the audience be provided with scripts so that they can read the play, either in advance or later, and then fill up the gaps for themselves.

This 'theatre in the round' (or 'square') is, to my mind, simply a nuisance. It has become fashionable to denounce the 'peep-show' stage with the familiar proscenium arch and curtain. But this denigrated architecture does allow the audience to see and hear the play in its entirety instead of straining eyes and ears to get glimpses and to listen to bits of speeches. I am such an old-world fogey that I do want to see the actors and hear the actors when I go to the theatre, and not to share 'audience-participation' in a hurly-burly. If you say that Shakespeare wrote for a platform stage I would reply that we have got a very sensible compromise in the apron-stages used at Stratford-upon-Avon and at the Old Vic. These stages give sufficient freedom of move-ment without compelling the players to act and speak in three directions, delivering one speech to one part of the audience and the next speech to another part. The 'peep-show' stage has sur-vived for three centuries because dramatists and players have found it acceptable: it enabled them to do their job and en-abled the public to appreciate that job. A long platform with audience right, left and centre frustrates them. Let the innova-tors sneer at 'peep-show' as much as they like: most of us go to enjoy the actors' use of voice and facial expression and I am sure that most of us do not like being frustrated in that just purpose of the play-goer.

Irene Worth is an actress with great emotional power. She can communicate intensity of feeling with a strong and vibrant voice. As far as I could see and hear her Alcestis, I was im-pressed and excited by it. But that, unfortunately, was not far enough. Thornton Wilder's play deserved, I am sure, a theatre of normal pattern; so did the players, especially Irene Worth.

The plays of the late Ugo Betti, well translated from the Italian by Henry Reed, had a burst of attention during the year. I saw two of them. SUMMERTIME at the Apollo was the lightest of light comedies about love in a village and picnic philandering in the Apennines. When I attended a matinée at Edinburgh during its pre-London tour the attractive Miss McEwan and Dirk Bogarde were communicating its airy humours to an audience, packed, I fancy, more for love of Dirk, Britain's Number One Film Attraction of the year, than from curiosity about Signor Betti. Mr Bogarde trifled agreeably and Miss McEwan trifled with a dewy simplicity. Michael Gwynn, as the local doctor, added a charming essay in bashful gaucherie. The play, being thistledown or produced as such, floated out of my mind and was gone with the wind, but the mountain air was fresh, a gentle stimulant. This kind of fanciful levity can be a yawnsome bore, especially at a matinée when yawning comes by nature. But Signor Betti and the players neatly dispelled the tranquil snooze that is so often chiefly disturbed by the crash of matinée tea-trays.

THE QUEEN AND THE REBELS was a much larger matter. The scene is a frontier where the rebels, now in command of a small country, are clamping down the chains of what is politely called a People's Democracy and treating any stranger as a spy working for Satanic Reaction. The rebels are hunting their de-throned Queen who has contrived to go underground and is in hiding as a peasant: so disguised, she is trying to get out of the country as an aeroplane passenger. The aeroplane is held up and its occupants are put under interrogation. There is a prostitute among them and she, having recognised the now doomed Queen, determines to take her place and face the firing-squad in order that the Queen may rejoin her child. Here is the old melo-dramatic Sydney Carton situation: the bad woman will do a far, far better thing than she has ever done. It is an old situation, but it was given new political urgency and a much more intelligent text and characterisation than melodrama used to possess.

The play depends on an assumption which struck me as very odd. The Queen had only been off her throne for five years, but none of the tough rebels seemed to know what she looked like. It is one of the habits, indeed one of the obligations, of royalty to be copiously photographed. Their features are more familiar than those of any film-star. The rebels rage against the ex-queen's stately appearances in the years of her power and splen-dour. Yet they cannot spot her among the aeroplane passengers, and are ready to believe it when Irene Worth as the prostitute pronounces that she is the hunted lady. If that can be swallowed, the play makes good theatrical sense.

Yet, even with Miss Worth's presence, it was less moving than it might have been. Under Frank Hauser's direction, she struck attitudes and orated when she might have been simple and poignant. Presumably in order to establish prostitute-status she wore 'tarty' shoes with heels so extravagantly high that she seemed to be walking on stilts, and stilts naturally make movement stilted. Thus handicapped in gait she found it difficult to be her natural, compelling self. The emotional appeal of her vibrant voice was diminished by a too powerful use of it. This actress can drive at the heart as few others can: but my heart, for once, remained unfluttered. The performance of Gwendoline Watford as the real queen was, on the other hand, extremely effective. In the contest between the quiet little victim of persecution and her flamboyantly defiant defender it was quietude that prevailed. Icily, impressively quiet too was Leo McKern as a persecuting and prosecuting Commissar: very rarely did he shout and always did he grip me as he imposed the horrible fascination of a human stoat among the rabbits. His part was well written as well as admirably rendered.

Plays, especially in the busy time of autumn, have to go where they can be fitted in. The Haymarket audiences are used, as a rule, to the English scene and to the comfortable comedy of our time and place. Signor Betti's tense and tragical lifting of the steely European curtain might have done better at another address and Miss Worth might have done better than well with another kind of direction; less than well she can never do.

Jesuitical

THE STRONG ARE LONELY
by Fritz Hochwalder, translated by Eva le Gallienne
Piccadilly and Haymarket Theatres

Since the Serious Theatre has depended so much lately on Classic Revivals this drama of religious controversy was welcomed and rightly so. Scarcity value may have over-emphasized its merits. On the other hand, the production was unhelpful and may have obscured some of its potential qualities.

The time of the piece is 1767. The place is a College of the Jesuit Fathers in Buenos Aires. Inspired and led by their

38

Father Provincial, Alfonso Fernandez, the Jesuits are building up a Utopian corner of a Spanish Dominion, protecting the Indians against exploitation by the slave-driving type of Spanish settler and rescuing them from poverty and even starvation. They are also rescuing Christianity from being a mumble of pious formulae and making it the basis of a Welfare State. But they are chargeable with arming the Indians and creating a separate community inside the Spanish realms: and that is intolerable in the eyes of the King of Spain, and of course the brutish type of colonial employer wishes them in hell.

The King sends his envoy, Don Pedro, to put the Jesuits in their place. This idealistic nonsense of theirs must be called off. Madrid has no use and no mercy for such deviation from its own ideas of Christian-Capitalist-Imperialism. Putting ideas into the heads of aboriginals! This is treasonable practice. But the Father Provincial, who has zealous and devoted priests on his side, defies Don Pedro and his dictates from Madrid. The Jesuits are doing God's work and God's work must be done, even if it means direct defiance of the secular authority. So far, so gallant.

But Madrid and Rome have more than secular power on their side. A wolf in sheep's clothing arrives on the scene, Signor Querini. The signore is, in fact, a highly placed Jesuit masquerading as a layman. He brings the fiat of the Order. It is no business of the Jesuits, he says, to play at politics, to be the architects of Utopia, and to translate Christianity into terms of liberty, fraternity and full stomachs for mere Indians. Let the Fathers preach salvation, not Socialism. The kingdom of Heaven is hereafter and is better approached, in the case of Indians, by prayer and fasting than by reasonable wages and well-fed bodies. Querini's doctrine is the familiar one of 'Pie in the Sky'. Here on earth Pie is for Spaniards only.

Faced with what he accepts as the word of God proceeding from God's ambassador the Father Provincial, who had stood up to the word of Caesar, collapses in an agonised but humiliating surrender. The seemingly burly, self-confident saviour of the Indians turns to a quivering jelly. The civil power of Spain he will defy: but against the Church and his own religious Order he will not say a syllable or move a hand. Reluctantly, but abjectly and absolutely, he betrays his Indians; to oblige Querini he abandons all his hopes, all his plans, all his humanity. One of

39

his priests has more gumption and determines to fight it out, but, betrayed by his own religious leader and faced with the military force of Spain, he goes to his death, leaving the Father Provincial to beat his bosom and salve his conscience with a lot of holy talk. Fortunately for the creature he does not have to survive long in his abasement. He stops a bullet when the guns go off and, if his soul finds entrance to heaven difficult, it is deservedly so. He has failed in his hour of trial.

At least so it must seem to the Protestant or to the agnostic. The play is a terrifying exposure of Roman Catholic autocracy working on the side of a ruthless white supremacy and a ruthless exploitation of the native Indians. The lay envoy, Don Pedro, is obeying orders from Madrid in a soldierly way and is allowed to show some dignity and the qualities of a gentleman. The commanding Jesuit, Querini, is merely cruelty incarnate, a human snake who injects his poison into the budding community of freedom and happiness and gladly sees it die while the Father Provincial is accepting his diabolism as the word of God. I do not know whether Roman Catholics deny the truth of Herr Hochwalder's story. The outline of the affair is certainly authentic. If the interpretation is also true to what actually occurred, it is an anti-clerical indictment of shattering force. If it is unfair, in part or in whole, they have good cause to protest, for nothing could show the Jesuitical discipline in a worse light. The Father Provincial has tried to behave with some humanity. But, because he is a good Jesuit before he is a good man, he has to recant and grovel and leave those whom he has raised from the depths of mundane misery to sink back into their hunger and their chains. It is a devastating treachery.

Here, then, is a notable indictment of a creed and of an Order. Is it a notable play? The title is a foolish one. The strong ones in the story are the many, the myrmidons of Church and State. The lonely figure is that of Father Oros who refuses to accept the betrayal of the Indians and is shot in cold blood for his honourable obstinacy, while his superior, the Father Provincial, is making his surrender. A play whose seeming hero turns out to be the craven servant of an abominable discipline is under handicap. High tragedy creates, or is supposed to create, some sense of human greatness in the ruin of a flawed nobility. But THE STRONG ARE LONELY leaves one only with a loathing of a form of religion that can thus disguise itself and become the tool

40

of cruel and self-seeking men. What has Querini to do with Christianity in whose name he destroys any effort to behave as the Jesus of the Gospels would have done?

I could not conceive why Donald Wolfit chose to play the Father Provincial. His versatility is beyond question. He can handle a wide range of parts admirably, but spiritual fanaticism is the one thing to which his robust and common-sensible presence seems alien. The Father Provincial first burns with spiritual ardour for his great experiment in making Spanish Imperialism humane; later, he is so much a man of his spiritual faith that, when the plenipotentiary of that faith orders him to abandon all his good works and to betray the miserable people who trust him, he accepts this nefarious order and grovels.

The part asks for a man of infinite dedication, a lean and hungry zealot. Mr Wolfit, with all his abilities, is not the actor for that part. He would have been happier cast as Don Pedro, the man of the world, the servant of Caesar who has at least some regrets for the foul duties that his office necessitates, a part which Robert Harris played well, but not so well, I fancy, as he would have played the Father Provincial. Ernest Milton was duly serpentine and venomous as the detestable Querini, but he was much hampered in his work, having to coil himself in a corner when, though silent, he should be clearly seen; for on the play of his features one should read the soul of Jesuitry and see the hinted shape of the icy cruelty that is to come. Still, with all its faults of presentation, here was a play with matter in it, a play for adults who are not terrified by the prospect of seeing problems of human behaviour presented in dramatic form with no irrelevant invasions of sex – not a woman in the cast – and with no shirking in its revelation of what devilry one species of religion can achieve.

The Problem King

RICHARD III
A film directed by Sir Laurence Olivier *Leicester Square Cinema*

The film of RICHARD III had even greater réclame than that of HENRY V. On the wings of Television it swept across the United States before it was shown there upon a thousand screens. Its dollar-earnings were so vast that it might have been several ship-loads of Scotch whisky. We were assured that it had gained for British prestige all that our diplomats and statesmen had been losing. Immediately after its showing, a friend in Philadelphia wrote to me that more people in America must have seen RICHARD III in one day than have seen the play's production in 'live' theatres down the centuries. The newspaper 'coverage' was immense. 'Now are our brows bound with victorious wreaths', observes Shakespeare's Crookback in the opening of his opening speech. They were indeed.

At any Quiz, Brains Trust, or parley of that popular kind I am accustomed to being asked, 'What would Shakespeare have thought of being filmed?' I am in no position to speak for the mighty dead, but, having made some study of the man's life, I suppose that my guess is as good as that of most. My answer is that he would have revelled in this profitable process. The text has, admittedly, to be cut. But he was used to having his texts trimmed, and that drastically, in the theatre, and he cannot have shared the belief fervently held by some of our Shakespeareans, that every word was sacred. (This point is further considered in my article in this volume called 'Harry in the Night'.) Moreover Shakespeare was certainly fond of money and much that he earned he saved and invested. He was of country stock and believed in the useful reality of 'real estate'. That he and his colleagues would have shrunk from selling film-rights for sums dazzling to their eyes is, to me, inconceivable.

After all, he was restless under the limitations of his platform stage, and protested at the mockery of mighty warfare by 'four or five most vile and ragged foils, right ill disposed in brawl ridiculous', which was all his company could produce. Would he not have welcomed the ample armoury supplied by Mr Rank, and the admirable service rendered to his battlescapes by Sir Laurence in HENRY V and now in RICHARD III? HAMLET gave less scope for the pictorial, but in HENRY V we had been as near as might be to 'the very casques that did affright the air at Agincourt'. Bosworth Field was said by some to be not so lavishly equestrian in its spectacle. But it was good enough for me.

RICHARD III, with more of helter-skelter and less of the finest poetry, with the meanderings from one murder to the next, with its luridness of character and its parade of 15th century panoply, was asking for film, especially for film in colour. Why should Shakespeare cavil at the mechanism which gave him, instead of denying him, the 'vasty fields' of a war? He lamented 'this unworthy scaffold' which the stagecraft and theatrical architecture of his time provided. Why then deplore cinemascope and all the magical rest of it? He would have insisted, no doubt, that his words, though cut, should be decently respected and he might have objected strongly to the drastic truncations and re-arrangements made by Orson Welles, who believes that a film should be a film first and foremost and considers a Shakespeare text to be a plinth for his skilful use and not a statue for his pious preservation. But to Sir Laurence's far more reverent methods Shakespeare could not object, while to that actor's own performance he must have responded with the admiration of one who was himself an actor, as well as an author.

The question of time arises. In our theatres we play Shakespeare at three hours' length (and sometimes more), but we have at least one longish pause or two shorter ones in which to rest the surfeited eye and ear and release the pent-up limbs. Sir Laurence made the film of RICHARD III to last two hours and three-quarters, with no interval. I make no question of the film's grandeur, but I do not think I am alone in finding this too much for enjoyment. The seating in most cinemas, as in most theatres, is naturally designed to accommodate as many people and take as much money as possible and the designers make the absurd assumption that all the patrons are of the same size. This bears very hardly on the large and fairly large and on the nearly arthritic seniors who, during a sitting of this length may begin to suffer the 'dry convulsions' and the 'aged cramps' which Prospero inflicted upon Caliban. Why not, by the way, divide theatre and cinema seating into large and small as well as near and far, and vary the prices accordingly? Space means money and might reasonably be bought at varying prices without loss to the house's 'capacity' takings.

Furthermore, the cinema makes an especial strain upon the eye, and I, for one, cannot pay more than two hours' incessant attention to the screen without optical weariness and aching. Many, I fancy, feel the same constriction and the same fatigue. I therefore prefer, in the cinema, a two hours' traffic of our screen; one hundred and twenty minutes make up the time-scheme expressly mentioned by Shakespeare in the prologue to ROMEO AND JULIET, whose full text can hardly be played in

43

less than three hours. The middle reaches of RICHARD III might have been shortened by Sir Laurence with advantage, but that was my only grievance as the Duke of Gloucester went his maleficent way up the bloody steps to a throne and along the road to ruin whose end was the ghosted carnage of Bosworth Field. The latter, incidentally, was notably un-English in aspect; but if he who cries 'A horse, a horse!' can only find his mounts and his cavalry 'supers' in sufficient and economic supply by making a trip to Spain, the excuse is good enough. We do not judge melodrama by the map or go to tragical-historical for accuracy in landscape.

The stars of our English stage had been assembled in galaxy. The knighthood was in force. Sir Ralph Richardson was admirably puzzled as poor Buckingham who so foolishly forgot to take his long spoon with him when he supped with the devil. Sir John Gielgud gave in the brief role of Clarence all the fine shades of our best Shakespearean voice while adding to the splendours of the Nightmare Speech:

'then came wandering by
A shadow like an angel, with bright hair'.

The promise of the hand of glory is manifest there, as in

'Their lips were four red roses on a stalk'.

(The magical play with the r's is perfect Shakespeare.) Such good things were not omitted.

The text, in the preparation of which Alan Dent was, as usual, a wise co-operator, received its proper honours; in this service Sir John was naturally prominent. Sir Cedric Hardwicke was there to play the crumbling Edward IV. That monarch was, we are told, a stalwart of 'bodie mightie', according to Holinshed, an over-eater in later years and 'corpulent', in youth 'greatly given to fleshlie wantonness'. Men aged more quickly then, and the shrunken and seemingly elderly invalid presented, though not according to Holinshed, was based, I presume, on other medical evidence. The much-vexed Queens had to be shown with some omission, but the team with Helen Haye, Claire Bloom, and Mary Kerridge, was excellent in force, poignance, and variety. Pamela Brown lurked behind the throne as Jane Shore, the sovereign beauty of the period, to whom Shakespeare made frequent allusion in RICHARD III without allotting her a part. It was surely reasonable to let the lady intrude her coaxing presence while remaining a vision without a voice.

44

Sir Laurence's Richard was less of a lurid monster and less an ogre of deformity than he gave us on the stage; no longer so melodramatically magnetic, he was the more persuasive. Is the conventional portrait of the 'cacodemon', which Shakespeare accepted, a scandalous and libellous falsehood? We are now constantly urged to believe that Richard III is one of the most foully maligned men in history. We are assured that he so excelled in humane government and kindly consideration of his family that he really merited the canonization which came to his traducer, Sir Thomas More. Shakespeare, of course, did not know that the Public Relations Officers of Henry VII may have been sedulously working to load every crime – as we are now told – upon the man whom Henry toppled off the throne. If Shakespeare had known this, the best he could have done was to preserve a tactful silence. Holinshed, an Elizabethan, was careful to describe Henry VII as 'more the angelicall creature than a terrestriall personage'. In the reign of Queen Elizabeth a play would not have been well regarded in which her grandfather was portrayed as far from 'angelicall' and as a usurper, a liar, a murderer, and actually responsible for the very atrocity by which Richard has been made infamous, namely the slaughter of the little princes in the Tower.

I can only claim a considerable ignorance of English mediaeval history: as a child I was brought up on the familiar vision of Richard as Shakespeare's fiend, the 'elvish-markt, abortive, rooting hog, the slave of nature and the son of hell', Richard the bottled spider and the hunchbacked toad. So it was an entertaining surprise to read 'The Daughter of Time' in which Josephine Tey, another pen-name of the late Miss Mackintosh who was also the dramatist Gordon Daviot, made a detective-story inquiry into the life and character of Richard and ripped to pieces the Tudor propagandists' portrait of a fiend incarnate. She triumphantly left the hunchbacked horror erect and stainless, almost, indeed, 'ensky'd and sainted'. The august historians and academic mandarins maintain that she is wrong. Miss Mackintosh is, alas, dead and cannot carry on the debate or protest her indignation at the conveyance to millions all over the world of the Tudor notion of Crookback. But there are many on her side, and I am sure that they must agree that, if the familiar, and possibly false, picture of the diabolic Richard must be kept in distribution, there could be no better distributor than Sir Laurence.

He gave to the film-figure a wonderful profile of the sly, self-confident evil-doer. I matched this again at the National Portrait Gallery with the anxious, considerate Richard there on display. 'Look here upon this picture and on this'. They were as far apart as the elder Hamlet and Claudius. Here is a problem king indeed. But the old portraits can be very problematical. For example, Henry V hangs in the Gallery, side by side with Richard III. The Henry portrait must be no less of a shock to those who have been brought up with the usual notions of a robust, romantic hero. Harry by day is a very different person from Harry of the playhouse night.

The painted head is long and thin: the expression gentle and ascetic. The attitude is demure. No young man of this aspect would be a likely toss-pot in the company of Falstaff, Doll Tearsheet and the malt-worms, or a joiner in impudent outrages upon the bourgeoisie. Nor can one begin to imagine him as the warlike king who 'assumes the port of Mars' and 'imitates the action of the tiger', who leads with valour as well as with rhetoric the assault through perilous breaches and clambers to victory on the bodies of the dead. Here is the face, almost, of a pale young curate; certainly the cast of thought is shadowing it o'er and giving it a pallid and a dedicated air. If its owner ever painted the town any colour, it was not red but off-white. This Henry might be a candidate for a monastery and this portrait of a would-be recluse would much better suit his successor, the sixth Harry, over whose crown the turbulent barons fought their tedious wars while he, in piety, was founding schools, colleges, and fanes, the Royal Saint of Wordsworth's famous sonnet on King's College Chapel.

Alec Guinness, commenting in a letter to Sir Sydney Cockerell on the criticisms of Gielgud's Macbeth, which blamed the actor for seeming insufficiently tough, wrote that, in his war-time naval experience, great fighters did not often look the part. That is also true of scoundrels who may be cherubs to the eye. So the portrait of Richard III is only supporting evidence for the kindly estimation of his deeds and for the granting of a certificate of good character. Looks, like hopes, may be liars, as Shakespeare himself knew when he made Duncan reflect: 'There's no art to find the mind's construction in the face'. So I shall leave the problem of the problem king for the historians to resolve: they will not be assisted in their search for exact historical truth by Sir Laurence's notable direction of the film and enactment of the past. But they will have much more pleasure from the (nearly) 'three hours' traffic' of his film than from three hundred hours of further delving in the archives of the Record Office.

Harry in the Night

HENRY V
by William Shakespeare   *Old Vic Theatre*

When Richard Burton joined the 'Old Vic' company in December to play HENRY V, both producer and players responded by finding their best form. The decoration by Audrey Cruddas, always a good contriver of the painted stage, relied on colour and grouping: we had only the hints of scenery, no embarkation fleet, no walls of Harfleur. 'Once more unto the breach' was delivered without architecture; a pattern of massed assault troops with their standards in centre-stage offered ample suggestion of the battle. A graceful map of the Channel and the rival shores made the early background: after that there was the sky and 'poring dark'. These were ample.

Since Shakespeare has, through the Chorus, expressly apologized for his lack of scenery and military apparatus, it is always silly to impose 'sets' of any kind on Southampton and the stricken fields of France. In this case the bare stage, peopled and caparisoned only by the surge of Shakespeare's battle-music and verbal brass, was abundantly filled. There was, however, one mistake. We are directly told to imagine the horses of the cavalry. Why then introduce into the 'French Lords' Scene' wooden steeds while the Dauphin rants about his Pegasus, that prince of palfreys, whose neigh is like the bidding of a monarch? The carpentered contraptions provided for the knights and cavaliers of Gallia only managed to look ludicrous. No doubt, it would break the heart of the actor playing the Dauphin if this scene were cut, but it is a tiresome interruption of the war and I note that in the short Quarto text, which probably represents one of the contemporary acting versions of HENRY V, it was drastically truncated.

Hereby hangs a puzzle, for me one of the many, great and fascinating puzzles inherent in the work of Shakespeare. The

Quarto text of HENRY V, in whose title the names of Agincourt and Pistol are included, thus advertising the 'hits' of the first production a year or so earlier, was printed by Thomas Creede for sale in Carter Lane in 1600. It is less than half the length of the Folio text of 1623. It omits ten characters as well as much of the discourse which impedes action. It is a fair conjecture, effectively argued by M. R. Ridley in his introduction to the New Temple edition, that there was a pirated replica of what had been enacted and would be re-enacted in revivals. This drastic surgery fits in with the famous phrase about the 'two hours' traffic of our stage'. HENRY V, as printed in the First Folio, could only have been got through in two hours with a wild gabbling of the lines which would rob them of their quality and meaning. The same is true of nearly all the major Shakespearean plays: MACBETH, of which the Folio text may be much nearer to an acting version, is an exception.

The puzzle is this. Shakespeare was essentially a man of the theatre: he knew the needs and conditions of pleasing the public: he must have known the discipline of the time-keeper. He was immensely busy, not least in 1599 when, before the return of Essex from Ireland in August, HENRY V took the stage. He was actor, 'sharer', as well as writer, deeply and profitably involved in all the affairs of his fellowship. He was a supremely practical man, as well as a supremely poetical man. Why then did he write at such length when he knew that so much of what he wrote would never be acted?

That would be easily explained if he had been careful to publish his work. If he said to himself, 'This is the play I wanted to write, the play I had to write, but the public would never endure so long a text and the players would never bother to learn it', and had then written at length for readers now and to come, he would surely have seen to it in his lifetime – as Ben Jonson did see to it – that his texts were carefully preserved in full. Perhaps he could not stop pirated and truncated versions of his successes being made and sold. But he could have arranged his own First Folio of complete texts and so had the due reward of his industry, which was sadly excessive industry if the players only wanted a modicum of what he poured out.

As it happened it is a mere, but infinitely blessed, fluke that we have the full text and, in the case of many of the best plays, any text at all. If Heminges and Condell had died soon after

Edith Evans and Peggy Ashcroft in THE CHALK GARDEN
at the Haymarket (*Angus McBean*)

Alan Webb and Ann Walford in MISALLIANCE
at the Lyric, Hammersmith (*Angus McBean*)

Shakespeare, if there had been another of the frequent conflagrations, one of which burned down the Globe Theatre in June, 1613, there would have been no Folio and the world would only have had the Shakespeare of the Quartos. Shakespeare, accordingly, is in the position of having written these lengthy texts, knowing that much of them would be cut and not caring whether they survived in printed form: in other words he poured out his glorious poetry in order to get it out of his system and to have the excitement, as well as the toil, of writing at length, whether anybody wanted the stuff or not.

At this point the anti-Stratfordian will inevitably intervene to say that Shakespeare never did write the stuff. It was by the great Anon., be he Bacon, Oxford, Derby, Marlowe, or any other of the score of runners entered for these stakes. But, if I am told that Bacon, or any others of the learned and lordly nominees, created Falstaff, Bardolph, Nym, Pistol and Doll Tearsheet, I must remain completely incredulous. The plays – and HENRY V is ample proof – were written by an actor who had knocked about the town and met the malt-worms and the rag-tag camp-followers who knew how to make profit from the rearward of the battle. But why that actor-genius was ready to write – and then let go – so much more than his fellow-actors wanted is a psychological problem which can only be met by saying that a man with a bellyful of words is going to be relieved of them, come what may.

What we had at the 'Old Vic' was most of the Folio text. There were a few welcome cuts and I was glad to be spared the archiepiscopal lecture on the State of Man and the moral to be drawn from the honey-bees, a passage wisely and naturally cut in the Quarto. But the same speaker was permitted the whole of his enormous discourse upon Salic Law: the courtiers were shown yawning, while he prated, but the comedy of this is insufficient to prevent yawns of our own. I suppose that it is a heresy to say that Shakespeare began HENRY V indifferently, risked considerable tedium, and was well served by the cutters. But it seems to be a case of Homer nodding so lengthily as to make us nod ourselves. By 1599 Shakespeare was master of his craft and had repeatedly shown that he knew the theatrical value of a quick start. It is the more odd that he should have so botched, with a wearisome loquacity, the beginning of HENRY V.

49   D

Once away, we travelled, under Michael Benthall's direction, with a proper speed. It had obviously been noted that the 'Ancient Pistol' and his gang were an important part of the original attractions, as the Quarto's sub-title attests. On this occasion they were given their chance and took it. Pistol is usually a bore. If he was a parody of the rival players down the road the joke is inevitably dead for us. But Richard Wordsworth contrived to make the swaggering grandiloquence congenial. Though I did not care much for the Bardolph, I found Nym (Job Stewart) excellent company. Nym usually goes for nothing, but the sad little scoundrel presented by Mr Stewart was intensely human and in excellent contrast with the alcoholic ebullience of the others. Rachel Roberts, too, as Mistress Quickly, now hazardously mated with Pistol, gave us an intensely human piece of companionable sluttishness and delivered the account of Falstaff's end with devastating simplicity and the right awareness that a passage which has become so famous should be delivered as though it were not famous at all.

And so to Harry, a curious stage-character, about whom, perhaps, Shakespeare never made up his mind. The turning-down of Falstaff can be explained as less than the ungenerous and even contemptible action it may seem: the old rascal had been warned by Prince Hal that condoning of debauchery and even crime could not go on for ever. King Henry would soon have his duty and discipline to enforce. None the less it was brutally done and both Pistol and his wife assert that the King has broken the heart of his old companion in mischief and so hastened his death. Harry is also snobbish and sanctimonious. After alluding to his army as 'we band of brothers' he reads out the English casualty list after Agincourt with a dismissal of the 'other ranks' as inconsiderable. This is ugly to our ears. A Duke, an Earl, a Knight, an Esquire – and then 'none else of name'. He is waging a selfish and inexcusable war of aggression. His prayer before the battle is a deplorable reminder to God of favours earned by pious deeds; he has expiated his father's crime; he has wept for and re-buried the murdered Richard II; he has built two chantries where masses are sung for Richard's soul; he has given doles to the needy, 'Five hundred poor I have in yearly pay'. Christian conduct, no doubt, but not nicely urged as a plea for divine aid in battle. He orders the killing of prisoners before the French slaughter of the English boys, who are guarding the luggage of the camp, offers him at least the excuse of claiming a corpse for a corpse.

But these things hardly touch the normal auditor in the heat of the play-house and amid the noise of simulated battle. To them he is the Happy Warrior, the Spirit of England in arms (never mind the origin and purpose of the war), and the Public Orator of the tented field, as valorous as orotund. His speeches in verse are martial music; in prose he unpersuasively argues his way out of responsibility for the carnage he has caused, but the argument is subtle and therefore not commonly noted, whereas the calls to gallantry are no more subtle than a brass band and therefore well calculated to stir even the laziest listener. Naturally the part goes to an actor who is already a favourite, one who has dash, voice, looks, and communicable passion. He wins his audience with his romantic rhetoric as easily as he thrashes the French army with the aid of God and wins the French Princess with the aid of a strong position and the inarticulate charm that comes with a smattering of stammered French.

Mr Burton suavely cloaked the nastier aspects of his Henry with the likeableness of his personality and the agreeable quality of his looks and voice. He certainly did not make the error of delivering the 'Unto the breach' oration outside the walls of Harfleur with the timid cough of an extra-mural lecturer. The lines came crashing over, as though they were round after round of artillery: then, having demonstrated his quality as a gunner, he shrewdly sapped and mined at our affections like an engineer. He was almost conversational in 'What's he that wishes so?' Rightly, for this is a talk with his staff-officers and not an address to the rank and file. The Ceremony Speech was rendered with great feeling and finesse. If I remember rightly, the romantic actors used to give these passages 'the full works', but Mr Burton is not a romantic: he drove into the meaning of his lines instead of gloriously posing and ranting on their surface. Something of the metrical value must be lost by this method, but, whereas our fathers cared much for the music of the verse, the audience of today is ready to concentrate on meaning if that be transmitted, as it was, by a performance in which the mind has its place. In the study one has plenty of reason for disliking Harry of Monmouth: in the theatre one surrenders to 'a little touch of Harry in the night' and Mr Burton's touch was sovereign.

John Neville delivered the Chorus speeches in a high, histrionic manner: why not? They contain high, histrionic stuff. I have heard them pattered in the 'throw-it-away' style of modern naturalism. That is absurd folly. This talk of swelling scenes, vasty fields, air-affrighting casques, port of Mars, and so on is not to be endured if offered in a fire-side, television style. Rant is to be ranted and Mr Neville was quite right to sound the tucket and beat the drum. He was hindered by a most unmilitary hair-do with a great pile of up-brushed forelock. Chorus must not thus resemble a cockatoo when he is soaring like an eagle over 'the high-upreared and abutting fronts' of 'mighty monarchies'. I have seen no better Fluellen than that of Dudley Jones.

Small Town

MORNING'S AT SEVEN
by Paul Osborn   *Comedy and Westminster Theatres*

The Comedy Theatre was re-opened, after necessary reconstruction and adornment, with the now almost inevitable import: but it was not an import of which one could sourly inquire whether its journey was really necessary. There was a case for producing MORNING'S AT SEVEN, though I could see no case for that particular title.

The scene may be described as Small Town, Depressed American middle-class. The characters are mostly senile and retired from their life-work: four sisters, *nées* Swanson, three married and one an aggrieved spinster, live and chatter in close proximity. One of the husbands is a professor Emeritus, trailing a few clouds of merit and some wisps of whimsy, for he has a bat or two in his scholastic belfry: another appears to be a kind of plumber whose life has been withered because he has failed to become a dentist. He is left with drills and forceps rattling in his bonnet. The third husband is comparatively sane, but he has had his guilty moments with the spinster-sister. Youth (or comparative youth) is represented by a moronic booby who has been 'going with' an eager, gay woman and has reached early middle age without the courage to marry her. His girl is a starry-eyed zany who believes the oaf to be an Apollo.

What happens? Very little. Everybody makes the obvious remark and bickers in the obvious way. Could anything sound more dismal? Yet out of nothing something came. Mr Osborn, without too obviously pitying this company of dolts, showed some affection for them and his comedy was genial where it might have been cruel. With strange skill he showed that the conversation of small-town failures, reported with no effort to throw in the wise-crack, can be made to hold the attention and arouse sympathy. In a way his play could be called a triumph of the conversational dull thud, of the bromide turned into a stimulant.

There was little action, beyond the comings and goings of entangled and quarrelsome relatives; there was nearly everything that a student of How To Write Plays would be taught to avoid. There was triteness which was not tedious and daftness which was not made unpleasant and embarrassing. It is one of the fascinations of the theatre that a man can win there by refusing to be theatrical. All the good counsel can be neglected and good theatre emerge in the end. It does not depend only on the actors, for this play was badly cast in some respects. The success here was won by a quite unabashed simplicity, warmed with a nice tolerance of the human silliness which is nobody's fault: these people never could be much in the world: they have given up trying to be anything much: they are, with the exception of the spinster, rumbling along to their end, some dottily, some with mild splutters of protest, some with docility, and all, save one, likeably.

The critics, spying sisters and frustration, muttered 'School of Chekhov'. There was no case for such high comparisons. The piece reminded me of the still-life realism that became fashionable in the more advanced English 'reps' after the Galsworthy and Granville-Barker epoch. The acting, with mostly English players managing pretty well to fit their voices into the American scene, was of mixed quality. Peter Jones, ejaculating the obvious and idiotic observations of the 'clot' without a spark of initiative, was admirably matched by the innocent inanity of Miss Tucker McGuire as the girl who thought this goose to be not only a swan but a bird of paradise. Among the elders Frederick Leister, Mona Washbourne and Nan Monro fitted best into the pattern of life's evening, seen from a small-town backyard. Margaret Vines, as the odd woman out, gave a memorable picture of an unquiet and revengeful spirit pent up in a thin parcel of nervous fidgets.

53

More Listeries

FRESH AIRS
A Revue by Michael Flanders and Donald Swann
Comedy Theatre

Messrs Lister and Adrian, creators of the very successful AIRS ON A SHOESTRING, contrived to do it again. The shoestring economies were not meagrely repeated: the production, slickly and prettily staged, may be said to have reached almost boot-lace proportions. The introductory item announced that this was to be a conventional revue: there would be no self-conscious eccentricity. The music in that case would be humbly agreeable and not imposingly atonic; there would be no airs on a foghorn. Max Adrian and Moyra Fraser would be themselves again, and so they were. A good time, it was hoped, would be had by nearly all and so it was. Words and music by Messrs Flanders and Swann were mostly admirable.

Immediately after the players' modest exposition of the scope of things to come, I had a few doubts. There was a stale and ineffective sketch about the hard treatment of authors by actors and producers: are we not all aware by now that the drama is the most co-operative of the arts and habitually prac-tised by people who are wholly incapable of co-operation? Nor was Moyra Fraser up to her own gay standard of mockery when she appeared as a sunflower and led us up the garden to no-where in particular.

But things soon mended. The House of Lords, eager for work at Westminster if paid for clocking-in and hurriedly joined by Lord Attlee, allured by the new wage-structure, made excellent company. It was a strong point in this entertainment that politics were not barred. The idea that the lighter show must always dis-cover its levity by laughing at the serious theatre has become tedious. There is a larger world in which to find targets and surely a larger audience which has heard of our statesmen. A feature called Volk Song was very much to the point in its com-mentary on Germany revived and re-helmeted: the satire here was sharp, quick, and justified, proper to a show designed for

54

adults and not merely for seekers of after-dinner triviality. So it was too in a neat song about the policies of the Tory and the Labour parties. How hard to quarrel about planks in the platform when both are using the same timber!

Incidentally, FRESH AIRS began at the civilised hour of half past eight. Revue is not to be taken on an empty stomach, the condition still forced upon us by the obstinate addiction to the 7.30 or even 7 o'clock opening. A later start may lose the bus-party from Luton: but there are some London play-goers still resident in London or lodged in its hotels who do not want to be bustled through a high tea or to seek their pleasure with only a drink and a snack rumbling sadly in a gastric vacuum. The five-thirty matinée, with a cup of tea behind and a proper meal to come, is an excellent device for combining the service of the eye and mind with that of the inner man. But Saturday is not the only day of play-going. A few more of the eight or eight-thirty starts would be more in accordance with the time-table of those living, or staying, in a capital and not driven to frantic fidgets by thoughts of the last bus.

Max Adrian, having initially commented on the fact that he is showing his age, proceeded to give himself the lie by much nimbleness of foot and more of wit. He has the right kind of gaiety for Revue, since he can be incisive without loss of geniality. What he debunks he does not insult. When he canes some public nuisance he seems to be saying to his victim, 'This amuses me more than it hurts you'.

Moyra Fraser has long limbs which she can use with wit, as though they were an excrescence of the mind. Having danced her way to fame in the orthodoxy of ballet, she now skips and scampers into another species of eminence, that of revue's tease and tomboy. She has the kind of large and rolling eyes which are said to speak volumes and the books, in her case, contain *contes drolatiques*. Her ditty on a partridge in a pear tree hit that bird fair and square. Rose Hill, in nice contrast, has a rosebud demureness, a sly humour, and an excellent voice. She was delightful as a lass who followed the domestic fashion of essaying to perform on the recorder. The young ladies of yesterday went to the piano: ours would a-flauting go and Miss Hill attempted and mastered her first pirri-pirri with such innocent joy that she must have tempted many another to hope that Hamlet spoke truth when he observed of performing with this instrument,

"'Tis as easy as lying: govern these ventages with your finger and thumb and it will discourse most eloquent music'.

The company was small and all its members had talent and chances. There were no chorines who could do nothing but show a leg and a smile, cut a caper and no more. When they had acting to do they acted and were neat in the trick of it. The level of singing was much higher than usual in revue. The chief academy from which the talent was drawn, according to a nicely informative and biographical programme, was the Guildhall School of Music. Since I spent much of my working life in Fleet Street hard by this nest of singing birds I used sometimes to wish its vocalism at a further distance. I forgive it now. It seems to teach acting as well as it does harmony and its Former Pupils at the Comedy Theatre were adding present mirth for the winning of present laughter.

Salute to Shaw

MISALLIANCE
by George Bernard Shaw   *Lyric Theatre, Hammersmith*

The Shaw Centenary Celebrations of 1956 began with a production of MISALLIANCE, an interesting choice since it is so rarely played. I have seen most of Shaw in revivals of varied quality, but stage acquaintance with the Tarleton family and the lady acrobat I had missed. It was nice to catch up with them.

MISALLIANCE has a mammoth preface on the subject of children and education. It is not an example of Shaw at his best. In one quality Shaw was here, as always, beyond criticism, that is in lucidity. He continually wrote much which would challenge disagreement; to be challenging and combative was his purpose; but he never wrote a line that was vague, indecisive, or obscure. He may have hit the wrong nail on the head time and again. But, at whatever nail he aimed that hammer-pen of his, he hit it hard and he hit it clean; there was no dull thud from any blow that he struck, but a clear and ringing sound. There is so much misty, muddled writing in our time that his clarity comes like an entrancing surprise. Can Shaw be imagined exclaiming to his public as a speaker, or to his readers as a writer, 'I think I know what I mean, but I can't express myself'? He would have regarded

56

that, as I regard it myself, as a disgraceful confession of incompetence. It is the first business of those who set out to say or write things to be efficient in communication. A cloudy, incoherent writer is failing in his primary duty to his public as well as betraying his own ideas by wrapping them in sentences that wander into a tangled incoherence.

Shaw was guilty in his MISALLIANCE preface of an offence which he rarely committed. He repeated himself: he would not lay down the hammer; he battered his nail until it vanished in the wood. The arrogance of parents who take up an attitude of divine omniscience and all-righteousness in the company of their children was part of his theme: the stupidity and brutality of our education was the rest of it. For more than a hundred pages he flogged the flagellants.

Shaw himself admits that he was spared the worst of it; he claims to have been mis-educated mentally; he does not say that he was maltreated physically. Of course all exceptional children have grievances against their teachers, who are, for the most part, ordinary people dealing with unlikely material. This is not to insult the teaching profession. The number of first-raters are few and these soon rise to exceptional positions in their calling or clear out to much better paid posts in other ones. The rank and file of pedagogues are tackling one of the hardest jobs in the world in discouraging surroundings with inadequate equipment and salaries insufficient to allow them a full and civilised life. We can, I think, fairly claim that most of our teaching is not so crassly or so cruelly done as when Shaw was a boy in Ireland and when the breed of Squeers and Creakle were still savagely plying their canes in England.

MISALLIANCE was written in 1910 and much of Shaw's attack was even then out of date. I was myself going through an English Public School, the kind of institution that Shaw conceived to be a mixture of Bedlam and Belsen. With all its faults of snobbishness and narrowness, it was not in that class at all. My curriculum was so intensely classical that one would have thought that mankind existed only between 800 B.C. and 100 A.D. But, after all, more good prose and poetry were written in those centuries than has been turned out in vast stretches of subsequent history and all the essential problems of ethics, politics, and metaphysics were clearly posed and cogently discussed by the ancient Greeks, who were starting from the alpha of

57

philosophy and reached the omega with miraculous speed. It is true that their works can be read in translation, but there is some advantage in studying the original for the reason that Ancient Greek is probably the subtlest as well as the finest sounding language invented by man. Shaw in Dublin seems to have acquired less Latin and still less Greek than Shakespeare in Stratford. But his own academic misfortunes provide no cause for dynamiting our seats of traditional learning. Of these he knew nothing by direct experience and heard much, I suppose, from the Socialists and 'odd men out' of his acquaintance who were likely to be misfits and disgruntled in any society where there was a conventional discipline and an acceptance of custom.

The preface to MISALLIANCE is very loosely attached to the play which has little to say about education. In one respect it seems to contradict the preface. One of the characters, Bentley Summerhays, who has been spared (or rapidly escaped from) the supposed factory of fools and bullies that was Shaw's idea of a Public School, and has been given the privilege of private tutoring, is certainly no advertisement for dodging the normal routine. He has become an egotistic, neurotic, and tedious nuisance and is properly snubbed and put in his place by Johnny Tarleton who is a Public School product. Johnny is made to seem what we now call 'a bit of a clot' as far as intellect is concerned, which is fair enough. But he has some common sense and good manners and is much less of a nuisance to society than is the conceited and insufferable Bentley Summerhays.

The play begins with a good deal of the palaver typical of the middle-aged Shaw who was beginning to mistake prefaces for plays and believed that disquisition is a suitable substitute for drama. I have no objection to a play which is mainly argument provided that the argument is strong in conflict and exciting in matter. Slap-brain can often be a civilised alternative to slapstick. But the talk here is not of Shaw's best and it is a welcome change when it is superseded by farce and logic in good mixture.

The scene is the Tarleton country-house at Hindhead. Tarleton himself is described as 'an immense and genial veteran of trade', and he is allowed to become one of the most agreeable of Shaw's capitalists. Shaw, we must admit, only grants him this mercy because Tarleton despises capitalism. The Roman Empress, Messalina, was said by Tacitus to grow tired of adultery because it was so easy. In the same way Tarleton has tired of making money because he has found it to be child's play. His underwear factory spins money as quickly and amply as it turns out pants and vests. So he has given his mind to wide, eclectic reading and has become a man of wide and random opinions and a walking quotation dictionary as well. He can cite a text for any of his notions. But he never booms lengthily or self-assertively. To his family he is a 'card' and to the audience, with his chuckling kind of wit, he is a dear. Roger Livesey was admirably cast in this role of a woolly bear with a far from woolly mind. He entirely confirmed my view, gained from reading the play, that Tarleton is very good company indeed. Ursula Jeans, as Tarleton's quiet, level-headed, and comprehending wife, who has to put up with her husband's nonsense as well as his sense, gave an equally charming performance of a serene and silvery quality. It would be a happy, as well as a stimulating, life in what house-agents call the Surrey Highlands if all its prosperous homes among the heather contained parents such as these.

Tarleton, incidentally, does to some extent link up the play with its prodigious preface, by expounding the difficulties of parenthood. The relation between the two generations is so difficult in most cases that there is no free communication of ideas and aspirations. Fathers and sons remain aloof, unsure of their contacts. 'You can't get over the fearful shyness of it', says Tarleton, and he brings in Charles Dickens and his letters to his family as an example.

'Read his letters to his family. Read any man's letters to his children. They're not human. They're not about himself or themselves. They're about hotels, scenery, about the weather, about getting wet and losing the train and what he saw on the road and all that. Not a word about himself. Forced. Shy. Duty letters. All fit to be published: that says everything. I tell you there's a wall ten feet thick and ten miles high between parent and child.'

There is much truth in that.

Tarleton's early conversation is mainly with Lord Summerhays, a retired Colonial Governor and scarcely as good a dialectician as Tarleton himself. Alan Webb in this part was bound to be over-ridden and was removed from reality by being absurdly dolled up as well as fluently talked down. Made to wear a foreign-looking beard and preposterous 'toff's' clothing, he arrived in Hindhead on a summer afternoon resembling an

59

Italian notable rather over-dressed for Ascot in a musical comedy. Why do producers go mad and run sartorially amok when confronted with the date of 1910 and thereabouts? An English gentleman with a Colonial Office career behind him did not go week-ending in Surrey and take a stroll amid the heather in the tails and grey topper of a vaudeville fop. Johnny Tarleton had to look equally ridiculous, appearing in tight knickerbockers over brown boots. I was an undergraduate about that time and I wore grey flannel trousers and shoes as any undergraduate would today. There is no need to play for 'costume' laughs in staging Shaw who could very well look after the laughs for himself. In any case, 1910 is not 1890.

Things liven up when a 1910 aviator crashes into the Tarleton greenhouse and emerges, somewhat surprisingly, without a scratch. Equally unscathed is his companion, a Polish feminine acrobat, wire-walker, and juggler with an intense pride in her profession. The lady immediately attracts Tarleton Senior, who is as ready to philander as he is to philosophise. One of the early escapades of his 'vie amoureuse' has produced an illegitimate son, of whose existence he has been unaware. The son is a most endearing character who has swallowed all the more obvious slogans of Socialism along with the clichés of melodrama and of sentimental fiction. Thus, earning his living as a badly paid clerk, he can pose as a victim of remorseless capitalism while, being 'a little basket', he can come with romantic retribution on his lips and swear, pistol in hand, to avenge his wronged, seduced Mamma. Donald Pleasence, as this inflamed ninny, belonging equally to the world of the Hyde Park soap-box and the pleasures of the old Lyceum, gave one of his best examples of comedy performance, which are always of conspicuous merit. The poor little wretch, with a cold in his head and no real stomach for the killing, is put by Shaw through all the hoops of farce.

He is first concealed, as though he were Mr Robertson Hare, in a portable Turkish Bath out of which he perilously clambers. He is then submitted to the glorious imperturbability of his intended victim who has the perfect retort for all his class-conscious chatter and his heroics of the righteous proletarian confronting the Wicked Sensual Plutocrat. So, with Miriam Karlin in fine form as the Polish diva of the circus-ring and Donald Pleasence snivelling and blustering, revolver in hand,

60

the play forgot all about its preface and soared from the ethics of education to the antics of entertainment. If MISALLIANCE is to be read, its preface should be looked into and skipped. If it is to be seen on the stage, the audience should not be depressed by its ponderous start. It does its own skipping and leaping later on.

The Gay New Days

THE THREEPENNY OPERA
by Bertolt Brecht. Music by Kurt Weill,
English adaptation by Marc Blitzstein   *Royal Court and
Aldwych Theatres*

Quite a League of Nations seemed to have been at work on this bit of old England. But no mention, you may notice, of John Gay. Not even a whisper of 'based upon'. You would think that Herr Brecht had himself written THE BEGGAR'S OPERA, many of whose characters and events, including Macheath, he has lifted and put to his own uses. Texts which are out of copyright can be legally plundered: but there is such a thing as courtesy: the programme contained names in plenty, down to providers of 'cigar-holder' and 'step-ladder'. But there was no room for a three-letter word, Gay. Herr Brecht, who prefers to work in Communist countries, evidently accepts the Communist dogma, 'What's yours is mine, what's mine's my own'. I should have thought that the promoters, who call themselves Peachum Productions, thus flaunting one of Gay's characters, might not have shared Herr Brecht's odd notions of property and propriety.

The period chosen for this re-hash of the old operetta was 'the threshold of the twentieth century', which meant crooks and slashers in bowlers and whiskers and their doxies in buttoned boots. The place was Soho. The story was the familiar one of Macheath's amorous removal of Polly Peachum from the Peachum home and of Macheath's subsequent betrayal, incarceration, and escape. Peachum equipped beggars for begging, hired them crutches, eye-flaps, suits of rags, cards proclaiming diseases and infirmities, and paintings for pavement use. Macheath, known as Mack the Knife, had his gang of toughs in Soho and his troop of girls in Wapping. In the programme we were faced with a frank and fearless modernism. The ladies of the town were labelled Whores. The adolescents could say 'Oo-er' to that.

The proceedings were mainly sombre. Late Victorian Soho was as empty of colour as any dingy slum, but it was full of noise. The music by Kurt Weill had a mixture of the menacing with the melodious: its theme song was hauntingly effective. The English text provided by Mr Blitzstein contained a lavish helping of heavy-handed indecency which was propelled at the audience in a heavy-handed way. Bill Owen brought a slickness of touch to Macheath for which role he lacked sufficiency of singing voice; but with him one felt that the actor had some objective in view: a glancing wit, a light sardonic vein were being attempted, and Gay's original had not been entirely forgotten. Bill Owen evidently felt that a sting of satire, a prick of wit should be felt, but what was Brecht satirising? And where was the wit? To announce that robbing a bank is less criminal than founding one may be called a fine satirical thrust at high finance and wicked capitalism. But to me such a 'crack' was only a dull thud made with a blunt instrument. Jocosity of this kind did not give Macheath much chance. I was sorry for Mr Owen.

Eric Pohlmann as Peachum showed a friendly kind of genial and adipose roguery. Daughter Polly was presented with agreeable charm by Daphne Anderson. But the rest of the cast had evidently been instructed to roar and gesticulate to the top of their bent. It was impossible not to hear them: it was equally impossible to hear what some of them were saying. I understand that Herr Brecht has a theory that actors should act actors acting and not humanity being human. If there is any value in this, I was unable to discover it. The result seemed to emerge as an orgy of boiled 'ham'. There were toy theatre figures and poses. There was rumpus galore. Amid the dingy scenic squalor was the 'blueness' of humour. Was the Censor of Plays charitably colour-blind when he read the text? All this had been critically hailed as 'immensely exciting'. Some far-off memories of Sir Nigel Playfair, Lovat Fraser, and Frederick Ranalow excite me still. I only got a yawn from this funereal shuffle performed on the dead body of the once entertaining BEGGAR'S OPERA. It may have been exciting in the Germany of the nineteen-twenties. But it is fusty fun in 1956.

Guthrie at Troy

TROILUS AND CRESSIDA
by William Shakespeare   *Old Vic Theatre*

It is a fairly common criticism of Tyrone Guthrie and Peter
Brook that they like the edges of the classics and not the heart
of them. They mount a play in a dashing spirit of invention and
delight. They devise new effects but I do not, as a rule, feel they
are in love with the old words. In Peter Brook's much (and
justly) acclaimed production of TITUS ANDRONICUS, while
most of the staging was ingenious, the best lines of the gory
tragedy were dropped; there are not many lines of quality to slip
through a producer's fingers. When I mentioned this to him, he
said, 'Well, they get in the way of the action'. But since many of
the most glorious lines and passages in Shakespeare are irrelevant to a strict development of the plot, this struck me as an
inadequate and ill-considered reply. Shakespeare himself was
notably inconsistent in this matter. When, through Hamlet's
mouth, he rebuked the gagging clowns for their interruption of
'some necessary question of the play', he himself then inter-
rupted that play by stuffing the text of HAMLET with fascinating
but irrelevant matter. Indeed, he did so in his scolding of the too
inventive Fools. What has the lecture which Hamlet delivers on
the state of the theatre and the malpractice of the mummers to
do with the 'necessary questions' of the play? The insertion is
invaluable to us if we are curious about the Elizabethan playhouse and its technique of acting. But it can hardly be called
dramatically sound.

I have no objection to cutting what is superfluous and maybe
tedious. There is superfluity of eloquence, not without weariness, in TROILUS AND CRESSIDA. Tyrone Guthrie's production at the 'Old Vic' gave the text, I think, in full, omitting only
the Prologue. But, to include all, he encouraged the players to
gabble most. There was so much scurrying through the text and
so much dropping of voices at the end of lines that, though I
tried to be 'all ears' as they say, and am not yet in need of a deaf-
aid, I found it at times very hard to keep up with the meaning.
This habit of throwing away the latter half of a line has become

63

à vexatious trick of the time. Because the old school of acting raised the pitch at the end of a line, the young school, so absurdly terrified of being thought 'ham', drops it and feels shame, instead of pride, in giving the final drive to a magnificent sentiment and a sounding utterance of that sentiment. In order to get through a full Shakespearean text in three hours, with two ten-minute intervals, it is necessary either to gabble or to cut. My choice is for judicious cutting and for careful speaking, with full insistence on delivery of the meaning in what is left.

It is useless to argue with Tyrone Guthrie, who is as obstinate as he is able. Having made my grumble about the gabble, I would salute his direction of TROILUS AND CRESSIDA as brilliant not only in pictorial quality but in witty arrangement of 'business' and of detail. It is a very difficult play to commend to a modern audience, especially if most of its members possess no special knowledge of Shakespeare's theatrical world. There is endless argument about its date, which does not matter: there is a contradiction about its early history. The first issue of the 1609 Quarto said that it was acted at the Globe by the King's Men, Shakespeare's company: the second issue contained an Epistle from 'a never writer to an ever reader' which called it a new play 'never staled with the stage' and 'never clapper-clawed with the palms of the vulgar'. This implies either no performance or only a private performance. Certainly it has been no favourite on the common stages. One has, in reading or hearing TROILUS AND CRESSIDA, the annoying impression that one is missing much topical reference, especially to the 'wars of the theatres' in which the King's Men and other companies were involved at the end of the sixteenth century. It is generally supposed that it was acted, either at the Court or Inns of Court, to audiences appreciating many a sharp thrust that has no point for us.

The play is a strange assemblage of material. The editors of the First Folio inserted it at the last minute and left it unpaged, between the Comedies and Tragedies. The writer of the aforesaid Epistle in the second issue of the Quarto obviously considered it a comedy, 'passing full of the palm comical' and went on to pour high praise on Shakespeare's comedies, commending 'their dexterity and power of witt' and never mentioning the tragedies. It is true that Troilus and Cressida are both alive at the end, and there is no tragedy for the woman since hers is too hard a heart for cracking: but there is agony enough for the

Aubrey Morris, Paul Rogers and Rosemary Harris in TROILUS AND CRESSIDA
at the Old Vic (*Houston Rogers*)

Wendy Hiller in TROILUS AND CRESSIDA at the Old Vic (*Houston Rogers*)

man in the betrayal of his love by this shameless little man-hunter who will eat a Greek as readily as a Trojan. As the story of a man's love it is essentially and memorably tragic, combining superb expression of passion and despair. As a picture of a good man caught in a foul pitch, fascinated to the height and flung down to the depth, it not only suggests the heart-break of the Sonnets but the splendour of their writing too. But as a story of the Greeks and Romans it is a sour, satirical comedy, with Shakespeare despising and deriding those classical heroes to the top of his bent. This gives the play a divided interest which, one may assume, has been a chief cause of its unpopularity. It is both a cry of pain and a sneer of contempt and the two are awkward mixers.

Moreover there are inserted some lengthy expositions of political theory which come very oddly on the tongues of the Greeks as well as being tedious to a modern audience. The long speech of Ulysses on the proper ordering of a community by the observance of 'degree' as the check to civil discord is of no use to 'the necessary question of the play' and reads as though it had been inserted to please the monarch, whether Elizabeth or James. It amplifies the social moral of the Histories and drives home the need for a strong central authority to curb the appetite for power among the nobles and leaders. 'The envious fever' of the ruler's subjects must be quelled. It is urged by Ulysses, in order to give this lengthy disquisition some relevance, that the Greeks are failing to capture Troy because their grandiose generals neglect observance of 'degree', Achilles being the chief offender. But this does not justify the size of the discourse which must have been aimed at the ears of a king or queen in the audience.

The portrayal of the Greeks as savages and buffoons has naturally been attributed to Shakespeare's desire to retort upon the classicists who were pert about his lack of scholarship. Chapman, translator of the 'Iliad' as well as rival dramatist, has been named as the target of Shakespeare's anti-classical outburst and the cause of his angry unmasking of the ancient heroes as a dreary set of thugs. It may be so: to the modern producer it matters little who exactly was the victim of the satire. His task is to make attractive to us this puzzling compendium of true love defeated by false lechery and of bitter raillery against the tin gods of the classical legends, tin gods accepted as demi-gods by the devotees of a classical education.

Tyrone Guthrie chose an Edwardian setting and wardrobe which Frederick Cooke brilliantly provided. This is one of the plays that best endures separation from classical costume: in its own time it was probably played (or meant to be played) in Elizabethan dress. Guthrie's Greeks appeared very much as modern Germans. This can be challenged, since Troilus expressly complains that he, a Trojan, must seem a boor to those Grecian devotees of the arts, good talkers, good dancers, and more subtle than his own rough self and own rough people. None the less, the Teutonic uniforms of the Greeks, with a little of Britain added in the person of Ajax, now turned into a perfect type of Edwardian military red-neck, as scarlet of face as of tunic, was a most effective device: the Trojans, a cohort in yellow, resembled the lifeguards of a Ruritanian state when the Hapsburgs still held sway. In its mockery of the military, TROILUS AND CRESSIDA has much in common with Shaw's ARMS AND THE MAN. Thus the Ruritanian touch was pertinent.

The details of modern, or at least recent, militarism, were introduced with sharply sardonic touches. With Admiral Ulysses in naval blue and an assembly of Germanic 'top brass' as the Grecian generals, the fun was neat and quick in a way that I think Shakespeare himself would have relished. Richard Wordsworth delivered the lengthy orations of the Admiral so cleverly as to keep them alive and to defeat their longitude. Achilles was very well presented by Charles Gray, looking like a prize-fighter gone to seed, with muscle turning to flesh, a puffy, dissipated monster, alternately petting and tormenting his favourite orderly Patroclus. The Trojan war-lords were seen as callow specimens of privileged caste. They drank and roared in their officers' mess like the students of 'Old Heidelberg' translated to high military rank. Both sides responded aptly to Shakespeare's description in his Prologue, 'The princes orgulous, their high blood chafed'.

Cast as the repulsive Pandarus, who takes an ugly, smirking glee in arranging the meetings of Troilus and Cressida, Paul Rogers showed us an Edwardian epicene, lisping his lewdness above the toggery of a dandy bound for Ascot. This was a glorious piece of work, revealing the ability of this actor to score as richly in cold, satirical comedy as in the heat of high, sonorous tragedy. His versatility is a continuous pleasure. It was a notable part of Guthrie's invention to make Helen's one appearance immensely amusing. Read as a piece of text, her scene is as feeble a piece of writing as ever came from Shakespeare's pen. But Helen, presented by Wendy Hiller, as a vapid Edwardian beauty playing a waltz at the piano, was superbly nonsensical, and the tiresomeness of the episode was most effectively concealed.

Rosemary Harris played Cressida as a minx of the same period, first in a riding-habit, and later in hobble-skirt. One had not visualised the walls of beleaguered Troy as particularly suitable for equestrian exercise, but somehow this Cressida with a hunting-crop seemed perfectly in the picture. Miss Harris gurgled with the plummy voice now fashionable among our younger actresses. Pandarus says of the creature, 'She does so blush and fetches her wind so short, as if she were frayed with a sprite. It is the prettiest villain: she fetches her breath as short as a newta'en sparrow.' Miss Harris was the prettiest villain indeed and abundantly supported the remark of Ulysses that 'her wanton spirits look out at every joint and motive of her body'. She was a bewitching and authentic 'daughter of the game'.

John Neville's Troilus had the right kind of bliss and torment and he showed, in the closing battle-scenes, that he can use his fine voice to the full. But in his love-scenes he suffered from the habit, already mentioned, of dropping the end of a line. Thus some of the exquisite passages about the excitement of lovers' meetings and the agony of lovers' partings were not given full effect. But this kind of production, so delightful in many ways, did not help him. The producer seemed to be less interested in the poignant pains of Troilus than in the derision of classical militarism. None the less, the atmosphere of lechery, at which Thersites keeps groaning and girning, was wonderfully well established. Paul Rogers and Rosemary Harris saw to that, while Clifford Williams, set to play Thersites as a scrubby Cockney pavement-artist, snapped and snarled at the way of all flesh.

I was sorry to miss the Marlowe Society's TROILUS AND CRESSIDA at Cambridge, which I am told was excellent. I am confident that the society's members gave the verse more justice than was done at the Old Vic. But I left Tyrone Guthrie's presentation with a feeling of great exhilaration. There had been a superb essay in theatrical high spirits and in delicious decoration. As one of the vulgar I 'clapper-clawed'.

Anouilh Dances

THE WALTZ OF THE TOREADORS
by Jean Anouilh   *Arts and Criterion Theatre*

There had been some doubts about the Censor's attitude to the public showing of this piece which had been greatly, as well as legally, enjoyed in the privacy of the Arts Theatre Club. Certainly it offers a frank, free-spoken picture of an incorrigible lecher, but to ban this honesty of naughtiness, while so much of the sly and sniggering exploitation of salacity can sneak by in one theatrical alley-way or another, would have been ridiculous. Furthermore, Hugh Griffith's performance of the amorous old general was as honest as his text: there was no intention to win laughter with a wink: if the deeds of this *vieux marcheur* were, to the godly, as dark as night, his declaration of his habits was as open as the day.

The central figure of the piece, General St Pé, is an elderly French soldier living before the First World War; if he had led a brigade or a division into that shambles he would probably have made an even more gory mess of the job than did most of his be-ribboned colleagues. One may hope that he was left to do nothing worse than muddle the supplies and seduce the serving-maids in a commandeered hotel at the base. In the false calm of that menaced peace he is writing his memoirs and finding concentration to be difficult. His mind, never of a serious and substantial quality, is easily diverted and there is trouble for him in the house: a more or less bed-ridden wife, who has come to detest him and will not leave him to please him, snarls her anger from the bedroom whenever occasion offers. There comes to visit the General a lady now in her late thirties or more. She has been dreaming of St Pé as her knight-at-arms for nearly twenty years. Had they not waltzed together when he was young and martial and she young and easy to impress? This pretty booby has been waiting and waiting while he, amid all his chambering, has never quite forgotten. The music tinkles in his sub-conscious, that suave old 'Waltz of the Toreadors'.

The lady arrives! The waltz re-tinkles. So the first act is a farce of re-union. There is music in the air. The melody pulses and

68

circles in the memory. But M. Anouilh has here shown his powerful comic invention and not indulged his usual taste for frailty of whimsical fancy. The story's complications are of the genially preposterous kind on which farce flourishes and the first curtain falls on what is known as 'a perfect scream'. After that the old tigress, the pent-up wife of a bad husband and the victim of many sorrows, has to be given a chance to show her claws and do her roaring. One must, of course, feel some pity for this ageing and infuriated back-room besom; to be married to General St Pé is to be the daughter of affliction, unless the victim has the necessary attractiveness and ability to be out and about, herself pursuing some retributive mischief. Madame St Pé is neither so alluring nor so agile as to be able to go her own amorous way: she can only make her tongue her whip, and crack it she does. Here, inevitably, the play changes its tune: there are no longer waltzes in the air. Struggle-music prevails.

In the end we escape from the verbal brawling of the battling seniors to the happier nonsense of the juniors. The oldest of all implements in the farce-writer's workshop is employed and the General's male secretary, a bashful boy, turns out to be one of his unsuspected sons; these, one may surmise, are to be numbered as a platoon, if not a battalion, and certainly not as single spies. After the necessary involutions of plot the General is left – engaging a new maid for the house-work, if house-work be all.

Such a tale could be sordid, but the writing and the direction by Peter Hall were sprightly. Nearly everything depends on the performance of the General and Hugh Griffith gave such cordial quality to the old scamp in his manoeuvres and confessions that the text went pirouetting to the music of old days instead of being bogged down in the squalor of marital misery. I was once told by a man renowned for his convivial fellowship and happy outlook on a smiling world that the line of Shakespeare's which he found most terrifying was 'To a dark house and a detested wife' and the psychologists can make what they like of this confession of a writer renowned for his felicitous expression of a care-free spirit. General St Pé has a dark house and a detested wife, and we heard the latter in full cry.

None the less, his tale emerged and sparkled as a comedy despite the sour interlude when Madame had her venomous say. For this success in the rescue of a potentially sad evening in the darkest of dark houses Mr Griffith was mainly responsible. The play is not long, but he was with us during nearly the whole of its length and as he prattled of his delight in carnal matters, the food, the wine, and the women of the waltzing world, he never let monotony impinge upon the gaiety of the memories. In fact, of course, the General was a deplorable example of human character, but it is the business of comedy, especially of the comedy which has a farcical impetus, to persuade us that the deplorable can be, for a couple of hours, delectable. The roll of the General's eye, his blend of gusto and grumpiness, his candour, and his eternally juvenile naughtiness went to the composition of a great comic character and not of a bad example properly to be pilloried in a play for Puritans.

Brenda Bruce intervened nicely as the lady from the past, who had been keeping herself for the formal re-union, old music on her lips and a light still burning in her eye. Could any French woman be so tenacious of fidelity? In effect, she made the happiest contrast with the General's total incapacity for a fidelity of five minutes' duration. Beatrix Lehmann played scolding Madame with a steely command of invective: the poor creature had once been a seductive singer, toiling on the fringes of Grand Opera, and I think that she must also have been metal more attractive than we were able, from Miss Lehmann's performance, to imagine. But the duel with her scamp of a husband was a major battle fought by a battle-cruiser in which the man, a mere frigate to this ironclad, could fire some effective rounds before retreating. As the young secretary Trader Faulkner was delightfully diffident in a home where defiance was the note. All in all, the background of domestic ugliness was sufficiently obscured by a foreground of victorious hilarity. The waltz kept tinkling and the text danced to its melody.

Life with the Liberals

THE MULBERRY BUSH
by Angus Wilson
Royal Court Theatre

The English Stage Company had been planned to re-open the re-built Kingsway Theatre, left a melancholy shell since the bombs of 1941. The Kingsway, a small house with a great past, had been the scene of some of my earliest, and happiest, play-going, and I

would like to have re-discovered it in a renewed life and recon-
quering its old prestige to which Granville Barker, as he then
spelled his name, contributed so much. But there were difficulties and so the E.S.C. set up its welcome shop in Sloane Square,
following still earlier tracks of Barker's. In fashionable drama of
the Pinero period and in 'advanced' drama of the Shaw-Barker
period this house had had its place in history. Recently made
prosperous with an urbane type of revue and now returning to
the more serious cultivation of 'straight' plays, the Court, which
used not to bother about announcing its regality, was obviously
a good site to choose for a new and possibly important under-
taking.

The English Stage Company opened its repertory with an announced programme of 'Doing New Plays'. Of the first four
pieces to be given one was a Broadway success, already played
at Bristol, and two had been played elsewhere in Britain; but to
quibble over the publicity would be petty. The use of the adjec-
tive English applied presumably to the acting rather than the
writing, for I observed that the fashionable Brecht, so highly
praised in London by many who have never seen more than one,
if that, of his plays, is on the list of attractions.

We began with Angus Wilson's piece, THE MULBERRY
BUSH, which had been produced by the Bristol 'Old Vic', and
this I found most interesting and under-valued by my fellow-
critics. It could do with a third edition, for its first act needed
clarification and its third needed more substance. Audiences do
not like being left vague as to which character is which in a
somewhat complicated family pattern, and Mr Wilson might
have been more informative about his domestic group of
Padleys at an earlier stage of the proceedings. But that was a
small technical point to set against considerable virtues of
serious intelligence, a quality rare enough in the theatre.

Angus Wilson has paid audiences the compliment of asking
them to face a reality instead of fobbing them off with the usual
types of lounge-hall comedy and their silly little sexual tangles.
His Padleys are an Oxford (or Cambridge) family and they
struck me not only as authentic but as representing a section of
society of whom the theatre sees too little. James Padley had
been Warden of St Rowland's College, but he has been more
interested in his own scholarship than in the affairs of his under-
graduates or the governing of an institution in which young

men are busily being youthful. He was essentially the Liberal Humanist Intellectual, a beneficent as well as a grave senior, not Reverend, since he was an agnostic, but reverend in a secular way. His wife was essentially the woman brought up in Liberal Feminism to believe that active participation in Public Life is the essence of the Good Life, which must be spent in the service of Good Causes. The mistake made, especially by Mrs Padley, had been to put the Feminism before the family and the Cause before common-sense. Placed in charge of youth, this admirable couple were most eager to look after Youth as long as it was an abstraction spelled with a capital Y and preferably located in the slums. But for young people as individuals, especially for young people in Oxford and in their own home, they had no eyes. Their last days in the Warden's House were a series of shocks: their complacent Good Citizenship was cruelly deflated. Another Liberal Deposit seemed to have been lost.

They were well-drawn characters, faithfully presented types of the comfortably and intensely conscientious academic class. I have known Padleyites all my life, especially among the middle-class Socialists who were so much more concerned with Problems than with people and who were all thinking (with the best intentions) about the Social Organism and quite ignorant of the humbler but numerous members of society and of their ways of life and feeling. (George Orwell horrified the Padleyites by going and looking closely at 'the workers' instead of making them the material of Blue Books and turning them into statistics.) James Padley had served his term as Warden and may have been edged out, reasonably enough, a little before his time was up. He was to be replaced by a man who was probably a far better administrator and, by Padley standards, far less civilised as a man. It is a pity that Angus Wilson kept the latter off-stage. The contrast was needed and the arrival of the brash successor would have helped him to amplify his third act. Thus we met the urgent problem, as to who should, in these years of State-subsidised and collectively 'bossed' education, be the Heads of Houses: the men of scholarship or the men who can cope with politicians and 'wangle' this or that? It is a point which Mr Wilson might pursue in another play.

We met the Padleys in the last days of their residence at the Warden's House. Amid the melancholy of packing up we realised the restlessness and resentment of the younger Padleys who had come to loathe the Padley Tradition of being so good, so progressive, and so helpful. A considerable skeleton fell out of the family cupboard. The model son, Robert, now deceased but once a model of Padleyism and the keenest of social workers, had let the family down; the truth was not known in his life-time, but he had in fact been what I suppose should be called in the jargon of today a Middle-Aged Delinquent. He had seduced (or been seduced by) a girl in one of his much-praised Youth Camps; to escape the shame, he paid a hard-up ex-officer in the Army to be his whipping boy; of course he did pay; he would not bilk. But for this shabby performance to emerge was not good news for his parents; and the arrival of another of Robert's ladies, a silly, affected creature, utterly without the Padley intellect, was another shock. Then a grandson, who hated the everlasting reminder that he is a Padley and must be therefore a model citizen, got violently drunk in the Warden's House of all places. A Padley as an alcoholic brawler at 'polite parties'! Bad news again.

There was certainly a good subject here and some of the characters were very well drawn, especially Mrs Padley who, I know, will go on sitting devotedly on Committees and Commissions till the end of her days. The dialogue was good too. Those criticisms which blamed it for being literary astonished me. One expects civilised talk in the Padley household, not the monosyllabic grunts which Noel Coward made the fashionable substitute for conversation. I would like to meet more Padleys on the stage and fewer of those types who can only make 'cracks' over cocktails. To censure as 'literary' anyone who does not make all his characters illiterate is a practice of great menace to the restoration of an adult English theatre.

But the play lacked architecture. It was a rambling building. The characters were, too often, denied effective scenes together. The story of Padleyism exposed and suffering for its victims could have been more tightly and effectively told. But it was a story that deserved to be told. For the players it must be said that they were grievously handicapped by the scene, arranged by Motley, and the production, directed by George Devine. The theatre had been equipped with an apron stage and a lofty grey background which will doubtless serve other items of the E.S.C.'s repertory well enough. But for a domestic play this sort of thing is fatal.

The room in the Warden's House had to be suggested by symbolic doors and beams. Wardens in our older Universities are handsomely housed. They live in some dignity. This skeleton of a home never looked like a place inhabited by the Head of a House in the academic sense. Furthermore, rooms in houses do not have apron stages, on which some characters step right out into the stalls. Stage-hands, placing or removing furniture in front of the curtain during the intervals, destroy all illusion in the case of a contemporary and realistic play. This kind of production gives the impression of a 'stunt' and of novelty for novelty's sake. Moreover the characters were often too far apart from one another. One got little sense of a family whose generations, though in dissension, were at grips with their problems and each other.

Even thus handicapped Gwen Ffrangcon-Davies gave a very fine performance of the old Mrs Padley as she saw the lights of her world going out and, unbeaten, was ready to kindle some more candles to the less than glamorous goddess of Social Reform. John Welsh, as her husband, was wastefully denied a chance until the end: then he took it in the properly quiet way of a scholar faced with actions and decisions. Rachel Kempson gave quality to a Padley daughter and so did Helena Hughes to a granddaughter. Mrs Padley, doing her Liberal duty, had taken in a refugee boy from Germany and let him grow up to be an idler and a mischievous pest. Christopher Fettes, in this role, and Kenneth Haigh, Alan Bates and Nigel Davenport in others showed that Mr Devine has talent at his disposal. I left with the feeling that Angus Wilson's play was more human than it had been allowed to seem, in that inhuman setting.

Twice to Elsinore

HAMLET
by William Shakespeare, directed by Michael Langham
Memorial Theatre, Stratford-upon-Avon
HAMLET
by William Shakespeare, directed by Peter Brook *Phoenix Theatre*

Stratford opened its 1956 season with a trip to Elsinore, a castellated harbour not visited by the Warwickshire team for many a year. This time there was no sign of luxury travel. Unwittingly, perhaps, but completely obedient to the Government which was enforcing economy with a 'credit squeeze', Stratford gave us a production of the utmost austerity. For scenery there was a vast black 'surround', mitigated by only one section of lighter shade. What was all very well for the battlements at night, was mourning wear indeed for the Castle's interior. If anything is true of the Court of King Claudius it is a callous refusal to mourn. The former king is only a few months dead, but 'heavy-headed revel', gluttony, and carouse are the practice. Yet Mr Langham insisted that the castle of Elsinore be staged in a manner reminiscent of the furnishings of a pauper's funeral.

The essential contrast of the play's opening, that of Hamlet, alone in his suit of woe, among the jovial gallantry and noisy wassail of the new wedding, was missing. For this Hamlet might have been wearing a shabby fragment of the Court's sepulchral hangings. As for wassail, there was hardly a cup to drain or cannikin to clink. The castle seemed also to be strangely short of furniture. Claudius may have murdered to get a throne, but Mr Langham was not going to have him sit on one – nor poor Gertrude either. They were continually under standing orders and were only allowed the most meagre of stools for the Play Scene. In her closet the Queen was permitted nothing so cosy as a bed or couch. I could see no point in all this insistence on a completely bare, as well as black, stage. The limit of concession to upholstery was the unrolling of a carpet by the Players: and this they hurriedly rolled up again. Does Mr Langham hate the Textile and Furnishing Trades?

But the black background had one advantage. With the forestage brilliantly lit, the actors were visible in the detail of their work. Facial play was never wasted. The spectators might become wearied by the unchanging sombreness of scene, but at least they could see all that was done and (another blessing) hear all that was said. I get so maddened by muted performance of Shakespeare and by refusal to attack the audience that I could forgive Mr Langham his Puritanical scorn of decoration because he insisted on the vigorous propulsion of the drama. Alan Badel's Hamlet was unkindly blamed for much – and somewhat unfairly, in my estimation – but none could deny its vigour and its vehemence. He was not one of the immobile mutterers who afflict our theatre. In Broadway English 'he shot the works' and, shooting, was well on the target as he had seen it. Nor was he crude in doing so. For he had studied the meaning of his lines intently and was using brain as well as body in the service of the part. Here was no attractive, heart-appealing Prince. But the Prince is only half a matinée idol. He has his coarse and brutal side and both Gertrude and Ophelia had occasion to feel the rough side of a tongue that could be smoothly noble in its eloquence.

Mr Badel is not an actor so graced by fortune as to be naturally 'the glass of fashion and the mould of form'. All the more reason, then, why he should take pains to give Hamlet a princely quality by care of his appearance. But, just as Mr Langham disdained the aid of scenic artistry, so did Mr Badel kick the haberdasher out of the Castle window. There were no Court knickerbockers on view: the order of the day was mainly for the narrow trousers (first cousins to jodhpurs) now affected, mostly in tartan, by young ladies. They are nicely described by the Dauphin in HENRY V. 'You ride like an Irish kern, with your French hose off and in your strait strossers'. Our Hamlet, thus straitly strosser'd and with an untidy doublet above his trews, looked as little as possible like 'the observed of all observers'. One critic described him as wearing a space-suit: to me he looked more like a 'bell-hop' attending a funeral. Not helpful, to put it briefly.

Yet with, and amid, much visual handicap, he gave a performance of intelligence and impetus. Declining to play for the easy sympathy that Hamlet can easily win, he had evidently decided that the Prince was not merely feigning madness for tactical reasons, but was driven to a real frenzy by the crimes of ambition and, more especially, of sensuality around him. He worked himself into a fever of fury against the world's unweeded garden. As the evening wore on, he sweated gall in his indictment of things rank and gross. He went into the ring with evil and fought the good fight. After having seen the curiously detached and disinterested Hamlet of Paul Scofield, I was the more grateful for a performance so deeply engaged and so emphatically shared with the audience. It seemed to me unlikely that the bus-parties and other travellers, who come from large distances to see a play of Shakespeare's at Stratford, would relish a production set with only cerements for its scenery: but they were certain of getting a real performance and not a routine stroll through a classic.

76

Harry Andrews, welcomed back to Stratford, made the King a handsome, swashing figure, not noticeably 'bloat' but with all the smack of a corrupt grandee. Beside him stood a particularly interesting Queen, played by Diana Churchill. She did not provide us with the familiar picture of a complacent bundle of sensuality: here was a woman who realised what she had done and what was stirring in Hamlet's mind: this taut, nervous, intelligent Queen fitted with a novel kind of intensity into one side of the play's psychological problem, and Miss Churchill's work was original and exciting. But one could not help wondering whether King Claudius would have cared so much for the possession of a woman with wits as keen as his and not appealing, one would have thought, to a sottish devotee of self-indulgence, savouring the more swinish pleasures of Royal Denmark.

George Howe is my ideal Polonius, a plausible Chamberlain, loquacious but not in his dotage. He was, as the average Polonius is not, a possible parent for Ophelia. This young lady was played in a way which made her seem a trifle 'mental' before she was driven wholly into ruin of the mind. A Laertes with plenty of spirit (Andrew Faulds) was matched with a Hamlet no less abounding of energy. The whole was an odd production and bound to annoy those in search of the customary Elsinore. It is right that the conservative taste should be given a jolt from time to time, and the jolt was applied with considerable vehemence.

The production of HAMLET which was honoured with the Moscow visit in the late autumn had some 'dates' out of London before coming to the Phoenix Theatre. I did not see it until later in its run, by which time the company, considerably hammered by criticism, seemed to have lost interest in the proceedings. There was very little attack in the sluggish performance which I attended, and Paul Scofield's study of a down-hearted Prince left me drowsy and down-spirited. The best item for me in this somewhat melancholy and soporific presentation was Peter Brook's use of a stage within a stage. On the acting side Mary Ure's performance of Ophelia was given particular value by its acute study of a mind in disarray, while Alec Clunes as the King was admirable in his show of grossness and of fury. The rest is better forgotten.

77

Fay Compton

STARLIGHT

by Michael Clayton Hutton   *Theatre Royal, Windsor, and on tour*

TABITHA

by Arnold Ridley and Mary Cathcart Borer   *Duchess Theatre*

That Fay Compton should not have been seen in central London during the autumn, winter and spring of 1955–56 was that region's obvious loss. Nor did the provincial and suburban audiences who saw her in the two pieces mentioned above have the chance to appreciate her artistry in plays of a memorable kind. When TABITHA 'came to town' Fay Compton had left it to be the star of STARLIGHT: her role in the former was taken over and played with great ability by Marjorie Fielding. But TABITHA's run at the Duchess was rather a brief trot and I do not suppose that, had Miss Compton stayed in the cast, there would have been a widely different result.

Mr Ridley and Miss Borer, creators of TABITHA, had explored territory once given most sinister population by Hugh Walpole, namely the cheap lodgings occupied by what used to be known as distressed gentlewomen, the time and place being Christmas in an English cathedral city. What the authors discovered there was nothing so macabre as THE OLD LADIES of Walpole's morbid fancy. In this case the poor dears on whom a churlish landlady raised the rent were involved in what might be called a slight case of murder. The complications of the story were steered clear of the horrific and the tangle of suspicion was kept amusingly intricate. The play got through an evening, but it did not rise above the usual level of its corpse-and-clue category, despite the admirable studies of hard-pressed and homeless gentlewomen provided by Janet Barrow and Christine Silver as well as by Marjorie Fielding. It was handicapped by brevity and I surmised that audiences might find it to be underweight for the money.

The late Michael Clayton Hutton was a vociferous dramatist with some brilliant streaks of achievement and many possibilities. Fay Compton, in his STARLIGHT, chose to play the part of Lydia Sheridan, a great actress who is feeling her years,

78

suffering for her follies of vanity and temperament, and now disastrously failing to please the public. We follow Lydia in the choice of a new play that is to save her status. It may originally have been a good choice, but we see her demanding such a foolish amount of alteration and re-writing that the young author's reputation will certainly not be made and Lydia's name will certainly be further tarnished. An old friend, a kindly and admiring dramatic critic, sagaciously played by Anthony Ireland, advises her in vain: the first night of Lydia's latest choice turns out to be, as expected, an unmitigated calamity. She may, of course, rise again and shine again: but one hardly believes that this feat of levitation is likely.

There was plenty of sad truth in this study of the old charmer who could not cope with advancing years and the changing tastes of a new audience. But the dramatist and the player together had made it too hard for our enduring: stars of this kind may be possessed by all the devils of egocentricity, but they have not won their position without a flamboyant kind of charm that gives allurement even to their absurdity. They mingle their selfishness with an intermittent and wildly extravagant generosity. Some evidence of this kind of likeable, even adorable, fecklessness would have carried Lydia into our sympathies and Fay Compton to a success. But it did not emerge in STAR-LIGHT, whose text could have been much kinder to both the actresses without the sacrifice of truth in the story.

Yet here is a chance to pay tribute to Fay Compton's glittering talents, rich beauty, and career of great diversity in professional achievement. James Agate used to counter high praise of Elizabeth Bergner by saying that she had shown the English public only one line of pretty pathos, whereas Edith Evans had proved her greatness in every kind of role from Lady Bracknell to Madame Ranevsky. But, if versatility be the test, Fay Compton surely carries off the highest honours of any. It is not usual for the most poignant of Ophelias to have been also the most enchanting of Pantomime's principal boys or for a superb performer of Regan in KING LEAR to be Prince Charming during the following Christmas. Fay Compton began as the golden girl of THE FOLLIES, was the sweetest singer of our lighter stage, and was soon leading in revue and musical comedy. Then she turned to the 'straight' way of drama, bewitched the town as Mary Rose, and was for years the reigning queen of light comedy at the

Haymarket Theatre. With her inherited gifts and her acquired technique she has always been able to excel in any role of levity or severity. She should have been established later in life, as she was earlier at the Haymarket, as an actress with a steady address at one good London theatre and with a policy to which her public could confidently look. Play-goers, I am sure, like their favourites to keep within a certain line of country, a broad line but not a line without limits. Our illustrious Dames, Edith Evans and Sybil Thorndike, have undoubtedly been equally prepared for comedy and tragedy, but they have not figured in musical comedy or strutted in the tights and thigh boots of Dick Whittington.

An artist, however eminent, cannot always choose work according to his or her will. There may be family obligations which necessitate the rejection of offers involving more glory than reward. It may be for such excellent and honourable reasons that Fay Compton has seemed to accept too many and far-flung invitations in her selection of roles. If so, she sacrificed that position of the highest standing to which her artistry has long entitled her.

Back to Belmont

THE MERCHANT OF VENICE
by William Shakespeare   *Memorial Theatre,*
Stratford-upon-Avon

The critics moan when mention of a new production of THE MERCHANT is made: but the public lifts up its heart and opens its purse. Here is a play with a surprise curtain to Act IV which had ceased to be a surprise three hundred and sixty years ago. But who bothers about a dead thrill? The play, undeniably, lives. It was long ago observed that 'the plot does not matter, except to bring in fine things'. THE MERCHANT provides the finery beyond question: even the Casket Scenes, intolerable to the professional play-goer who has seen them until he aches, continually afford delight to the many. The viewers of Commercial Television have been rejoicing in a close parallel to the Belmont Suitors' dilemma of agonised selection while watching Mr Michael Miles and the contestants in the Take Your

80

Irene Worth and Leo McKern in THE QUEEN AND THE REBELS
at the Haymarket (*Angus McBean*)

Dirk Bogarde and Geraldine McEwan in SUMMERTIME
at the Apollo (*Armstrong Jones*)

Peter Bull, Timothy Bateson, Peter Woodthorpe and Paul Daneman in
WAITING FOR GODOT at the Arts and the Criterion (*Houston Rogers*)

Estelle Winwood and Leslie Caron in GIGI at the New (*Angus McBean*)

Moyra Fraser in FRESH AIRS at the Comedy (*Houston Rogers*)

Pick programme. Will the poor wretch before us, who might have had fifteen pounds in ready notes and resolves to spurn the cash and take his chance with a casket, find inside only a bus-ticket or a shoe-lace? Or will he decide upon the lucky buy and open a chest as plentiful in gifts as was Pandora's Box of old? The game never tires. Shakespeare, as the man in the street would say, was 'on to a good thing'.

There can be no wonderment now about the result of Shake-speare's Casket Scenes or the Venetian Court verdict. Yet, in the theatre, these episodes have a miraculous power to yield eternal pleasure. I do not think that the majority of contem-porary play-goers, after the first night, attend a production of this play simply in order to see, and assess, the performance of Shylock's or Portia's part. They go to see a play and they enjoy it to the full. Even if they went under compulsion and as often as critics must, it is a nice question as to how soon they would decide the outing to be an odious drudgery.

I am not so bored with Belmont as are some of my colleagues nor do I share the common loathing of Bassanio that is now the expected thing in academic quarters. M. R. Ridley, editor of the New Temple Shakespeare, holds that Bassanio competes with Claudio and Bertram for the distinction of being the poorest specimen of a man to be discovered among Shakespeare's comedy heroes. Mr Ridley maintains that Bassanio gives not the least indication of anything that can be called love for Portia, and so he regards Bassanio as nothing but a caddish and con-temptible go-getter. But Bassanio is as eloquent about Portia's virtues as her beauty: it is true that he is eager to marry an heiress, but it is by no means evident that he would have pur-sued any heiress however little he liked her.

It is surely worth noting that the marriages of young Eliza-bethan noblemen were carefully planned by their parents or by themselves with an eye to landed property as well as with an ear for the pulsing of an amorous heart. Lord William Herbert, who became Earl of Pembroke and may have been the male recipient of Shakespeare's Sonnets, refused to marry Mistress Mary Fitton, the Maid of Honour who had borne him a child. He went to the altar instead with one who brought with her a degree of wealth as necessary to that young and profligate Earl as was Portia's fortune to the spendthrift Bassanio. But did the Eliza-bethans regard Pembroke's conduct as contemptible? The mentality of the modern gentleman was not theirs: marriages were a part of social policy. And so with certain types and classes they have remained. I do not believe that any member of Shakespeare's own audience would have regarded Bassanio as detestable because he wanted to pay his debts by his marriage. Even if he had been frank about loving Portia only for her ducats, they would not have thought his conduct strange. But in this case there was no need for such candour about gold-digging. He deeply admired the virtues as well as the vision of his Goldilocks of Belmont and she made no secret of her regard for Bassanio as the ideal husband. So why all this contempt of the Venetian whose qualities were so appealing to his lady? It was a love-match, with lucre abundantly attending. What happier?

It can be argued that Bassanio, when he borrowed from Antonio to pay for his courtship-journey to Belmont, lied to his friend. If everything depended on the right choice of casket, there was no need to make a grand show of elegance and so Antonio's money was obtained by false pretences. Surely that is pressing the case against Bassanio too hard. Did he know that the casket business was going on? He tells Antonio that many 'renowned suitors from every coast' are besieging Belmont and that he wants to hold a rival place among them. There is no statement that luck will decide the issue. Naturally he does not want to arrive as a pauper short of a clean shirt. All that can be said against Bassanio is that, in order to reach Belmont looking like a handsome fellow, he borrowed over-much and put too great a strain upon the fortunes of his friend.

But the opinion of our time has been so much schooled to regard Bassanio as a conscienceless cadger and a matrimonial money-grubber that the actor in the part rarely gets critical justice. I did not see sufficient praise among the notices of the performance of Basil Hoskins in this role: he had the right looks and carriage and did his wooing in good voice and fettle. He had a radiant Portia in Margaret Johnston and, if Bassanio can ever be admitted nowadays to deserve the Lady of Belmont, he deserved her.

In direction Margaret Webster, with Alan Tagg as her decorator, relied, wisely, upon romance and no nonsense. Of course the plot of THE MERCHANT is, on the Belmont side, a farrago of pretty implausibities. Hence it can be classed as fairy-tale stuff for which a fantastical treatment can be justified on the stage: Portia's home seen as a doll's house, with Morocco as a gollywog, has been one notion of the way to handle it. But a certain amount of realism, with colour and grace attending, will do very well: one needs just enough of moonshine and starlight to illumine, but not to flood, the garden where Lorenzo makes harmony of the harmonious universe. This was properly supplied and naturally the production gained in popularity with the Stratford audience owing to the contrast with the austere and colour-starved presentation of HAMLET which had just preceded it.

There was general relief at the discovery that Stratford had not gone into perpetual mourning, that romance could ride again, and that a painted stage was not taboo. Miss Johnston's Portia was charmingly established in the happy picture: she jested with ease, loved with conviction, and pleaded in Court with the right mock-gravity. We have to accept the Elizabethan convention that lovers and close acquaintances cannot recognise each other if there be some slender disguise, but this nonsense is only tolerable if it comes with a smile. A Portia gravely striving to be realistically the masculine lawyer will never convince: Miss Johnston was right to play the Trial Scene with a playful assumption of the learned legalist, and to keep a smile beneath her spectacles.

Shylock usually comes first in any notice of THE MERCHANT, but my interest in the character of the much maligned Bassanio led me to the Gentiles' camp before I came to the ghetto. Emlyn Williams disappointed the First Night House by the balance and modesty of his performance; he had studied Shylock exactly, as a man both wronging and wronged, with the result that he played neither for warmth of sympathy nor for extremity of hate. He had carefully planned, I think, every phase of the character and as an actor of high technical accomplishment he put his plan into careful and considered action. To be equally just to the sufferings and the sadism of Shylock is to deserve, and surely to win, the praise of those who give the play a careful study. It is also to risk losing the acclaim of those who want the lightning flash to play upon the butcher's knife. Shylock has been, down the centuries, a joy for the lovers of histrionic thunderstorms. There is a feeling that the Jew should be large, if not in stature, at least in impetus, and that he should make the play his own, whereas it is, by length of part, Portia's and, by title, Antonio's. The refusal of Emlyn Williams to seize his audience by the throat from the start and his resolve to play the part fairly and in just proportion lost him some votes. If he had played Shylock less well he might have got far better notices.

Gold in the Glen

THE ORIGINAL JOHN MACKAY

by Alastair M. Dunnett   *Glasgow Citizens' Theatre*

The Glasgow Citizens' Theatre wound up its season of 1955–56 with a Highland comedy. Its author, Mr Dunnett, had recently left a journalistic chair in Glasgow for another, and more illustrious one, in Edinburgh. Since there is a traditional aloofness between the two great Scottish cities, it was pleasant to meet in Glasgow a play by the Editor of *The Scotsman*, that old, strong voice of Edinburgh. It remains for the Gateway Theatre in Edinburgh to repay the compliment by staging a play by the Editor of the *Glasgow Herald* or, if the latter be a less versatile writer than Mr Dunnett, by one of the *Herald* staff, which must surely be able to put a playwright into this field of agreeable rivalry.

Mr Dunnett's Mr Mackay was a crofter in a glen where, at least in the play, the sun never failed to shine and no midge or cleg flew in to puncture human skin and deflate human felicity. The worst arrival was an English author with a taste for the Celtic twilight and a pen for the writing up of all things quaint and beautiful. He discovered John Mackay and found his life and sayings to be rich and marketable stuff, if suitably treated for the delectation of the general reader in other lands. So Honest John of the lone shieling was turned into a kind of tribal hero, in whom the Gaelic virtues of the rude forefathers of the clachan still abode. What Mr Beecher, the wandering author, presented to the public was a Davy Crockett of the Kailyard. Scotland's own S. R. Crockett, powerful writer of historical-romantical stories until he took to boiling the Galloway pot and became excessively the servant of sentiment, might have made something rather sticky out of John Mackay: but it would have been nothing so odious or so financially rewarding as the achievement of Mr Dunnett's Mr Beecher.

84

The dramatist has, however, given a new and amusing twist to the Kailyard story. His John Mackay turns out to be no dreamy Gael, unpregnant of his cause, but as tough a salesman as could be found in any Croft with Green Shutters. The English writer had exploited him. Why should John not exploit himself? This he resolved to do: and this he had the capacity also to perform. So he started to do his own writing as the whimsy Gael for the benefit of English readers. Mr Beecher's 'John Mackay' book had been sold to the extent of 65,000 copies. Mackay's Mackay book did even better, a sad blow to Mr Beecher. What right has a crofter to rise up and be his own author?

But John had more in his plans than profitable scribble: in a year or two there was a John Mackay distillery: there was also a flotation of John Mackay shares: in the midst of all this the auld croft had its face lifted and became the 'Auld Croft Hotel', with a cocktail bar in which ladies from London drank Martinis when they were not telephoning to their stock-brokers.

Here was a happy and a novel rendering of the usual Highland play upholstered in heather mixture. Good talk was laid on by the local and lazy Highlanders, a gillie and a stalker well played by George Davies and yet another of the local clan, Fulton Mackay. Neil Gunn, a Highlander of the North East and most knowledgeable about the crofts and crofters, assures me that Highlanders are not the idle fellows of the comedy tradition: they are quite ready for a hard and long day's work. I accept the advice of the expert. But, if the claim that an incurable inertia is the occupational disease of those living in the glens be maintained for purposes of comedy, then these two players are the right men to press it.

At this point of John Mackay's triumph in financial tycoonery, Mr Dunnett tried a new tack. His hero developed a conscience: he began to despise himself, to renege, and to renounce his unabashed commercialism. Financially, that was fatal. Before long the Mackay shares had fallen so low that they were described as lying about the floor of the Stock Exchange. The audience had now to regard John as schemer turned saint.

But saintliness can have its material rewards. When the shares were worthless an American Mackay, prospering in California but loyal to the clan, heard what was happening and set the trans-Atlantic telephone busily at work. Together he and John bought up all the shares at trash prices and started to build up the Mackay Business all over again. I may have misunderstood Mr Dunnett and may malign him by regarding him as cheerfully cynical. But it did seem to me that his Mackay was going to make more money out of his conscience than he ever did from the lack of it. The original Mackay backers in the City had apparently lost all when aid from the Far West enabled John to rise on the ruins of this investment. But we could, I think, assume that John Mackay was now going, in his renewed prosperity, to be a good citizen as well as a good industrialist and that he would devote some of his old energy and his new-found capital to the rebuilding of industry and farming in the Highlands.

There was some confused writing at the end of the play and I suspected that cutting had been done in a hurry. A new draft of the concluding passages might be a great improvement. But THE ORIGINAL JOHN MACKAY deserved a welcome: it had originality of mind and it had style in the dialogue. A tactical mistake was made by dividing the stage into two, with the interior of the croft, later the Auld Croft Hotel, on one side and the Highland scenery on the other. This meant that the centre of the stage was often wasted and that the more important passages, that is the 'indoor' ones, were played in cramped conditions and with the actors relegated to a corner. Richard Mathews has served the Citizens' Theatre well as a director of their operations, but this time he was working under handicap. I may be old-fashioned in disliking a setting thus partitioned, but I would wager that the actors would be on my side in preferring one full-sized room for their performance to a small room with the view from its windows thrown in for decorative purposes.

Mr Dunnett will have learned from this experiment, learned especially that a leading character, such as his John Mackay, needs plenty of scope to display his leadership. Andrew Keir has been a pillar of the Citizens' and he did all he could with Mackay: but he was hindered by lack of effective episodes of conflict. His crisis of conscience was recounted more than dramatised. Mr Dunnett surely should not have bothered to bring in a love-interest unless he was prepared to give it more life and plausibility. Nora Laidlaw, as the lady involved, made the most of a scanty chance to fashion a real person out of a shadowy character.

But I would not stress the play's faults at the expense of welcoming its virtues. The Scottish Theatre has a body of keen

86

and capable writers, including Robert Kemp, Robert Sellar, Moray McLaren, Alexander Reid, Donald Mackenzie, and now Alistair M. Dunnett. With Henry Sherek come from London to give them scope and to supplement the work of the resident repertory companies when their seasons have closed, there is abundance of vitality on the creative side. The problem is to make audiences more aware of what is being done. The audiences that I see in Scotland do not contain enough young people and I doubt whether the Universities are as ready as they might be to find in the theatre a lively forum for the critical presentation of the nation's current doings and desires.

The President of an undergraduate society told me that one cause of diminished social activity in the Universities is the presence of the TV set in the students' lodgings. It is a sad look-out if the stale comicalities of English drolls on the screen are sufficient to satisfy the appetite for entertainment existing in the youth of Scotland. A play, it is often said, is not a play until it is acted and the response of its audience is enormously important for more than the necessary considerations of finance. The new Scottish dramatists must be given the assurance that they are not only giving Aunt Bella a chuckle and a cosy evening: they must feel they are touching, to anger perhaps as well as to enthusiasm, the makers of Scotland's tomorrow.

The Steaming South

CAT ON A HOT TIN ROOF

by Tennessee Williams *Published by Secker & Warburg* (12s 6d)

Trailing clouds of critical rapture, garlanded with Pulitzer laurels, and dripping with blood, sweat, and sex, Mr Williams's CAT ON A HOT TIN ROOF found the British Public ostensibly protected from any infection by contaminated imports owing to the saving presence of the Lord Chamberlain. The reason for the veto, presumably, was that the story concerned a frustrated wife who demands her due of intimacy from a husband who is supposed to be a homosexual and certainly behaves with an aloofness improper and discourteous in a normal man. (Discourteous? Is that fine word 'courtesy' within the vocabulary or the cognisance of Tennessee Williams's characters?)

It seems to me idle to pretend that marriages are never made miserable for this reason and hypocritical also to claim that such affairs are better not revealed and discussed in the theatre at a time when homosexuality is investigated by committees and commissions at the highest levels of Church and State. The Lord Chamberlain may reply that the story is coarsely told and that is true: its characters belong to a squalid, but fairly wealthy family, in the Deep South. They scream and squabble at the tops of uninhibited voices and discuss their sexual relations with the vocabulary of a barrack-room. If the business of the British Censorship is to protect our ears from such grossness of vocabulary and from some completely irrelevant bawdy, which Mr Williams has thrown in for good (or bad) measure, the Censor's officers could hardly refrain from getting out the blue pencil. But how ineffective is all this vigilance! The futility was sufficiently pointed out in the great protest against Censorship made fifty years ago. And here am I, not only with Mr Williams's text before me and legally entitled to give it to any acquaintance of any age, but with two variants of that document's last act provided in order that nothing be left wanting. No one is going, I am confident, to demand the gaoling of Messrs Secker & Warburg, the prosecution of any bookseller stocking the book, and the destruction of the volumes now available. By the time this notice is printed the play itself may be legally available in the full horrors of performance to all who pay a trifling subscription to join a play-goers' club.

The clubs' membership will doubtless swell dropsically since 'there's nowt like muck' for fertilising box-office soil. I am not sneering at Mr Williams when I talk of his play in terms of muck. His characters are sons and daughters of the soil in the Mississippi Delta where passions appear to run high and language low. There is a stench of sweat, liquor and lechery constantly in the thundery air. It is not for persons like myself who know only the Eastern coastal strip of the United States to announce that Mr Tennessee Williams is making the atmosphere too hot and sticky or even that cotton-bosses of the Delta are not so crude as he colours them. This is his region and it seems that he feels that he must get very close to us and tell us all about it.

He has prefaced his text with a meandering piece of pretentious balderdash about the artist called, sentimentally, 'Person to Person'. He starts off by remarking 'Of course it is a pity that so much of all creative work is so closely related to the personality of the one who does it.' Why a pity? What sort of quality, what value would creative work have if it were not related to the maker's personality? We are then told how blessed it is to talk 'person to person' for the reason that 'We are all sentenced to solitary confinement inside our skins.' Next, 'Personal lyricism is the outcry of prisoner to prisoner from the cell in solitary where each is confined for the duration of his life.' To this I would answer that, if confinement there must be, solitary confinement is the only tolerable form of it to a civilised person. To be locked up with a crowd of others and denied all privacy is hell absolute. If hell absolute can somehow be rendered even more horrible, it would be by outbursts of personal lyricism on the part of all one's fellow prisoners. Nobody, who happens not to be in gaol or an asylum, is sentenced to solitary confinement in his skin; nearly everybody is far too uncontained for general comfort and convenience. Don't we all want a lot more silence in the world? But that is not the opinion of Mr Tennessee Williams who announces that 'There is too much to say and not enough time to say it'.

There is not too much to say. If the world's authors, so busy everywhere for about three thousand years, have not said everything there is to be said, except on matters of factual and scientific discovery, what have they been up to? The business of the writer becomes harder and harder for the very reason that it has all been done so often and so well. To find something new to say about nature, human or scenic, becomes more nearly impossible. The early English poets, for example, were lucky; they had a virgin field and then Chaucer and Shakespeare came and ploughed up most of it. We cannot get away now with nice simple stuff about April and her showers sweet. Our contemporary poets have to twist their metaphors and images as painters and musicians twist their forms, straining after violent contortions, in order not to echo their predecessors, and the result may seem to many affected and tiresome.

But what are the poor devils to do? The artist's agony, Mr Williams, is certainly not that there is too much to say and too little time, but that, as the years roll by, more and more great men and women have already done the saying job that youngsters want to do – and done it, probably, so well that no more is needed. That will not, of course, stop people writing, nor will the fact that selling paper and ink and printing with them are now the most remunerative sections of the Book Business. But do not let us delude ourselves with the sentimental twaddle poured out by Tennessee Williams in his Preface about our all being prisoners in need of releasing a mutual sob and getting rid of the song in our hearts.

The art-lovers need not worry. Artistic creation will go on for a host of reasons, the chief of which is that the artist is a creature of vanity; if he were not he would keep his mouth shut and his hand still. Enough people may be interested in what he does to keep him just above the starvation line. But there is no logical necessity for all this saying of things so often said and of making songs so often sung. The excuse of a new idiom for a new time is partially valid and in any case it would be a dull world if there were no egoists piping up and no new voices telling the old story. To write in this way is not to be a Philistine or against art. A man is not against beef-steak because, loving it, he stops eating when he has had enough. And that there is already enough of books, music, painting and all the rest can be discovered by anybody who uses his rights as a citizen to enter Public Libraries, Art Galleries, Museums, Concert Halls and subsidised theatres, some of which excursions will cost him nothing and the others much less than indulgence in a little drinking and smoking.

Mr Williams has asked for this wordy riposte by spoiling a good play with a bad prologue. When he lays off his pompous chatter about personal lyricism and settles down to work, he shows that he can do it. His people come bursting into life; they are not the kind of people one would expect to be popular in refined circles, either Bostonian or British. In short, they are crude and carnal and talk what Hamlet called 'country matters'. The mixture of the sentimental with the brutish which is now common in life and letters is a chief characteristic of the themes and lingo of Tennessee Williams. The characters, a family of land-owners and cotton-growers in the Delta, wear their hearts on their sleeves and are constantly practising what might be called indecent exposure of the elemental emotions. They hate and howl, but in the midst of all their toughness and roughness they speak of each other in baby-talk terms, Big Daddy, Big Mama, Sister Woman. Even grown-up sons say 'Big Daddy' to their termagant father, as though he were the kind of woolly bear so cosily played at times by Roger Livesey.

90

Big Daddy in this case is a dying man with property to bequeath and Tennessee Williams accepts the common view that agrarians and avarice are inseparable. The family gather round. Where will the money go? Big Daddy is a bouncing, roaring type, as free of tongue as close of his own secrets. His daughter has married a crafty lawyer in Memphis and has bred freely: they have a fair claim to plenty of aid. His son, Brick, is married in name to a woman called Margaret; but he has had too strong an affection for a man friend to be a loving husband and to beget a grandchild for Big Daddy who has a large appetite for fertility. Margaret is the angry cat on the hot tin roof and can caterwaul at the miserable Brick as cruelly as his father bellows at him. Brick's refuge is the bottle and he is hardly ever without a glass in his shaky hand.

One need not betray the end. One point is that all these characters are able to clutch the reader by the scruff of the neck and drag him along. Tennessee Williams, who writes wish-wash when he starts to theorise, is a dramatist and writes with simple strength when his characters are giving tongue. He may be accused of overdoing the barrack-room touch in conversation and certainly he at times drags in more barrack-room than is demanded either by character or by circumstance. Any reader will surmise that the piece acts excitingly, and that is the report of all who have met Big Daddy, Big Mama, and caterwauling, tin-roof Margaret in the uncensored American theatre. By all means let the piece be praised for its urgency of writing and close-packed conflict of a violent and vituperative family, praised also for the scenes in which the wretched Brick defends himself for his seemingly indefensible conduct.

But there an end. There is little humour, no beauty, no civility, and no subtlety in these people and their brawlings, nothing but the stark and elemental interlaced with curious streaks of the sentimental. For a play to be good on its own lines is good enough. There is no need to start discovering superlative genius. Mr Williams has made himself look silly in his Preface: we shall do him wrong to make his genuinely powerful play look silly by over-praising it.

Mr Guinness Goes Gay

HOTEL PARADISO

Translated by Peter Glenville from the French of G. Feydeau
and Maurice Desvallières   *Winter Garden Theatre*

It was a good idea, and certainly well rewarded by the public, to
revive the Palais Royal routine and so let us renew acquaintance with one of those Parisian hotels whose scene-maker has
dealt exclusively in bedsteads, doors, and cupboards – the kind
of hotel where there is likely to be a cuckoo in every nest. To the
Hotel Paradiso, in the year of 1910, came M. Boniface, the meek
little builder, running from the storm and thunder of Madame
Boniface's matrimonial manner. The poor fellow did not, of
course, make a lonely bolt for a calmer world: hand in hand
with him came a simple, gushing, enthusiast for liberty, Madame
Cot, the wife of Boniface's pompous neighbour, M. Cot, the
architect. Inevitably this errant couple had a large following,
since it is one of the rules of farce that the whole cast must arrive,
whether in innocence or on mischief bent, at the same time at the
same hotel.

The only absentee was Madame Boniface, who was having
blameless adventures of her own: that was a pity, because
Martita Hunt was magnificently sniffing and snorting and
bridling and booming in that lady's part. However, the actress's
long (and to us regrettable) rest in Act 2 brought her back in
Act 3, refreshed and even more vehement and voluble, to cope
with the unscrambling of last night's eggs.

To the Hotel Paradiso, where M. Boniface and Madame Cot
were seeking their little bit of hard-earned heaven, came his
business friend with four yelping and clattering daughters, his
servant-girl with a student of philosophy (Spinoza), and M. Cot
himself. The last had been called in by the manager to investigate
a faulty water-tank; this had been deemed to be a more likely
source of strange noises than a covey of ghosts would be. Add,
for good measure, a Duke and his Lady, a Turk, and a page with
an eye for keyholes, imagine all in motion on a stage which
reveals the goings-on in sundry apartments and on assorted
stairways, and you have a fair idea of the assembled company

92

and of the ballroom in which, as the anxious M. Boniface, Alec Guinness leads the dance. We are back in the period of Anouilh's WALTZ OF THE TOREADORS. The music this time is more suitable to the polka, gallop, and Lancers. But the idea of the taurine arena did enter my mind. Alec Guinness, with his delicacy of comic touch, in the midst of all this? While other histrionic bulls go raging round the china-shop of farce, would not the acting of Guinness resemble a piece of china in a bull-ring? It did, but the china was not smashed. Here was a most charming example of how to humanise mechanical situations and to bring a touch of creative fancy into the rigmarole of farcical rampage.

Peter Glenville's translation was not always in period. Europeans of 1910 did not speak American and inquire of each other how they 'made out' last night. But his direction was vigorous, inventive, and made the most of a very strong team of players. Whoever invented the 'business' – the original French authors, Guinness, or Glenville – the result contained some ingenious notions. When M. Boniface was being described to the police as a man of some height, the way in which Guinness dwindled to a shrimp was a perfect piece of physical comedy. His resort to a chimney for a hiding-place and his emergence as a black-faced sheep was also a fresh form of escapade to me, while Irene Worth's rescue from discovery by the jamming of a huge top-hat, like a tea-cosy, over her entire head was another novel fabrication of tomfoolery. Incidentally, this excursion into the tough-and-rumble of farcical storms, pursuits, concealments, and mendacities must be a new one to Miss Worth, whose year has included everything from ancient Greek to modern Italian tragedy, as well as this pirouette in the Paris of 'oh-la-la'. She went robustly into the battle of the bedrooms with a make-up and a wardrobe that were right in period. Her frilled blouse, with a tight high collar, was to me an adorable reminder of what attractive feminine visitors to my boyhood's home were accustomed to wear.

The principal pleasure was, of course, Alec Guinness's performance as Boniface. Film-goers are accustomed to Guinness in frivolity, but play-goers are used to Guinness in solemnity, as Hamlet or Richard II, as the sad, wan Fool in LEAR, or as the tormented ecclesiastic in that grim play of totalitarian savagery, THE CARDINAL. On this occasion he was mixing, in the theatre, his 'Ealing comedy' film-manner with a veteran form of stage-routine. He alone in the cast had the opportunity to insert some nearly realistic performance. While the others had to thunder or gesticulate, scream or be otherwise preposterous, he could be an actual specimen of the hunted husband. Thus at times he could direct his acting rather higher than at the tickling of ribs: he could point it at the heart. Not for long: he knew that Hotel Paradiso was not to be confused with Heartbreak House and that his function was mainly to put the audience in full chortle. But such laughter can be all the more effectively won with an occasional reminder that the victim of the hurly-burly is, in the last resort, a human being.

It would be absurd to say that Guinness was wasting his time and talents in this uproarious *galère*. The most devout remembrancers of Irving agree that among the topmost flights of his performance was his 'Jingle' in the dramatised version of *Pickwick Papers*. (Mention of Dickens reminds me that one of my happiest glimpses of Guinness's stage-work was as Herbert Pockett in his own adaptation of *Great Expectations*.) If our French farceurs have not provided him in HOTEL PARADISO with more than the ordinary figure of Mr Henpeck endeavouring to emerge as Mr Rooster, he has translated that normality of farce into something that abides in the mind, something individual and remarkable. While Frank Pettingell imposingly strutted and intoned, while Douglas Byng amusingly strutted and stammered, while Martita Hunt and Irene Worth took the measure of the vast Winter Garden auditorium and threw their voices and persons accordingly into loyal service of a good, rowdy night, Alec Guinness could keep still to conquer.

A few days after the opening the huge house was packed and appreciative. One naturally did not want so great an actor to remain engaged for a mammoth run and to be entered for years in this kind of steeplechase. But that was a point for him to settle. Meanwhile he was all that any man could desire as the centre-piece in the antique antics which Peter Glenville had so shrewdly deemed to be worthy of salvage from the dusty play-shelf.

Two points were noticeable about the text, which, I believe, has had its English versions before, both 'straight' and musical, under the title of A NIGHT OUT. One was the neatness of the workmanship. Usually we can expect the third act of a farce to

94

be ragged stuff and to reveal some despair of a neat finish on the author's part. But the French craftsmen really did tie up all the loose ends with exceptional deftness of contrivance. The second notable feature was the innocence of the whole affair. A French farce, fun in a series of bedrooms, would not this, of necessity, be dismally, repetitively 'blue'? Not at all. There was no pursuit of the risqué line and the nocturnal capers of M. Boniface were, in the end, as blameless as a cultural excursion to the Louvre.

Whisky - Priest

THE POWER AND THE GLORY

Adapted by Dennis Cannan and Pierre Bost from the novel by Graham Greene   *Phoenix Theatre*

The scene is Mexico, 1930. The Clerical Reactionaries have been routed. The Revolutionaries are in command. The People have been liberated, which means that they are forbidden both to practise their religion and to satisfy their normal impulse to consume alcohol. Priests are proscribed. To arrange a mass may be a capital offence, since that involves the presence of both faith and wine. The story is of a priest who defies the proletarian dictatorship, makes desperate and dangerous efforts to collect the sacramental wine and to celebrate the mass, and dies in the end for loyalty to his creed.

But it is well known to authors that saintly heroes are never such 'good copy' as are those with some taint of human frailty. The priest in this case has been quite copiously a sinner: he has been and remains a drinker and he has had a child by a peasant woman. He is shabby, shuffling, and as little romantic as any seedy cadger at the street-corner. So really we are back with one of the oldest of melodrama's ever-appealing veterans, the Wrong 'Un Who Does The Right Thing. The play's last scene is yet another version of THE ONLY WAY. When the priest risks and loses all, returning from safety to give absolution to a dying drunkard, he, like the once so popular Mr Carton, is doing a far, far better thing than he has ever done.

Nowadays, of course, the scamp turned hero does not announce the fact with the beautiful vocal tones once employed for the purpose by Sir Martin Harvey. But his great exit is none

95

the less an oppressive cliché. One might protest that so expert a hand as Mr Greene's could surely have worked upon a character less faded and events less banal in order to make a story; but at least he gave the familiar yarn a fresh setting and established the squalor now so much relished in our notions of a play. Peter Brook obviously had his fun, and most effective fun, in transferring Central America to the Charing Cross Road. In the countryside the drums were beating; in the town the police force boomed and bellowed: the dentist's surgery, where the play began and ended, was exquisitely sluttish and the few implements employed by that depressed tooth-tugger seemed incorrigibly septic: the glimpse of a Mexican hotel, in a town tactfully left anonymous, was not such as to stimulate the tourist industry of that country.

The part of the sodden whisky-priest was played by Paul Scofield who, in portraying the plucky vagrant, gave him the humility of an ill-treated dog and something of an animal growl in the voice. Grubby, gnarled and graceless as the fellow looked, he was the vessel of an inner grace and through the coarse clothing and rough demeanour so necessary to keep him in disguise among the rabble and unnoticed by the police there shone the light of a queer, unquenchable courage. The Noble Sinner of a myriad melodramas he might be: but Mr Scofield did give the old hokum a new look.

The 'good new play' for which the public vaguely clamours was not to be discovered in all this. There was a lively production by Peter Brook, with admirable lighting laid on by Strand Electric, that benefactor of so many producers. There was, indeed, a striking performance by Mr Scofield. But the story, as is the way of novels dramatised, ran thin. It suffered from a lack of well-built scenes and from an excess of small parts, some of them quite inadequately played. There was no secondary role of sufficient size or quality. The women's chances were inconsiderable.

One-part plays have had their occasional triumphs, but they are difficult to present to the best advantage. I did not weary of the whisky-priest and his misdeeds, misfortunes and meanderings, but I did wish that we were not always being introduced to new cross-sections of the Central American public, with whom it was impossible to strike up a firm acquaintance. The best chance of creating a sizeable and memorable character went to a Lieutenant

Clive Morton and Wendy Craig in MR KETTLE AND MRS MOON
at the Duchess (*Wilfrid Newton*)

Daphne Anderson and Bill Owen in THE THREEPENNY OPERA
at the Royal Court and the Aldwych (*Kevin MacDonnell*)

Dora Bryan in THE WATER GYPSIES at the Winter Garden (*Houston Rogers*)

Richard Burton and Zena Walker in HENRY V at the Old Vic (*Angus McBean*)

of Police, but the actor was not to be able to put the right degree of metal into this fanatic. Paul Scofield did provide the audience with an abiding point of interest and thus gave some strength and a centre to a piece in great need of them. But the fundamental weakness could hardly be obscured; I refer to the staleness of the notion that there is something eternally and inevitably attractive about the good deeds of bad men and in the spectacle of a sottish cleric who is obviously going to heaven after all.

Miss Robson

THE HOUSE BY THE LAKE

by Hugh Mills   *Duke of York's Theatre*

We are, at mid-winter, in what seems to be the area known to Estate Agents as the Surrey Highlands – or at least the Surrey Lake District. Oh to be in Frensham now that Feb. is there! For then the ponds will be frozen and, with a thaw just coming, guilty persons, taking short cuts across the ice, may vanish under water – or be deemed to have so perished.

Colin Holt, financier, certainly merited this kind of dismal drenching, if not a fatal dip at the end of his flagitious career. He had treated his family well at one time, but now, in his troubles, roughly and meanly. He had for neighbour a brother, Maurice, who was a gifted mesmerist: Maurice, a doctor, had blotted his professional copy-book by mixing hypnotism with medicine and both with the investment of a patient's money. He was living moodily by the lake without much visible means of subsistence. With him were his sinister sister as well as Janet, his long-suffering wife. (Maurice was not remarkable for the geniality of his conjugal manner, and his sister was no smiling angel in the house.)

For various reasons of family finance it became necessary for Maurice to be rid of his bad brother, Colin. Poisoned coffee would see to that, and the weather suggested that the corpse might very well go into the cold storage so conveniently provided by the frozen lake outside the door. But unfortunately Colin's financial misdemeanours had already attracted the attentions of the police; a detective lurked about the lake-side. This sleuth oddly and continually took the liberty of entering Maurice's house by the window instead of calling at the front door and his pursuit of Colin the crook was bound to lead to the chase of Maurice the murderer. In any case his wife, Janet, was becoming suspicious of the goings-on. This was natural enough, since her husband always bundled her out of the room when he wanted to talk family business (and murder) with that black-a-vised sister of his. The way in which ex-Doctor Holt treated his poor Janet would have made any woman wonder whether she was not herself destined for a place in that natural ice-box, if the frost continued.

The outcome of all this was obvious. It had been carefully 'planted' that Maurice could hypnotise any patient who had agreed to be put in a trance by him at some previous time. He had mesmerised Janet when he had rescued her long ago from the suicidal misery of her ill-starred youth. Now that Janet knows him to be a murderer and is likely to betray him, why not hypnotically persuade her to kill herself? You may have guessed that he had reckoned without that detective who always came in by the window. Windows in drama of this kind more often let in the Law than they do the light.

Here, with little element of surprise, but enough allure of the gruesome, was the kind of play that managers accept, the kind of play that gets generously cast, the kind of play that usually reaches the West End and 'gets along' when it gets there, and probably has a sufficiency of 'rep' and amateur rights to follow. Andrew Cruickshank was the right actor for mesmerical Maurice: he carefully avoided any Svengalist melodramatics. He cast his spell on poor Janet with a sulky but resolute quietude, just as he had brusquely planned his criminal operations amid terse and sullen conversations with his sister. If one is going to collide with a homicidal hypnotist amid the lake-side scenery of the Home Counties, doubtless he would be just the morose, but not too suspiciously macabre, figure that Mr Cruickshank presented. But I could not feel that the right lady for the persecuted, spell-bound Janet was Flora Robson. Still, without her, the play might, I suppose, never have got to London. The climax of the piece is Janet's submission to and reaction to her hypnotic husband. The play-goers would know that if anybody could vibrate the strings of sensibility in a scene of this kind, it would be Miss Robson.

We all know what that great actress has; she has strength, and therefore the kind of suffering that she can best present is that of a primitive nature stretched on the rack of an unheeding and incomprehensible world. But Janet in the play is not primitive: she has her wits about her, but she is like a fluttering bird in the domestic cage dominated by her sinister husband and sister-in-law. Miss Robson does not resemble or suggest a fluttering bird: she has, inescapably, an air not only of power but of the common sense that will use that power to good purpose. I never believed that her husband could put the 'fluence' so simply and so rapidly on the robust and rational wife whom this casting bestowed upon him. But of course Miss Robson, though she did not look the part, knew what she was doing and how to do it, and so was the leading attraction at the Duke of York's Theatre.

At present Miss Robson seems condemned to hob-nob continually with homicide. Shortly before this she had been brandishing no less a weapon than an axe. It is true that in THE HOUSE BY THE LAKE she committed no violence, but she was housed once more with crimes and criminals and so the public could be increasingly inclined to feel that any piece with her name on the bill will be of a macabre description. This is unjust to a versatile, as well as a profoundly moving, talent. Miss Robson can be gay, radiant, and conversational on the best Shavian lines. I have not forgotten, for example, her charming performance as Lady Cecily Waynflete in Shaw's 'CAPTAIN BRASSBOUND'S CONVERSION' at the Lyric Theatre, Hammersmith, and I shall look forward to a time when the name of Flora Robson outside a theatre does not necessarily signify that there are only dark deeds and condign punishments to be met with on the stage within.

Don Wharn

DON JUAN and THE DEATH OF SATAN
by Ronald Duncan   *Royal Court Theatre*

Plays, as I have remarked in my general review of the year, have tended to get shorter and shorter: even 'the two hours' traffic of our stage' is whittled away by a couple of lengthy intervals. But, in Ronald Duncan's case, the English Stage Company offered full measure. It provided two pieces which included thirteen scenes and lasted well over three hours. The E.S.C. thus not only displayed unusual bounty in the matter of amount: it also displayed this generosity while fitting four new productions into a period of a few weeks and sensibly including a native practitioner of verse drama in our time. Mr Devine has proved himself to be a man of urgency, as well as of doctrine, in the theatre. Furthermore, his journey into Mr Duncan's Spain (and Hell) was ingeniously staged and most cleverly lit.

More than fifty years ago A. B. Walkley challenged Shaw to write a Don Juan play. MAN AND SUPERMAN was the superhuman response. Shaw realised that, while men presented solely as lechers and Lotharios are bores, the Promethean and Faustian types, the rebels against the laws of God and man, have always tended to be popular. The conventional moralists are satisfied by the thought or the spectacle of the punishment coming to these wayward antinomians: the unconventional relish the idea of authority defied. So Shaw carried his Devil's Disciple from 18th-century America to contemporary England and turned Don Juan into John Tanner, Member of the Idle Rich Class and author of *The Revolutionist's Handbook*. Ronald Duncan, coming fifty years later to this theme, has examined the Don as a figure of romance in his own 18th-century Seville: in the second play he pursued him into a very modern hell where the company included Byron, Wilde, and G.B.S. By doing this the dramatist set himself an impossible task, which was to provide conversation good enough for three such masters of the spoken and the written word. He could not, of course, succeed: but he made a brave shot at it.

His first play observed the legend of Seville's indefatigable lover and of his single defeat and displayed the appropriate qualities of gallantry in gesture and in phrase. It threatened at times to become dull, but was saved by writing that had a sinewy style and by acting which, in the persons of Keith Michell as Juan and of Rosalie Crutchley as Ana, combined energy and elegance. Mr Michell's work at Stratford-upon-Avon had introduced him as a fitting heir to the almost forgotten romantic tradition of English acting in the 'costume play'. He has sonority; he has stature, carriage, and the right dash: he was thus a well-qualified Juan. (Why not, by the way, pronounce Juan as Ju-an? In this case I am for the Churchillian way with foreign names. The dreary talk of 'Don Wharn' had a suggestion of lamentation for me: do not the more melancholic sea-birds re-utter, Wharn, Wharn, Wharn? Do not the pains of the aching gum or anguished belly set children, and adults too, making Wharn-like noises?)

When, in the second play, Juan has got to hell, ruled over by a highly ecclesiastical Satan, he listens to the chatter of his successors and finds it discordant and disagreeable. Why not return to modern Spain? There he finds that the Anglo-American inmates of a luxurious and modernly decorated hotel make love without passion and are Laodiceans in lechery. In this sad world there are no jealousies because there are no ecstasies, and no glory of guilt because there is no sense of sin. His Ana has become a hard-bitten journalist, married to a 'please-the-public' novelist. There are no raptures, no splendours, no swordsmanship here. What can the fiery Don make of love in such a cold climate? To brandish a blade is meaningless and futile. Don Juan has discovered the true nature of hell; it is remembering the past; heaven lies in forgetting it.

Play-goers may have preferred the latter piece, in which Mr Duncan writes prose about his new inferno, to the former with its poetry about the old Seville of seductions and of duelling. But Miss Crutchley and Mr Michell did lift the fatal episode with Ana to a level which, if less than tragedy, was more than 'tushery'. In the second play Rachel Kempson handsomely presented a picture of the modern wanton who was a lover by routine, as little enthusiastic as a worker in an 'automation' factory, while Michael Gwynn was amusingly canonical as a Right Reverend Satan. Some of it went on excessively long and trimming of the text would have been helpful. This Seville had need of its barber. But on the whole I was grateful for Mr Duncan's conducted tour of world and underworld.

Amateur Final

BRITISH DRAMA LEAGUE FESTIVAL OF COMMUNITY DRAMA

Final Performances.   Scala Theatre

The National Press takes little notice of the amateur actors: it is understandable that occasional performances, having no run to follow and being of dubious quality, should be overlooked. The local Press will probably review them. But, since space is often found in papers of national standing for professional productions of a minor order and of very limited appeal, it is strange that the National Festival of Community Drama, especially in its Final stage, should not attract more attention. The number of newspaper readers in some way affected is much larger, I fancy, than most London editors imagine.

This year's Competitive Festival of one-act plays, organised by the British Drama League, drew nearly 1,100 entries from England, Scotland, Wales and Northern Ireland. Of these Scotland was the most prolific in proportion to its population, supplying 421 teams. All this productive effort is quite separate from a large number of other local Festivals to which competing companies of amateurs come with either short or full-length plays. Some of the best amateur societies do not care for the competitive spirit and dislike the travel and trouble involved in entering for tournaments of the kind: they prefer to do their own work in their own headquarters.

What is obvious to those who know anything about the amateur theatre in this country is the astonishing extent of its operations and the very great number whom it attracts both as members of the audience and as partakers in the production. The Amateur Drama is not 'news' in the Fleet Street sense: but news and views of its work probably interest far more people than some folk in Fleet Street realise. Mr Edward Hulton, however, holds a different opinion. Believing strongly in the value of the amateur drama and the quality of its achievement, he readily associated *Picture Post* with the Festival of 1956, giving excellent publicity to the work of the teams and welcome awards to those surviving the early rounds, awards most useful in meeting the ever-soaring costs of travel as well as of production.

The British Drama League's nation-wide Festival usually reaches its final stages at the Scala Theatre in June, after initial rounds have led to Area Finals and Divisional Finals. The organisation necessary for this demands much labour from the local committees and from the enthusiastic individuals most concerned: the staff at National Headquarters has also a big job on its hands, which this year became bigger than ever because there were two tournaments instead of one. On the afternoon of 16 June, there was the Final of the English Section, won by a society called 'The Dramatists' of Stoke-on-Trent, and in the evening the Final of the National Event in which the Stoke-on-Trent company competed, as English champions, against the winning teams of the Scottish, Irish, and Welsh sections. This was won for Scotland by the Greenock Players.

Naturally adjudication of the performances given in plays of entirely different kinds must always be extremely difficult and must at times yield results extremely disappointing to the competitors and most surprising to the lookers-on. How to match good work in costume and poetry against good work in modern prose, how to decide between a neat contrivance of comedy and a powerful presentation of a serious or a tragic theme? The adjudicators are specialists and usually well-known in the professional theatre. They do their best to fulfil an almost impossible function. It would be much easier if all the teams had to perform the same test-piece, but that is unpopular with the teams, who naturally want to select a play according to their various tastes and their talents: it is also calculated to drive the audiences and judges into the depths of boredom and distress.

I had on the occasion of this last Final to watch two performances in a day by the Stoke team of THE BESPOKE OVERCOAT by Wolf Mankowitz, now a very popular piece of Jewish sentimentality which I had already seen played on the professional stage – and filmed and 'televised' as well. I must confess that I crept out to avoid the second dose; a judge who had to watch this piece (or any other) repeated a score of times in rapid succession would certainly need psychiatric treatment at the close. So the competitors' offerings are inevitably different and the adjudication inevitably 'chancy' as the result, however scrupulous may be the judge or judges and however exact the scrutiny.

What many people fail to realise is the astonishingly high level of achievement in these Festivals. It is true that a company which has carefully rehearsed a short play and got through several rounds before it reaches the Scala in June ought to have its presentation of the piece fully polished and ship-shape beyond a doubt. But, when that allowance has been made, it remains true that the acting seen at the Amateur Finals is well up to the standard of our better professional repertories and considerably above that of the worse. This large claim was fully justified, in my opinion, by the National Final, whose Howard de Walden Trophy was won by Greenock.

First came Wales, represented by the Brecknock Little Theatre. Their play was called PROFILE and its author was T. C. Thomas, a dramatist who has helped other Welsh teams to victory and has a very happy knack of using Welsh humours and Welsh-English idioms and accent. But on this occasion he did not exploit that considerable advantage. His story was one of those macabre, back-from-the-war tales of a battle-scarred man who discovers that the woman whom he seeks cannot see his hideous deformity as she has been blinded. To this essay in austerity and suffering Welshness was incidental and strong sincerity of performance most essential. It was firmly directed, well-lit – the play's event is nocturnal – and expertly performed. The judges, Barbara Couper, Denis Carey, and Peter Forster did not have to declare their placings after announcing the winners. If they had, I should have expected them to allot the second place to Brecknock.

It must be remembered that this was a new (or comparatively new) play and I think that more emphasis should be laid in competitions of this kind on the desirability of escaping from routine favourites which the players can have previously seen professionally performed on stage or screen or on TV. The Stoke-on-Trent team with THE BESPOKE OVERCOAT were treading, with advantage, on familiar ground. Furthermore, there is another problem for the judges in deciding how to value a play depending for its main effect on one or two parts as against one which demands an 'ensemble' production and a team of varied and well-balanced capabilities. The two chief actors of the Stoke company were certainly most efficient in transmission of its racial quality, but the piece did not put much responsibility on the others or demand co-operation in a difficult theatrical pattern.

104

Northern Ireland, represented by Bangor Drama Club, went hell-for-leather at Eugene O'Neill's grim piece THE ROPE. (It was a curious occurrence that during the day the Welsh team spoke in English, the Irish in American, and the English in English-Jewish: only the Scots were loyal to their native lingo and accent and the 'braid Scots' volubly delivered by the Greenock voices was so extremely 'braid' that even an Anglo-Scot in the Scala audience could frequently have been gravelled for lack of Doric.) It would have been quite easy to let the melodramatic side of THE ROPE topple over into the laughable. But the acting had a firm grip on the medley of greed and homicidal passions seething in Eugene O'Neill's rough types on a rough shore. One actor at least, Colin Blakely, had the looks, power, and assurance to catch the eye of a film-director if any such had the unlikely prescience to be scouting round among amateurs.

Greenock won with THE REVE'S TALE adapted from Chaucer by Colin MacLean. This mediaeval caper demanded great animation and nimbleness of action from the players; the production, by Colin Brown, was most cleverly contrived to let the action flow as Dougal Sim the Miller was tricked by his wife and daughter. The costumes took the eye: the acting was so vivid that all could follow the detail of the plot, even though the ear might be baffled by strange words and intonations: the timing of the complicated intrigue and bustle of the story was most expert. The whole affair had a confidence in attack and an assured expertness of touch that fascinated the audience. The average member of that packed assembly must have wondered during the first five minutes whether any of the spoken word was going to be intelligible in any degree. But the Greenock gusto proved richly infectious: the old Chaucerian jest went jauntily on to gain first place, and few can have thought the judges' verdict was a wrong one. This was indeed an 'ensemble' effort. All the team had makeable parts and all made good, lusty use of them. I pick the word 'lusty' advisedly: the story of the trickery is not an essay in the stricter morality.

I found the long day at the Scala both stimulating and consoling. I was never more convinced that the unprofessional actor can justify the fine name of amateur by killing for ever the silly belief that 'amateurish' is a synonym for the slip-shod performance and for the crudely ambitious flounderings of people impelled mainly by a shallow exhibitionism. The amateur at his

105

best is one who proves himself to be a lover, as the name implies, of his chosen craft and exercise. Both the B.D.L. Festival Finals revealed this kind of energetic affection for the art of acting. Careful preparation had been made: but the study of technique had not produced a dry exactness of performance. There was obviously pleasure taken in a thing worth doing and worthily done. The Scots, naturally, with their choice of a robust comedy, had the best opportunity to display gusto of spirit as well as mastery of craft: and, to the full, they rapturously took it. A supposedly dour and self-suppressing people has lately taken to dramatic self-expression of the liveliest kind – and on an imposing scale. (Witness the number of Scottish entries and the still larger operations of the Scottish Community Drama Association.) Greenock, which has lately built for itself a first-rate little Arts Theatre, was well rewarded by this victory. The other three nations will be on their toes to win back the Trophy next year.

Enter a Bawd

GIGI
by Colette and Anita Loos   *New Theatre*

Not having been a student of the novels of Colette, I cannot say from my own knowledge whether Anita Loos correctly interpreted the emotional tones of her 'Gigi' story. One more in touch with the French writer assured me that Colette could tell a squalid story with some reconciling tenderness. The play of GIGI has plenty of squalor before it moves to a sugary finish. The main part of it reveals the efforts of a schoolgirl's mother, grand-mother, and great-aunt to 'launch' the child in life; by 'launching' they mean turning the girl into the call-girl of a wealthy young owner of motor-cars and mistresses. These elders have all been in the business of *cocotterie* themselves, two with only moderate success. But the great-aunt has had a rewarding place in the world of the Higher Prostitution and has collected enough jewellery from one man or another to prove that love's labour was never lost in her case. This raddled harpy has at least the merit of being frank and she sets about the training of Gigi in the way a girl should go (*i.e.* wrong) with complete candour,

106

steely cynicism, and a certain amount of rancid wit. We meet this kind of harridan in English classics of the Tudor and Restoration Theatre. Our ancestors had a word for her, a short, blunt, and powerfully dismissive word, 'bawd'.

Gigi herself is seen as a gawky schoolgirl with a half-petulant, half-pathetic charm. She is getting too old for her go-to-class tartan dress and long button-boots. (The period of the play is that of the first telephones and motor-cars in Parisian life.) Her mother is now a failed soprano, having failed also in the family profession. But she still gets small parts and keeps her voice in practice. (Over-much fun, perhaps, with the topnotes of this too ambitiously melodious Mama.) Granny is the buxom relic of a love-affair with a Spaniard and cares, no doubt efficiently, for the cooking in the home. The bawdy great-aunt lives apart, in her own luxury. It is not a nice family circle in which Gigi does her scholastic home-work and is given further education for a career deemed likely to pay quick and plentiful dividends.

The chances are, I suppose, that in actual life Gigi, having been coaxed into the life of profitable vice, would have satisfied a plutocrat, earned big money, and so brought home the wages of sin to satisfy her avaricious and unscrupulous elders. But that would not do for the American and English stages. And the public, having so enjoyed a RELUCTANT DEBUTANTE, would surely rejoice in a RELUCTANT PROSTITUTE. Gigi has to protest that she wants to be a good girl and the young Midas who at one minute is callously trying to buy Gigi as his mistress (and is put to some hard bargaining by the great-aunt), turns round and says that his heart is pure, his purpose honourable, and will the sixteen-year-old girl consent to be his wedded wife? Needless to say, Gigi, dewy-eyed but smiling, consents.

This supposedly happy ending might be as horrible to any sensitive person as is the proposed selling of Gigi's body by her disgusting relatives. Could a girl of sixteen rightly decide to pledge her life, not to a Romeo, but to a Lothario, on the assumption that the rip is now going to be reformation's masterpiece? The issue was neatly burked in production by casting Tony Britton as the plutocratic rake. Mr Britton arrived in pursuit of Gigi looking so little French and so little rakish that he might have been standing for election to the M.C.C. – and getting in! Never did a fresher-faced, cleaner-limbed specimen of God's

Englishman, as pictured in the serial stories of women's maga-
zines with a four-million sale, come with a more handsome innocence before an audience. Of course Gigi would be able to
marry in confidence a husband so obviously equipped to be a
model of spotless gentility.

The cunning of enlisting Mr Britton, though it must have been
completely unpersuasive to anybody who gave the character of
the rich playboy a moment's thought, was bound to please the
less reflective and more numerous play-goers. It was equalled by
the cunningly contrived writing and casting of the part of Gigi.
The French ballerina and Hollywood Film Name, Leslie Caron,
inevitably won the hearts and applause of the audience and got
past the critics too. I say 'inevitably' because here is a role in
which no young woman of any talent could fail to score. The
long-legged schoolgirl with the simple antics of a filly in the
field, the schoolgirl beset by the bawdy temptress that is her
great-aunt, the child doomed to a life of shame and then, thanks
to her obstinate purity of heart, winning both her marriage-lines
and a fortune – what can go wrong? But Dorothy Tutin could
have romped home in this exercise even more easily than did
Mlle Caron, who was handicapped by the fact that her speaking
of English was not always completely intelligible. But she had
the right kind of puckish, plain-pretty charm and she never
risked underacting. The young lady was engaged for a part
which needs a performance, and suitably she performed. So Gigi
won her way out of the Bawds' Nest into matrimonial bliss and
the public, with the orange-blossom almost dropping from the
proscenium arch at the final curtain, could forget the odious
great-aunt and forget also the fact that the unscrupulous lover
of Act 2 was very ill qualified to be the Perfect Husband of
Act 3.

As the Bawd who had done Big Business in her time and
means to do even Bigger Business with a child for sale, Estelle
Winwood presented a terrifying old besom. Supposed, or so I
suppose, to be amusing, the part is surely too ugly for British
taste and the scene in which the old lady shows her medals in the
form of jewellery enough to fill a Bond Street window failed to
amuse. At Gigi's home Ena Burrill was a formidable Granny
and Kathleen Michael a devastating soprano. The efforts to
make light relief from her unquenchable vocalism were somewhat laboured, doubtless at the producer's orders. Peter Hall,

directing, was obviously at his wits' end to get some blameless laughs amid so much that was squalid in the story; only in part did he succeed.

John Clements' Year

THE SHADOW OF DOUBT
by Norman King   *Saville Theatre*

THE WILD DUCK
by Henrik Ibsen   *Saville Theatre*

THE RIVALS
by R. B. Sheridan   *Saville Theatre*

John Clements, in management at the Saville, became one of the theatre's C.B.E.s in the Birthday Honours List of 1956. This was well timed for he had just given London three productions of high quality and representative value during the previous twelve months. In using the word 'representative' I mean that the work of three centuries and three nations was put on view. Modern was mingled with classical. There was a new English play of social realism, then a fine example of Ibsen at his ripest in his play which ridiculed the Ibsenites, and lastly a Sheridan revival in which John Clements himself was at the top of his own fine range of performance.

To those who keep asking 'Where are the new playwrights?' I suggest the name of Norman King as one satisfactory reply. His piece THE SHADOW OF DOUBT had, I was glad to note, a satisfactory run. It had a topical subject: it was tautly written: it provided good acting parts. The central figure, played by John Clements, was a man of science who was not a man of the world. This gifted dreamer thought that, with the war well over, it was the business of a liberal-minded expert to share his know-ledge with the world, for which piece of virtuous innocence he found himself in prison and with a future sombrely over-clouded.

Such men are not, indeed cannot be, left unwatched upon release, for the law and the Government must, in such grave cases, be arbiter of the thing done and cannot be confident of blameless notions in the past and of blameless conduct on the morrow. The sufferings of the scientist in the play were the penalty of his silliness, in the ancient and honourable sense of

109

that word when it meant simplicity; he had never purposed treachery. But those who, despite their professional brilliance, behave like 'silly sheep' in politics will find that such sheep are easily herded through Traitor's Gate by counterfeit shepherds to whom the crook is a natural implement and symbol.

Here was a play that met Hamlet's requirement: it was an abstract of our time and it was all the more effective because of the plausibility of the setting in a shabby flat in a manufacturing town. Place and persons both struck true. A cast which included Raymond Huntley, Patrick Barr, Henry Hewitt, and Jane Baxter as well as John Clements provided the best kind of English performance in a play about assorted English types, ranging from a Whitehall vigilant to the agent of another nation.

In THE WILD DUCK Ibsen may be said to have handed out all he had got. There is symbolism for those who hate a plain statement in any work of art and love to wonder what means what: there is satire for those who relish the spectacle of a supposedly noble and hard-working papa being shown up as an insufferably selfish, greedy, and lazy chatterbox: there is pathos in the light that failed in little Hedwig's eyes: and there is the spectacle of the dramatist who had himself been counselling ruthless unmasking of frauds and exposure of lies turning round to explain that this advice can be disastrous. Gregers Werle, insisting on holding up the Banner of the Ideal, on shattering harmless illusions which he took to be poisonous lies, and on proclaiming Truth-At-All-Costs, is simply an over-zealous Ibsenite. Ibsen realised that he was beginning to produce fanatics of the kind by his own zest for overturning the pillars of society and prising open the shutters of dolls' houses. It needs a great campaigner to turn and criticise his own campaign. Ibsen had this greatness. For that reason, as well as for half a dozen others, THE WILD DUCK with its frank declaration that some illusions are, after all, essential to human happiness, is one of the greatest of the world's great plays. It is wise, it is honest, and it is both immensely touching and richly amusing.

Again, the cast was a strong one. The arrival of Angela Baddeley to play the mother of Hedvig, the girl of whom she had given such a moving picture in her own girlhood, was most welcome. Dorothy Tutin as Hedvig naturally drove deep into the heart of one's compassion. Michael Gough had the right foolish fanaticism for Gregers, and Laurence Hardy could not have been bettered as the drunken doctor who is the dramatist's own messenger and intersperses the tippler's hiccups with the salutary common-sense of one who knows the ways of human misery as well as the frailties of the human body. Emlyn Williams joined the company to play that rich humbug, Hjalmar Ekdal, and failed, in my own opinion, to do it richly enough. He seemed too thin, too meagre, too active, for the insatiable eater of tit-bits and for the lounging and complacent depender on the work of his family. Of course, Emlyn Williams is very rarely an actor to fumble: but I think that on this occasion he missed his usual certainty of touch. That was odd, since Hjalmar is an obvious cousin to the great Dickensian frauds about whom Emlyn Williams knows everything.

The production did not make the most of the opportunities, but Laurence Irving's setting, as in the case of THE SHADOW OF DOUBT, was exactly right in its composition of the scene and suggestion of the atmosphere.

THE RIVALS was received with rapture and drew very large audiences. I was chiefly delighted by the Sir Anthony of John Clements, a ramrod in figure, poppy-red in colouring, and as explosive as a major firework, yet never outdoing the humanity of a choleric codger. There were two Jack Absolutes during the run. I saw Richard Johnson, who had recently given us such an acutely drawn cartoon of Warwick in SAINT JOAN. He now brought a charming ease of style and a witty, self-confident calm to the pretences and excuses of the young rogue. Sheridan's Jack is an impudent puppy to his father, but this Jack would have won a first prize as an elegant and intelligent thoroughbred in any Dog Show of the shires. On the night of my visit Athene Seyler seemed to be out of form, possibly out of health. For her Mrs Malaprop was sadly devitalised and, unless that dear dragon delivers her lines with genuine gusto and with immoderate energy, she dwindles into a curious ineffectiveness. Illness regrettably kept Kay Hammond out of Lydia's part which Gwen Cherrell played with a kindly compliment by providing a neat Kay Hammond imitation. Paul Daneman, condemned to be the sententious and tiresome Falkland, made light of the sentence by making Falkland's flow of soul sparkle with comedy as well as run deep with sighs. Acres was inadequately played and Fag was over-played, but William Mervyn's Sir Lucius came to the rescue. I sometimes find the trip to Sheridan's Bath

111

less than rewarding; but this time there was, among weaknesses, a Sir Anthony who lifted the whole performance at his every appearance.

Dubious Counsel

HOW NOT TO WRITE A PLAY

by Walter Kerr   *Published by Reinhardt* (21s)

Mr Kerr of the New York *Herald Tribune* is one of the most important and powerful of American dramatic critics. He has taught in drama schools: he has directed plays in important productions. He writes in the brusque, blunt, and confident manner of American journalism. He holds strong opinions and does not stop to consider that there may be replies to his contentions. On he rattles, always immensely readable and often, in my opinion, immensely contradictable.

He takes the line that the American theatre is nearly dead because it has failed to give the larger public what it wants: that, in his view, is strong drama of situation with no intervention of ideas. His chief bugbear is the play with a theme, or even worse, a purpose. Accordingly he censures the social realism, with the posing of problems, which came in with Ibsen and the Ibsenites: the secondary victim of his disgust and derision is Chekhov and the Chekhovians, who give us static pictures of frustrated people continuing to be frustrated. He can hardly deny that the world is full of social problems baffling all of us and of individuals who cannot solve their own problem of how to escape from their own stagnation. What he vigorously asserts is the reluctance of the majority of people to be interested by plays about political and moral issues or by plays in which the characters are drifting about instead of driving forward.

In support of this he points out that plays of this order do not have long runs on Broadway, whereas stronger stuff with no appeal to the mind, or musical comedies with their violently animated capers, have run for years. This appeal to box-office figures (and to box-office figures only) is crude and disastrous logic. One might as well claim that because more people prefer jazz music to classical music the Symphony Orchestra is a failure and ought never to be assisted to continue: further, on these

John Clements and Laurence Harvey in THE RIVALS at the Saville (*Houston Rogers*)

Richard Burton as Iago and John Neville as Othello at the Old Vic (*Angus McBean*)

John Neville as Iago and Richard Burton as Othello at the Old Vic (*Angus McBean*)

Peter Ustinov in ROMANOFF AND JULIET at the Piccadilly (*Denis de Marney*)

lines, it can be insisted that a National Gallery of painting is an unjustifiable institution because the great majority of citizens pass it by or regard it as a cultural 'must' to be got through with haste and forgotten with relief. Is there to be no consideration of minority opinion? Is everything in the world of the arts to be settled by the counting of heads, many of them empty?

Mr Kerr is on doubtful ground when he asserts that the American theatre, which is mainly the New York theatre, is moribund. The season 1955-6 has been a lively one for all types of drama. Nor does that theatre always lose fatally by the post-Ibsen or post-Chekhov type of play. Such plays continue to be written: also they continue to find 'backers' and, if the 'backers' take more risk than do the promoters of bouncing 'musicals', surely that is to their credit. The runs of the plays which Mr Kerr detests are not always brief nor is the investment always disastrous. He ridicules, for example, the lack of punch and speed in the plays of John Van Druten, but it is incontestable that the author has had many long-running successes even though his method may be mocked as 'The Slow Road to Nowhere.'

Mr Kerr writes with a smart flick of the wrist and, when he sets out to punish a dramatist who does not conform to Mr Kerr's idea of what the public wants, he does so with a neat and witty castigation. But he does not, because he cannot, demonstrate that a mass-vote is a proper test of quality whether it be in politics or art or entertainment. He is contemptuous of 'little theatre' productions simply because little theatres are little, which is rather like despising a members' social club because it is not a public restaurant with a thousand tables. Little theatres do have small audiences and run into financial trouble. (So, often, do big ones with big 'musicals'.) I cannot agree that a thing is not worth doing unless the doing of it satisfies millions of more or less moronic patrons. It is not intellectual snobbery to maintain that the few, if indeed they are as few as Mr Kerr claims, are being futile in backing their own fancy and defying the mass-vote of the multitude.

We live in large communities dominated by what Mr Priestley calls Admass, *i.e.* the provision through the new mass-media of films, radio and television of centralised entertainment in which a handful of star-artists are monopolising the attention and the admiration of millions simultaneously and acquiring almost divine status in the opinion of those millions. Because these hordes like to sit at home at no cost absorbing Admass products instead of making or discovering variety of recreation and showing some power of choice and appetite for novelty, the theatres suffer loss of patronage. Does that prove the theatre to be useless and effete? To satisfy a thousand reasonably intelligent people is not as profitable as to satisfy a million morons and may result in financial loss. Agreed. But will the drama be essentially healthier, except in finance, if every playwright has to consider all the time how to gratify moronic taste?

One would think from reading Mr Kerr that the mob is an assembly entirely composed of the judicious and that its verdicts are always good tributes to quality. For him, it is the mob that makes the masterpiece. 'Molière perfected himself by coming to grips with the common appetite.' Shakespeare wrote fine plays because he loved money and wrote for the groundlings. What nonsense this is! Shakespeare wrote for the Court and Inns of Court wits just as much as for the groundlings. The highbrows adored him. We are told that University students kept pictures of him by their beds. Naturally he wanted to please the noblemen who protected the players and gave private and well-paid performances in their houses. To be played at Court was to be twice as well rewarded as to be played in a public theatre. Shakespeare threw in bits, no doubt, to bring in the groundlings; but they paid very much less for their places at the play than did the milords in the galleries, and, since Shakespeare was normally interested in money, he naturally had his eye on the good payers.

Mr Kerr's habit of generalising (and generalising from ignorance) is astounding. 'No great play ever came from what might be called a minority theatre. All of the work we prize most highly was born of the commercial, or at least competitive, hurly-burly and in the presence of a mass-audience.'

Did the tiny Abbey theatre of Dublin, created by an English philanthropist Miss Horniman, by Lady Gregory, and by W. B. Yeats, ever provide a mass-audience? Yet it produced THE PLAYBOY OF THE WESTERN WORLD and JUNO AND THE PAYCOCK. Did the Irish people ever back or applaud their dramatists? They rioted against Synge and made O'Casey prefer exile with the supposedly brutish oppressor of his country, England.

114

Incidentally another Irish exile, Bernard Shaw, had all his earliest and best plays produced in minority theatres and at special performances.

When Mr Kerr mentions Greek drama he speaks of Sophocles and says that the Greek theatre was not a sober and high-minded affair, but 'garish, musicalized and shatteringly robust' with a noisy audience not above throwing stones if displeased. The Athenians' Festival of Comedy may have been on the convivial side, but Sophocles was not a comedian. The great tragic Festivals, the Dionysia, where Sophocles won twenty first prizes, were solemn religious ceremonies with the priests of Dionysus presiding and judging the productions. The tragedies themselves were more like religious services than secular entertainments. If Sophocles had been told that he worked for a theatre 'garish, musicalized, and shatteringly robust', he would indeed have been surprised at this description of his stone auditorium, sceneless stage, solemn and restrained eurhythmic movements, and chorus of hymns chanted to thin flutings and pipings.

What happened in Athens does not greatly concern the present state of the theatre. But it does show that when Mr Kerr bangs the desk he may be going to speak the thing that is not. I am rarely to be found on the side of the more elevated Egg-Heads and the most choice of the Chosen Few in matters of the arts, but Mr Kerr's devout addiction to the mass-vote drives me to believe that minorities can sometimes be right.

Yet if Mr Kerr cannot be read with any confidence for facts or for a philosophy of the arts, he can certainly be read for fun. And, since discussions of the theatre often become a trifle dismal, he should be read accordingly. It is always a pleasure to meet a writer who is wholly incapable of being a bore; being a critic, he will not mind being thus criticised – or will he?

Ustinovia

ROMANOFF AND JULIET

by Peter Ustinov   *Piccadilly Theatre*

Peter Ustinov, unlike most of our dramatists, understands that politics exist; he will not bore us, we know in advance, with just another tinkle on the eternal triangle. He knows that the affairs of the world are not simply affaires of the worldly. He also credits his audience with enough intelligence to understand and even relish political satire. And rightly so. One of his previous plays, about Love among the Colonels, was a triumphant success: his product of 1956, which might be called Eros in the Embassies or Love among the Diplomats, seemed likely to be no less of a triumph. It had the same ingredients, a pleasantly sharp wit, a pleasantly free fancy, and a pleasant ability to stage immediate and mundane realities, *i.e.* Power Politics, in the kind of fantastic setting where one might look for song and dance.

In a personal address to the audience the actor-dramatist introduces 'the smallest country in Europe'. Since he does not name it, let us call it Ustinovia. It has been invaded, overrun, and liberated with tedious iteration down the centuries. It is at present more or less free to pursue its entertainment of tourists in musical comedy surroundings. But even Ustinovia has now to be courted by the Great Powers who would have it join either the Western or the Eastern Bloc. On one side of the Central Square of the tiny capital is the American Embassy, on the other the Russian. Between them is Peter Ustinov, enacting the elected potentate of Ustinovia; at one moment he is a General, dressed or rather bedizened as though to appear in a revival of THE MERRY WIDOW; at another he is solemnly garbed in the topper and tails of a Cabinet Minister with the business of the Foreign Office on his hands.

He must keep the peace between a taut and nervous American Ambassador and a large, heavy-fisted, stentorian Russian. To the bitter political suspicions of these two has been added the deplorable arrival of the tender passion among the parental portfolios. Young Romanoff, the son of the Russian, has entranced, and is entranced by, Juliet, the daughter of the American. So the tragic situation of the Montagus and Capulets of old Verona is renewed in the chancelleries and on the balconies of up-to-date Ustinovia.

Peter Ustinov has his own way of composing and performing in the theatre: he is quite ready to address the audience directly in contempt of realism: yet he does not carry anti-realism so far as to disdain natural and witty dialogue naturally spoken. Thus he does not make guys of his Russians and Americans: they are close enough to actuality to be the genuine persons of a likely story and not just the useful puppets of a satirical surrealism.

116

To the Russian, presented with the right massive squareness by Frederick Valk, he allots not only the usual dread of deviation and the familiar eagerness for confessions of that crime, but also a moving speech about the dawn of the Revolution. In his eloquence we can vividly see pale, fierce faces of the rebels who knew for what they fought and believed in what they knew. That surge of the free spirit is poignantly contrasted with the mechanisation and even the enslavement of the mind which has been, so ironically, the reward of that revolutionary victory.

The dominant note, however, was comedy; there was the eternal tragi-comedy of the lovers in divided camps and the present political comedy of the Powers also in division. Between these human icicles of the Cold War the ruler of Ustinovia, the peace-ensuing General, went hastily padding. His task was to play for time till tempers cooled and also until, by a trick, he had got the young couple safely wedded. That *fait accompli* could accomplish also a political appeasement among the sour seniors and, since this was a fairy-story in the cloud-cuckoo-land of Ustinovia, it eventually managed to do so. We were not asked to believe it, but merely to enjoy it: and this, on the night of my visit, we certainly did.

The heart of the matter, of course, was Mr Ustinov's own performance. As the Ruler he spoke directly to us, simple and suave and sweet. Could a General be gentler, could a Diplomat be more coaxingly the dear, paunchy, avuncular fuddy-duddy of this performance, so childlike and bland on the surface, so well aware, below the surface, of the foibles of humanity and of the way to play on them? There was high comedy as much in the writing of his part as in its delivery. I should have thought that the young lovers might have been more strongly cast, but both the Ambassadors had the right kind of service from Mr Valk and John Phillips while David Hurst as a spy, and Delphi Lawrence as a spy on spies, added humorous character to the strength of the Russian team.

It can be said of Mr Ustinov that he takes the theatre very lightly and offers charades with himself as compère rather than plays with himself as a strenuous author-dramatist. I heard someone say that he is not a dramatist but a doodler, and that his acting is a form of doodling too. This was not said in censure: the implication was that he doodled most delightfully and that his decorated margins or note-pad scribbles are as rich a contribution

117

to our theatre as any well-considered, long-worked-over script. I agree. Peter Ustinov must go his own way and, certainly in a play such as ROMANOFF AND JULIET he tip-toed engagingly into our sympathies with his mixture of personal patter and professional craft.

Many members of the audience must have left the Piccadilly Theatre most eager to spend a holiday in Ustinovia, if only they could find it and provided, of course, that the General was still there to discuss his nation's past sufferings, present amenities, and future political alignments. They would insist too on attending a public ceremony graced by the deaf and doddering archbishop so nicely introduced to us by Edward Atienza and presided over by Peter Ustinov in full military fig. Above all they would require the General to be their personal guide and courier, lecturer on local history, and 'Spa Manager'. Mr Ustinov, the Peter factotum of our theatre, could easily be all.

The death of Frederick Valk, which occurred shortly after this review was written, deprived both Mr. Ustinov's play and the English theatre of a great talent, voice, and personality.

Two Dames in a Garden

THE CHALK GARDEN
by Enid Bagnold   *Haymarket Theatre*

It was surprising that this piece, which immediately became the season's 'play-you-can't-get-into' was first produced in New York. For it is as English as our South Down chalk and as native as our governess-companions were in the age of the golden sovereign. It is as English as somnolent judges who should have retired ten years ago and drowsily remain; as English, too, as fantastic old ladies who have the oddest tastes and forms of behaviour but are perfectly normal in their addiction to gardening – or to seeing that somebody does the gardening for them as commanded. Can it have been rejected here and then recovered for the London theatre after it had been acclaimed on Broadway? If so, it makes me the more surprised when our Henry Sherek tells us, elsewhere in this volume, that managers are all agog to pounce, with the speed of panthers, on any 'good play' in sight.

Of course no play is a 'good play' until it is acted and acted well. Superlative performance, such as THE CHALK GARDEN received, will hypnotise an audience, including the professional members of it, into overlooking faults which may be serious. But, after rubbing my eyes in order to shake off any effects of this histrionic mesmerism, I could not discover any sufficient reason for regarding the piece as meriting a place on the 'reject' pile of typescripts in the managerial office. It contains one large improbability, but most of the world's great plays, beginning with OEDIPUS REX, are based on large improbabilities, and life itself is continuously stuffed with the unlikely and the almost impossible event. When I am asked to believe that the dumpy, solid, taciturn and immensely respectable woman, whom we first meet applying for the job of governess in a Sussex home, was once sentenced to death for murdering a relative, I can remark that this is a tall order, but I cannot call it an impossible command. And since Dame Peggy Ashcroft played the part, anybody's disbelief may be most easily and willingly abandoned. It is never, by the way, stated whether the governess was actually guilty or not. The lady herself remains uncommunicative.

Such a discovery, coupled with the fact that the Judge who passed the sentence is meeting her at lunch, suggests a drama of tense situations and a return to the old technique of the 'strong curtain' crashing down upon the Woman at Bay. (In case you may wonder how, after the sentence, the lady was at large again, it must be explained that there was a reprieve and a life-sentence which was remitted after fifteen years.) The fascinating feature of THE CHALK GARDEN was the way in which the play was sustained in the air, almost in the air of comedy, above the melodramatic arena into which it might easily have fallen. The production by Sir John Gielgud and the leading performances by Dame Peggy Ashcroft and Dame Edith Evans did effectively keep the action moving on its tight-rope of high comedy, despite the grim quality of the previous events.

Mrs St Maugham, who owns the house with the chalk garden and the view of the Downs, has been a silly creature all her days, and a bad mother into the bargain: she is also one of those irascible relics of the Edwardian domesticity which took 'domestics' for granted. Yet the play would perish if we did not like her follies and her nerves and her mixture of gaiety and tantrums; to make her likeable Enid Bagnold has contributed some agreeable aspects of character. But it is Edith Evans who takes the part by the scruff of the neck and forces Mrs St Maugham to be endearing in her gusty moods as well as irritating by reason of her general lack of sense and ample presence of caprice. In this kind of 'rescue work' Edith Evans is supreme: she has only to make her first entrance from the garden demanding to know where her teeth have been left to persuade an audience that an evening with Mrs St Maugham will have its dowagerial delights of the frank and the whimsical combined. The old party, thus presented, is not only 'a card'. She is the queen of trumps.

Beside her, as the governess selected to take charge of a child not so much 'difficult' as insoluble, is Peggy Ashcroft. We do not know at first about the long imprisonment. The woman we meet might be just a curious specimen of the shy, the stubborn, the incalculable spinster who comes along in answer to an 'ad'. But with her knack of significant intimation the actress soon lets us know that she is a mystery and her performance becomes an inspired series of Enigma Variations. Yet, as I said, the background of long and terrible suffering is never permitted to overshadow the part or the play. How the governess, when accepted, comes to cope with Mrs St Maugham's unbiddable grandchild and also with the obstinate soil of that lady's chalk garden – for she knows even more about horticulture than she does about juvenile psychology – is the matter of the story. Before long one is believing every word of it. In short, one is in the mood engendered by good plays, the mood which can simply be described as wanting, desperately wanting, to know what happened. Plays which can do that trick and create the curiosity are fairly defined as 'good plays'. At any rate, they become the 'plays-you-can't-get-into', at least during the first year of their run.

Felix Aylmer, cast as the Judge who so unfortunately turns up to renew an old acquaintance of the judicial arena, was away when I saw THE CHALK GARDEN. I had to imagine the serene richness of character which he gave to the part; my imagination, working on happy experience of Mr Aylmer's exquisite essays in ripe humanity, was pleasantly employed. George Rose contributed a very shrewd performance as the kind of male help that a Sussex home might get nowadays, a neurotic, a 'character', half weakling and half wag, a tail-wagging spaniel of a chap who enjoys giving service but also enjoys being temperamental and having his own little cry.

120

But, of course, it was the two women who made the play: the remark in this case does not demean the authoress. Dame Edith, with commanding magic, propelled the personality of an absurd old lady over the flower-beds of her chalk garden; and Dame Peggy – the honour is well justified but how odd the words sound! – at first tight-lipped and jerkily-moving, like a wibbly-wobbly pudding on its plate, then emerged as the woman with a will and a mind as well as with a past. It was a new line for her, and her touch was as sure with Sussex chalk as ever it had been with Grecian marble or Shakespeare's many-coloured earth.

Charades in Castle Crazy

CARDS OF IDENTITY
by Nigel Dennis   *Royal Court Theatre*

Mr Dennis's novel about brain-washing, a tale both sinister and smiling, was much acclaimed a short time ago. I began it with pleasure and, though I forgot to finish it, I did, because of this brief acquaintance, manage to understand what the first act of the dramatised version was about. This was a feat somewhat baffling to play-goers who had not done their home-work. So in the theatre I once more began CARDS OF IDENTITY and I was there till the end; but there were moments in the middle when I could have forgotten to conclude the exercise, as I did when reading the book.

The English Stage Company has wisely been encouraging in-telligent novelists to share their intelligence with the theatre. The novelists have a duty to respond by paying some attention to theatrical method. Angus Wilson in THE MULBERRY BUSH had troubled to do that. But Mr Dennis had not. His ideas, put forward gaily and forcefully, may obviously be an asset to the stage. But he really must consider his audience. In the case of CARDS OF IDENTITY he swept his characters unexplained into a Castle Crazy called Hyde's Mortimer. This was a country house where Captain Mallet and his allies in hypnotic treatment were destroying the personalities of the neighbours and other victims in order to turn them into servants, gardeners, and sources of revenue. Having shown Mallet at work, Mr Dennis then whisked us into a meeting of a senile Brain-Washers' Club where we were entertained by irrelevant characters devised in mockery of the B.B.C., the College of Heralds, and the religious writers who parade their Sense of Sin, flourish their Guilt Complex in the face of the public, and find that this kind of exhibitionism pays remarkably good dividends.

That was all very bright and breezy for a while, but some of it was over-long and much of it had insufficient relevance to the activities of Captain Mallet and his fellow 'trick-cyclists'. In the third act the story did swing back to this rogue and his confederates, but the conclusion was so weak as to be a confession of dramatic incapacity.

I do not know whether Mr Dennis has closely studied Ben Jonson's 'The Alchemist': if so, he might have profited by that model. For the situation is very much the same. Some cozening swindlers of Jacobean London get hold of an empty house and there sell the secrets of their supposed alchemy which are to provide health, wealth, and happiness to the dupes who will pay for this bogus magic. In CARDS OF IDENTITY the sharpers are also established in a vacant house and employing the magic of our time – which is the hocus-pocus of psychotherapy and hypnotism. These are used by the impostors in order to alter people's identities and turn them into dupes and serfs. The difference between Jonson and Mr Dennis is that the former kept up a sustained and well-told story, which the latter despairs of doing. Accordingly his contribution to the theatre is more a series of sketches for revue than what is known as a play.

Very amusing in some places, brash and tasteless in others, especially in its presentation of a drunken priest whose jests about the Cross were bound to be resented by many, CARDS OF IDENTITY could certainly give the English Stage Company a publicity line. 'This is the kind of play you won't see anywhere else.' But this uniqueness is not necessarily a sure appeal to the play-goer's mind and pocket. However, Mr Dennis has obvious assets: his mind darts round and into modern follies with speed and penetration. What he needs is a producer with a large blue pencil. He further must acquire the willingness to put himself in the position of a play-goer who has not read his books and can fairly demand some initial intimation of who's who and what's where and why.

There was a strong company assembled. I suppose there was deep policy in casting that delightful actor, Michael Gwynn, whose personality speaks benevolence and gentleness before his lips have said a word, as the heartless scoundrel who is Captain Mallet. Joan Greenwood played the Captain's lady, a parallel part to that of Doll Common in 'The Alchemist': she did so most amusingly, but also with so much affectation of a plummy kind of speech that at times, while the noise she made was audible, the exact words were indistinguishable.

George Devine, as the whisky-priest who glories in his life of sin and in its unabashed philosophy, 'I Stink, therefore I Am', had an enormous soliloquy and delivered it with comic force, skill and relish: but it would have been far more effective at half the length and with certain of the phrases most likely to vex the faithful omitted. Tony Richardson's production used the text as well as might be: but he really should have insisted on some clarification and re-writing to remove the confusion of the audience and to let the dramatist, speaking more clearly, speak to more advantage.

Birth of a Debutante

by WILLIAM DOUGLAS HOME

One evening in the summer of 1952 (or was it '53?) I was sitting, toying with a cocktail, in my father-in-law's flat in London. He was reclining in an armchair, casting a tired eye over the evening paper, and recuperating after a long day in the City, where we like to keep him working as an insurance against the failure of any of my plays. Also in the room was my sister-in-law who in that particular year was, as the expression has it, 'coming-out'. That evening she was also going out, and in the course of time the telephone rang from the Porter's Desk downstairs.

'There is a gentleman waiting downstairs for Miss Tessa', said the porter's voice. 'Thank you', said she, replacing the receiver, and picking up her bag.

My father-in-law laid aside his evening paper.

'Why don't you ever bring your young men up here, Tessa?' he enquired.

'Why, you don't want to meet them, Daddy, do you?' she replied.

'Well, I'd just like to know whether they are black or white', said he.

'They vary, Daddy', she replied, and left the room.

With that, my father-in-law picked up his evening paper again, and I picked up my cocktail, and I picked up something else as well. An idea for a play.

I didn't know it at the time, but looking back on it now, it is clear to me that as a result of that small slice of dialogue there was planted in my mind the seed which later blossomed into what is unmistakably to date my most successful play. But please don't imagine that I rushed into the lift, hot with inspiration, and then via my car to my study, where I poured the steaming phrases on to sheets of ice-cold foolscap till, my muse expired, I sank exhausted on the study floor and moaned for brandy. It wasn't like that, thank goodness. No, not at all, for don't forget that I didn't know that anything had happened at the time. Indeed, for months afterwards, I went around with no apparent change in my normal demeanour.

124

In other words, I presented to the world my habitual expression of surprised vacuity, which has always put my friends in mind of an agricultural simpleton, struck on the head by a frosty turnip falling from a cart.

Moreover, I continued to bewail with the regularity of a teething baby my inability to think of a plot for a play, while, at the same time, tidying up all rejected manuscripts with a view to trying them out on unsuspecting Managers in order to keep my Bank Manager at bay. For baying he was. Indeed, never in my chequered financial career had he bayed quite so loudly or for quite so long. The reasons for this were many, the chief among them being that THE CHILTERN HUNDREDS as a means of livelihood had almost run its course, while its successor, THE MANOR OF NORTHSTEAD, had not yet appeared. Moreover, in the interval, apart from serving up several financially unsuccessful plays, I had also got married, as a result of which I had been blessed simultaneously with a very small family and a very large overdraft. In fact, not until we were at the height of our financial crisis, when we were living in love and charity with a neighbour (that is to say, we loved him and he was charitable towards us in that he charged us not one iota of rent) did the birth of THE RELUCTANT DEBUTANTE take place. And an inauspicious birth it was, resulting as it did from the unpleasant union of an overgrown overdraft and a bad attack of catarrh. For, having retired to bed one morning in the late autumn of that year (or was it the next?) with the feeling that at least six Bank Managers were sitting on my chest, I took a notebook from the coverlet and wrote down, out of the blue, the words 'Jimmy and Sheila are sitting at the breakfast table'.

Why I decided to write a play about a debutante at that particular moment I shall never know, nor why I decided to start with her parents at the breakfast table. All I know is that I did start like that, and that the time was ten o'clock, and that by twelve-thirty, two-and-a-half hours later, which period is all my poor overtaxed brain can stand at a session, I had written roughly but fairly completely what is still Scene I of the play.

The next morning, catarrh or no catarrh, I stayed in bed again, and wrote the second scene, which was rougher and a great deal shorter than the first, because exhaustion was now setting in. And on the third morning, almost at a standstill now, I wrote the third scene up to where my new-born debutante

125

returned at 3.0 a.m. to find her parents sitting up for her. And there I stuck. Not just temporarily, not in the sense that a man who gets his car bogged up to the axles in mud, and then goes for a tractor, is stuck, but really properly, totally, utterly and completely stuck, with my bonnet pressed up against a blank wall, my reverse gear gone, my batteries flat, my radiator boiling over, my petrol tank empty, in five feet of snow, with no tractor or signpost in sight, and no map. And there, in that position for a year I stayed. I do not mean that I stayed, as it were, in the car all that time, madly jerking the gear lever backwards and forwards. That was to come later. No. Like a sensible fellow I abandoned the car, only making a disinterested mental note about where I had left it with a view to retrieving it if possible when the thaw set in. In other words, I replaced the notebook on a shelf in my study, and left it there. Quite honestly, I would have thrown it away if it had not been that my wife asked me to read what I written to her. I did so, ashamed, degraded and depressed. And when I had finished I remember that I shut the notebook and said, 'It is a lot of nonsense, irrelevant, flippant, useless, featherweight nonsense'.

'It's funny', said my wife. 'How can it be?' I said. 'No plot, no body, no substance, no ending, nothing'. 'It's still funny', she repeated. So instead of dropping it into the waste paper basket, I decided to appease her, and I dropped it on a shelf instead. And there, for well over a year, it stayed. Indeed, its only journey in that time was in a Pickford's van where, with all the rag, tag, and bobtail from my study it travelled to our new home in Hampshire, where it was unloaded on to yet another shelf, and there it stayed for six months more. Then one week-end, when all the remaining theatrical ammunition in my study had been primed and fired into the auditoriums of various London theatres with varying results, when Mr Butler and my Bank Manager were, between them, quietly squeezing me to death, I took it down again and read it to some week-end guests, and strange to say, they laughed.

'Sycophants,' I said to myself, 'or if not sycophants, just canny: determined not to alienate the host until the wine has been selected for the evening meal'. But after dinner, when the reading was continued, they still laughed, and then I started working, and if anybody thinks that play-writing is not work, let him try it. Day in, day out: week in, week out: month in, month out I worked, first in the house then in the garden, on the foreshortened little body of my prematurely born and sickly little literary child. And as I worked I said to myself, 'It won't do, this play. There is nothing in it,' and always a shadow seemed to fall across the roses and the hollyhocks, and in my imagination I heard my Bank Manager's voice: 'It won't do – your account', it said – 'There is nothing in it'. And I bent again to my task. All through that summer I worked on it until one version was finished. I didn't like it, and I wrote another version, and I liked that even less. But rather than have nothing to show for my labours, I labelled the first version 'Play A' and the second, 'Play B' and sent them to my agent, Kitty Black, with a note attached, which plaintively enquired which version was the right play – if it was a play. Back came the reply 'Version B'. 'Well, bless my soul,' I cried, 'she thinks it *is* a play'.

Then more weeks in the garden, weeks of worry when I thought the play would only last about an hour, and feverishly wrote a 50-minute Act, which I had typed, and then rejected, only saving one or two of Jimmy's choicest cracks. Soon the moment came when I couldn't even read the play any more, let alone write it. I hated it. It bored me, and I asked my wife if I could burn it. 'No', she said. And so, instead of burning it I put it in an envelope and sent it off to E. P. Clift, to whom I had already promised my next play, and as I sealed it up I felt like someone who has sent a serious-minded friend a present of a joke cigar. In fact, I felt ashamed. Indeed I felt so bad, that as a palliative to my conscience, I despatched another copy off to Archie Batty, who was once my agent, and had given me invaluable advice about THE CHILTERN HUNDREDS in its pre-production days.

But meanwhile, unbelievably, Paul Clift decided that he liked it, and still more incredible, Archie decided, with some reservations that were easily adjusted, that he liked it too, and all in a moment the play was placed. The embryo, the nonsense, the thick wad of typewriting, the work that I was still ashamed of, that I still wished I had burnt, had been accepted by a London Manager, and was to be produced.

I took the car and hurried up to London to the office of Paul Clift, and there I met his new partner, Producer Jack Minster, and to my profound amazement he vouchsafed that he had read the play and liked it very much. Poor man, I thought, poor embryonic Manager whose hard-earned cash is going down the drain with this ill-favoured product of an overdraft and a catarrh.

Well, then we started casting, and they sent a copy off to Celia Johnson, and once again my heart was in my mouth. Three days I waited, during which time I learned that her agent shared my own opinion of the play, and then I could wait no longer. I went to the telephone in my father-in-law's flat, that flat in which the play was first conceived, and called her up. 'Have you read that play yet, Celia?' I said. 'Yes', she replied, and then there came a pause of possibly two seconds, which seemed like an eternity to me, and then I heard her voice again. 'I think it's very funny', she vouchsafed. 'Come down to dinner.' 'Thanks', said I. That evening my wife and I arrived at Nettlebed. 'It's very funny,' Celia repeated, 'but it wants things doing to it'. My heart sank. 'Just little things', she said, and I breathed again. 'Will she do it, Peter?' I asked Peter Fleming, her nonchalant husband. 'You know Celia', he smiled, as he lit up his pipe. I didn't at the time, at least not very well, but naturally I nodded, sagely. Anyway, she did.

Home we drove that night, stopping off at a call-box for a suitably muted triumphal report to Jack Minster, and the next day I started on the 'little things'. They took two days, and as my secretary insists on living down in Cornwall while I live in Hampshire, they were typed by the young daughter of my mother-in-law's Italian couple, and returned to Celia within a week. And shortly after that we signed her up.

By now I was beginning to think the play must be a little better than I thought it was, for even my mother, who is a sterner dramatic critic than any of that salaried fraternity, had said that it was funny when she read it. Then came the day when Anna Massey read the title-role, with no acting experience of any kind, and ultimately got the part: and with Jack Merivale coming up from Worthing Rep. and Wilfrid Hyde White coming down from Thirsk Races, the four leading roles were filled. Then came rehearsals which, contrary to my usual custom, I visited about once a week. This change in my normal routine was occasioned by the complete confidence I had in my Producer, Jack Minster, whose approach to the play was wholly attuned to my own. It is, I think, impossible to over-estimate the importance of the Producer's role in the theatre. I have a theory

Gillian Lind, Marjorie Fielding, Christine Silver and Janet Barrow in TABITHA
at the Duchess (*Armstrong Jones*)

Anthony Nicholls, Emlyn Williams and Basil Hoskins in THE MERCHANT OF VENICE
at the Shakespeare Memorial Theatre, Stratford-upon-Avon

Margaret Rutherford, Robert Morley and Violet Farebrother in A LIKELY TALE
at the Globe (*Angus McBean*)

Paul Scofield, Robert Robinson and Harry H. Corbett in THE POWER AND THE GLORY at the Phoenix (*Armstrong Jones*)

that dramatic critics would be well advised to seek for the cause of a play's failure less in the Author's writing than in the Producer's handling of rehearsals, for he it is that calls the tune, and if it differs, ever so slightly, from the tune the Author played, it then becomes inevitable that a false note will struck. Better, I would say, that a bad tune should be played well than a good tune badly.

However, Jack Minster played my tune, and when he demanded a re-write of any particular passage during rehearsals I, under protest, played his. And then we came to Brighton for a try out. We opened on my son's third birthday, and the Curtain fell on Scene I, and the audience broke into frenzied whispers and Jack Minster leant over the back row of the Circle and he whispered in my wife's ear and my own, the two words 'Honey Dew'. And from that moment I knew that the little, stunted creature that I had brought into the world two years – or was it three? – before had now become a strong and popular grown-up.

From Brighton we travelled to the Cambridge Theatre and the First Night. There, before the Curtain rose, I took the precaution of giving my father-in-law a box of cigars as an act of appeasement in case he objected to the portrait of himself he was about to witness from his Box. I could have saved my money. He was pleased – and so was everybody else, myself, the actors, the audience, the critics, the Ticket Agencies, the public, the Metro-Goldwyn-Mayer Film Company, and even my Bank Manager.

Well, that is the story. What is the moral? To those of you, whatever your profession, who have succeeded in ploughing through this intensely personal account of the birth of a project, and have noted how the anguished despair and lack of confidence of the parent – none of which has been exaggerated – led ultimately to what I may call, without conceit because it is a fact, phenomenal success, I would suggest that it is embodied in the two words which Terence Rattigan once spoke to me over the telephone when I told him I was bogged down badly in my current work – 'Press On'.

Antipodean Report

by Sir Ralph Richardson

I have recently returned from a theatrical tour of Australia and New Zealand, which was instructive as well as agreeable. Economically, also, we did extremely well. For theatre people, 'there is gold in them thar hills', so, if for no more interesting or exciting reason than that, I gladly respond to the invitation to write something about our journey and the conditions awaiting others who may take plays to the Antipodes; it is, therefore, both a Market Report and a Vote of Thanks to good hosts and audiences.

But before I start, there is a thought even more interesting than the above for us all, both inside and outside the theatre. This was brought home to me in that theatrical tour. Australia is a very large place, and, as seen on the atlas, I did not dare to doubt its immensity. But you have to be there to get the feel of that vastness. I would never challenge the size of the sun, but until I saw Australia I had never realised its dimensions, and I had insufficiently realised that when you get a very large country, it contains a large number of people, and those people have a large number of thoughts not always thought of by us. What struck me so forcibly on my visit was something of which the atlas gave no hint, namely that the Australians and New Zealanders thought a great deal about us in Great Britain, a great deal more, I should say, than we think about them.

They think all kinds of things about us; of course, some of them are nasty thoughts and naughty thoughts, but there are a great many people on that other side of the world who are thinking good, kind, and affectionate thoughts. I felt rather embarrassed to think that I had not realised it before, and as an Englishman I felt very happy that we were receiving these good, kind and affectionate radiations from afar, because I felt that on every side they were most valuable and I wondered what I could do about it in the future. All I have done so far is to send some good thoughts back, but I am uncertain as to how that may benefit Australia and New Zealand.

130

The plays we took on our theatrical tour were THE SLEEPING PRINCE and SEPARATE TABLES, both by Terence Rattigan. SEPARATE TABLES was the big hit of the London theatres when we departed and, incidentally, it still remained so after nearly two years. We thought that our hosts would like to see the very latest success in London which they could not see for themselves. So we chose THE SLEEPING PRINCE to go with it as it made a strong contrast in settings, one splendid, the other drab, one gay, the other dramatic and partly tragic, and the fact that the two plays had been written by the same author put, as it were, a frame around them, and we could then call our programme 'companion studies'.

I had the good fortune to appear in these plays with an extremely good cast. Only my wife (Meriel Forbes), myself, Daphne Newton, and our director, Lionel Harris, were exported direct from this country. But we were joined in Australia by Dame Sybil Thorndike and her husband, Sir Lewis Casson, and the rest of the company were recruited out there by the wise selection of our director who went out before us. They were a splendid team, they did their work excellently, and they were the most hard-working, conscientious and delightful set of people to work with.

My wife and I and Daphne Newton had rehearsed in London with 'ghost' actors reading in for them; Dame Sybil and the Australians had rehearsed there with 'ghosts' reading for us. We all met in Perth in March 1955 and rehearsed together in flesh and blood. Our employer and manager in Australia was Mr Garnett Carroll. It was he who made the offer to us in London to come out, saying that he would sponsor the enterprise, leaving suggestions regarding play and players to us.

After rehearsal we opened our plays in Perth. We had the advantage during rehearsal of the presence of our author, Terence Rattigan, who was so keen on our project as to pay us this visit. Mr Garnett Carroll has a very large playhouse in Perth. It is most suitable as a cinema, but it was awkward for us. We had to strain somewhat, but that is not always a bad exercise at the beginning of the study of performances and I think we were heard. We did extremely good business. The seats sold for rather a high price; I think the stalls were A£1 5s 6d and there is very little entertainment tax to be paid. Generally speaking, I think I am right in saying there was nothing unusual in the box-office taking A£1,000 a night in the cities we visited. This is very good going.

If one goes out by boat, stopping at so many foreign ports, and then takes the last, long trip from Ceylon to Perth, it is quite astonishing to find that at the end of the journey one has apparently arrived back at an English county town; there is a very Victorian air about Perth, with its charming and innocent community. We went up into the hills to spend the day with a professor from the University of Perth. They call it a 'free' University and I believe that nobody pays any fees. The professor had built himself a bungalow which he visited occasionally. It was in an isolated spot. 'Is it all right', I asked him, 'to leave this place with all your things? Won't somebody come and break in?' 'Good Lord, no!' he said. 'You know I left my home in Perth this morning for the day and I would never have dreamed of locking the door.'

They say in Perth that they are farther away from the next town than anywhere else in the world, and that there is not an inhabited island anywhere which is so far from a neighbouring community. But the people of Perth struck us as very bright, aware, and certainly most agreeable folk. They make a delightful audience to play to.

After what we had considered to be our 'try out' at Perth, we moved on to Melbourne. There Mr Garnett Carroll possesses a delightful theatre built in the golden age of theatres, about 1885; it has a beautifully shaped auditorium, which is perfect in size and has plenty of gold in the decorations. We played for ten weeks in Melbourne to excellent business.

One is asked to a great number of functions, starting in the morning before lunch when tea is served; one is invited to lunch and after lunch tea is, of course, served. The most unusual cup of tea I can remember was one night at the trotting races. At about 9 o'clock I was invited to the Stewards' Room, and a whisky and soda leapt to my mind; but, inexorably, there was some splendid tea and hundreds of scones and cakes! I am afraid I sadly shirked my duty in appearing at the functions; perhaps there I could have shown a little more how grateful I felt that the people of Australia had the kind thoughts of us in Great Britain. But, to tell the truth, I put in so poor an appearance and was so ill at ease when tightly packed among a great many people, however kind, that I felt that I was the worst possible advertisement both for my theatre and for my country. Dame Sybil and Sir Lewis Casson, along with their great theatrical talents, possess brilliant social gifts and they gave themselves with the utmost generosity and swallowed each cup of tea to the last, with grace and apparent appetite.

After Melbourne we played ten weeks in Sydney at the new National Theatre in which we gave the opening performance. This is a theatre paid for by private subscription and it is hoped that an Australian Drama may arise from the efforts connected with this building. It is situated in a rather out-of-the-way and slightly dingy part of the city, but it has a splendid auditorium. For years past it has been a second-rate cinema and I believe that it was purchased on favourable terms, rather like picking up a good violin in an old junk shop.

I was delighted to play at this theatre and felt it was very easy to speak in. When I was going to the theatre in a taxi one night the driver said to me, 'How do you like it out there at this New Elizabethan?' (That is the name of the theatre.) 'I like it very much', I said, 'it's a very nice theatre.'

'You don't say?' said the driver.

'Oh yes', for some reason I went on, 'very nice theatre to play in, very nice to speak in.'

'You don't say', said the driver. I said no more.

'I drove two old ladies home from the Elizabethan last night, mister', the driver turned round to inform me, 'and they were saying, in this cab, that they couldn't hear a word you said.'

The rest was silence!

Wherever we went and whatever we did, we had the advantage of the powerful and energetic presence of Garnett Carroll; this was very important to us and it helped us greatly. Garnett is not the kind of manager who is pictured with a big cigar and with his feet up in the office; he physically does the hopping about on his own feet, and he does what it is supposed he might do; he manages. He could always make me laugh, and there are times on tour when that can be the best tonic in the world. At the Elizabethan one night he had been to see us in our rooms after the play and we arranged to meet later for supper. He said he had his car and would go on ahead. We left in five minutes to find a little knot of people waiting for us outside the stage door. Carroll was there talking to them. We passed by and we got into the car that was waiting for us. He stepped to the side of the

kerb, he raised his hat in respectful salute, he bowed as in re-
cognition of passing great ones, he permitted himself a discreet
but respectful little clapping of the hands. Then he turned back
to the little gathering at the stage door. 'Great, great artists', he
roared.

A lot of things astonished us in Australia; if you like being
astonished, it is really worth a visit. One thing we found unusual
was the number of young children who came to our plays, which
we did not think very suitable for the young; further than that,
there were many infants in arms brought into the theatre. For
them we had no entertainment value whatever and they snarked
and they cried and they yelled. This was most disturbing; so we
had to announce: 'No infants in arms', and told the management to admit none such. We settled down to one or two peace-
ful performances, then at one matinée, when we had hardly got
going, there was a wail, long drawn out and gurgling. We looked
at each other; 'someone had blundered'. Next, there was a more
powerful and sustained infantile trumpeting. This tailed off, and
then down, turned into a ghastly rattling, and ended, at last, in
silence! We were alarmed. At the end of the scene we sent the
stage manager to find out what could have happened. He found
the mother who said to him 'Yes, I did bring baby, but in case
he should make a noise and disturb the play, I brought his rattle
to keep him quiet!'

After playing ten weeks in Sydney, we proceeded to New
Zealand, where we played in four or five towns.

Our experiences in Australia had led us to high expectation of
the interest that we might arouse in New Zealand and our
management were agog. The result was a little disappointing; we
did well enough, but there was not the busy buzz at the box-
office that we had hoped for, the advance booking was rather
weak, and the barometer of our trade shot up and down in un-
accountable ways.

But the whole adventure was extremely interesting and
bracing to us; we returned the richer in many ways. The plays
which we took were good enough to maintain our own respect
for them, no matter how many times we played them over.
Indeed, I did not feel that I had by any means scraped the
bottom of this excellent barrel. We were never ashamed of the
manner in which we were able to present them for, as I have said,
we had an admirable cast and our management maintained the

excellent production laid down by Lionel Harris. The theatrical equipment was excellent also and the standards high, wherever we went. This, to my mind, is a matter of great importance.

What memory our visit has left with our hosts I am unable to say, but I know that I shall always have 'good' thoughts and gratitude for their many kindnesses to us.

Paris Season

by Thomas Quinn Curtiss

Paris with its 70 playhouses rivals London and surpasses New York in amount of theatrical activity. Over 150 plays of all kinds and origins were staged in the French capital during the 1955-56 season, but investigation proves that plays from abroad and revivals of the classics and of what may be called semi-classics dominated in the success category.

The contemporary French dramatists were busy, but versions of British work were more popular. There were new plays by Jean Anouilh, Marcel Pagnol, Marcel Aymé, Jacques Deval, André Roussin, Michel Duran and Jean Bernard Luc. Yet none of these displayed the drawing powers of Peter Ustinov's Love of Four Colonels, of the Somerset Maugham – Guy Bolton comedy, Theatre (adapted by Marc-Gilbert Sauvajon as Adorable Julia), or of Bernard Shaw's Pygmalion; all three in their second year here. French revivals were better supported than French novelties. A decorous revival of Rostand's Cyrano de Bergerac (with Pierre Dux as the large-nosed knight), and return engagements of Jacques Audibert's Le Mal Court (with Suzanne Flon repeating her original performance as the high-minded princess who learns about life from court intrigue) and Armand Salacrou's Histoire de Rire (played by Danièle Delorme, Yves Robert, Marie Daems and Pierre Dux before he withdrew to don the cloak and sword of Cyrano) outdistanced the new native plays in popularity.

Anouilh's Ornifle, a gaudy caricature of a gifted poet who sells his talent for worldly gain and turns into a repulsive sensualist, was acted with flamboyant vigour by Pierre Brasseur. There were helpful performances, too, by Jacqueline Maillan as his meek, abused secretary, symbol of her cruel master's sleeping conscience, by Louis de Funes as the crass man of commerce and by Anouilh's daughter, Catherine Anouilh, as the dreamy maiden whose innocence tempts the corrupted poet. Ornifle was coldly treated in the press, but the public disregarded the critical verdict and the highly-coloured satire ran out the season.

136

Marcel Pagnol, internationally famous for his picturesque comedies of the Marseilles waterfront and the cynical TOPAZE, defended the Biblical traitor in a long and often incongruous dramatic apology, JUDAS, which aroused discussion but failed to appeal to the paying play-goer. There were moderate successes for some well-known names. André Roussin's latest was L'AMOUR FOU. This concerned a middle-aged bachelor who behaved like a schoolboy when he fell in love with a middle-aged married lady. In Marcel Aymé's fantasy, LES OISEAUX DE LUNE, a provincial schoolmaster was granted powers to transform tiresome humans into birds. Jean Bernard Luc provided a rather stilted romance, LES AMANTS NOVICES, while Michel Duran's JOSE studied farcically the effects of a jazz singer's sudden fame. All these met with a fair measure of popularity.

The veteran boulevard playwright, Jacques Deval, contributed a three-character triangle comedy in UNE CHARMANTE SOIREE, but though Michel Simon, now a popular cinema player, undertook the leading role, it failed quickly. But a three-character triangle comedy written by a novice, Claude Magnier, scored an immediate victory. This was called MONSIEUR MASURE; it starred the *chansonnier* comedian, Gérard Sety, and was much enjoyed.

Three other new dramatists made their débuts during the season and all three received warm welcomes from the critics: first Colette Audry who with SOLEDAD contributed a tense, effective melodrama of love and intrigue in a Fascist state. The second was Pierre-Henri Roux, whose drama about a ruthless middle-class mother, A CORPS PERDU, had the advantage of Valentine Tessier in a star part. The third was Louis Velle, author of A LA MONNAIE DU PAPA. This was a farce in which a budding novelist, disguised as a university student, took up residence in a bourgeois household with the object of satirizing its members.

The Madeleine Renaud – Jean-Louis Barrault Company occupied the Marigny for the better part of the winter. It relied chiefly upon revivals, which included Giraudoux's INTERMEZZO, Chekhov's CHERRY ORCHARD and Feydeau's OCCUPE-TOI D'AMELIE. In addition there was a production of the Hellenic masterpiece, the Oresteia trilogy, and Lope de Vega's LE CHIEN DU JARDINIER was also added to the repertory. Monsieur Barrault himself enacted a new play by Jean Vauthier, LE PERSONNEL COMBATTANT, a long monologue about the agony of a struggling author, at the Marigny's second playhouse, Le Petit Marigny.

The Comédie-Française, in the course of the year, staged a brilliant presentation of Molière's LES FEMMES SAVANTES. Marivaux's LES SERMENTS INDISCRETS, Diderot's EST-IL BON, EST-IL MECHANT ? and Corneille's LA MORT DE POMPEE were also among the classics. On the modern side was Jean Cocteau's LA MACHINE A ECRIRE (written in 1941 and first performed in 1942), a curious drama in which the hypocrisy of small-town life is exposed by a flood of poison-pen letters. Naturally the Comédie took great pains to commemorate the 350th anniversary of Corneille's birth. Accordingly it gave eight of his dramas, LE CID, CINNA, LE MENTEUR, LA MORT DE POMPEE, SURENA, PSYCHE, NICODEME and HORACE. As a contemporary epilogue to these ceremonial salutations there was a brief and entertaining playlet by André Obey which showed the great poet in his study receiving the news of his posthumous fame from a messenger sent by the modern world.

The Théâtre National Populaire – minus Gérard Philippe this year – had as its new productions Molière's L'ETOURDI, Marivaux's LE TRIOMPHE DE L'AMOUR and Victor Hugo's MARIE TUDOR. After its annual engagement at the theatre of the Palais de Chaillot it went on an extended tour which included a short season at the Palace Theatre in London. The mime Marcel Marceau, fresh from his triumph on Broadway and on American television, reorganized his company and presented a new programme of pantomime plays at the Ambigu.

Among the successful importations were a new version of Gorki's THE LOWER DEPTHS at the Théâtre de l'Oeuvre, and Emlyn Williams' SOMEONE WAITING adapted by André Roussin. François Perier appeared and was liked in LE SEDUCTEUR, derived from an Italian original by Diego Fabbri, an amusing comedy about a philanderer who tried to bring some order into his love-life and thus lost both his wife and his mistresses. Constance Colline's adaptation of Peter Blackmore's MIRANDA (LA DUCHESSE D'ALGUES), a witty piece of nonsense (and an old favourite on English stage and screen) recording the adventures of a doctor who installs a mermaid in his home as an in-patient, was again a hit when revived at the Théâtre des Arts. Gaby Sylvia once more delighted the public with her performance as the trouble-making lady from the sea.

The most important event of the season was the Third Dramatic Festival of Paris. This brought to the Sarah Bernhardt Theatre representative companies from 17 nations playing in their own tongues. Among the most impressive of these were the Piscator troupe from Berlin in an Epic Theatre production of WAR AND PEACE and the Kungliga Dramatiska Teatern from Stockholm in Strindberg's THE FATHER and Chekhov's UNCLE VANYA. Among other distinguished Festival visitors were the Popular Theatre of Morocco in a Molière-Beaumarchais programme and the Schauspielhaus of Bochum in Goethe's FAUST and Sartre's LE DIABLE ET LE BON DIEU. The Theater in der Josefstadt from Vienna contributed von Hofmannsthal's DER SCHWIERIGE, and the Compagnie Morelli Stoppa brought from Rome Goldoni's LA LOCANDIERA, while the Oslo National Theatre offered Ibsen's WILD DUCK. The English-speaking theatre was represented by the Dublin Players in CANDIDA, the London Theatre Workshop in Hasek's GOOD SOLDIER SCHWEIK, and the Birmingham Repertory in Shaw's CAESAR AND CLEOPATRA.

Playwrights

by HENRY SHEREK

Constant Hot Water is the Theatre's natural element. Our drama is continually scalded and scolded by all sorts of people who may or may not know something about it. But, as is sometimes said, 'there's nothing wrong with the Theatre that a good play won't cure.' This sounds trite, but it is one of the few sayings in common use that are true.

The opposite view is that the star-name is all that matters. Much has been said and written about the British Theatre relying chiefly for its success, at least for its financial success, on these names. This is also, up to a point, true. But I believe it to be only a passing phase, a phase which good plays will cure, curiously enough, by making new stars in the medium of flesh and blood entertainment and not through other and mechanical media. Good actors may cover up the badness of bad plays, but good plays can, and do, make good actors or make actors, already good, better.

There are many actors and actresses well able to fill theatres in the provinces who can give only a very poor account of themselves in plays in which acting must be learnt as a mixture of art and technical exercise. These have achieved national and sometimes international renown in the easier form of appearing in motion pictures; but this does not help in the more difficult and harder-to-please milieu of the West End, where it is essential that the play itself must be good.

The essential basis of a healthy theatre is therefore still the playwright and in this we, in this country, are having a very thin time indeed just now.

The reasons are manifold and are not the fault of the wicked manager, who is always and absurdly drenched in the Constant Hot Water laid on, as I said, to the much-abused theatre. Would any manager turn down a good play if he is lucky enough to have one submitted to him? In these sparse times even one good act out of three will send an intelligent member of the species – and there are some – scuttling off to find the author and offer him a fairly large sum for an option on his play. The manager's hope, usually vain, (and there's one of the rubs), is that the writer will then proceed to work on his script and thus improve it.

I think it was George Kaufman who said that a good play is not written but re-written, and this marks the fundamental difference between the American and the British playwright. It is most difficult, if not impossible, to get the latter to do much further work on his creation. Very often it is because he is just 'denkfaul', sometimes it is because the British author seems incapable of returning to something that he considers to be finished. He has in the meantime been at work on film or television scripts and will not, or cannot, switch his mind into reverse. Many a time a playwright has said to me: 'I really can't go back to it, old boy. It's cold fish as far as I'm concerned. It's your worry now, but don't you dare to change a word or I'll sue you.' That is – well, scarcely co-operative.

It is customary to play a few weeks in the provinces before London 'to get the play right'. To regard this as necessary is an absolute fallacy. If the local critics abuse the play, the author says: 'After all, old man, you are not doing the play for the provinces but for the different kind of audience in London. If they had *liked* it here, I would have been worried and agreed with you that I should do some re-writing.'

On the other hand, if the notices are good, the playwright says: 'Seen the reviews, old chap? Absolutely splendid. They prove that you are wrong in asking me to alter a word of the script,' and he goes off to order a fat supper at the manager's expense.

There is another weakness of the British playwright. He cannot realise that it is impossible to write well of any subject that he does not understand thoroughly. The essence of good writing is truth. By this it is not meant that any Criminal Court Judge can write another WITNESS FOR THE PROSECUTION or that the murderous inmates of Broadmoor can dash off a few of the DIAL M FOR MURDER kind, but a playwright has only to stay for a few weeks in, say, Tanganyika to think that he can write a telling play about the intimate problems of the people living there. He has probably only heard the view-points of the people with whom he stayed. He does not pick up much from the District Commissioners or similar types that he may meet at the local British Club.

141

Many American Colleges have courses in play-writing. These are apt to elicit sneering remarks over here. 'How can you *learn* play-writing?', a fairly successful British playwright once said to me. 'Why not?' I answered, and the author drifted away muttering, 'Un-British cad.' That is hardly a specimen of illuminating dialogue, but just as bad are to be found in many plays that I read.

The cure? I do suggest the value of Chairs for Drama at our Universities. By this I do not mean only at Oxford and Cambridge, where the Drama is fairly well taken care of, but more particularly at the Universities in the big industrial centres and in the capital city of Edinburgh. Apart from instruction, we desperately need more support for our repertory and club theatres, not only from the public, but from public bodies. There should be a larger grant for the Arts Council or some other body to distribute intelligently in order to encourage promising playwrights and to get production of approved plays by them. Personally, I could do with a little less Opera and Shakespeare centred in London, if, with the money saved, help and hope could be given to intelligent young writers who are more often found north of the Trent and particularly north of the Tweed.

It is worth noting and gladly acknowledging that the British Broadcasting Corporation has given more encouragement to young writers to work for their television service than has been given by the theatre in decades. This means, however, that the work, however good, will probably only be performed once. It is the opinion of most managers that, after a television transmission, it is not a commercial proposition to put a play on in the theatre. This is still 'not proven'. But if it is true, it does not further the art of the theatre, nor does it teach the young playwright the various technical obstacles which are much easier to overcome in television where the camera need only take in the actors speaking. This is an important point. One of the great faults of amateur playwrights is that they very often leave characters on the stage for long periods with nothing to say, and the director does not know what on earth to do with them. The author also seems to be quite unable to get them off or find words to get them going.

Let me repeat that one really first-rate playwright is more important to the present and future of the theatre than all the stars showing off in revivals.

142

The Treasury is not much interested in the so-called 'living' theatre and refuses the tax-exemption which might help to keep it alive. But a successful and popular playwright is an asset abroad as well as at home and the cost of discovering and cherishing the new makers of plays would be easily repaid by their subsequent value as dollar-earners.

PLAYS PRODUCED

IN CENTRAL LONDON

July 1st 1955 – June 1st 1956

A dash after the first date indicates that the play
was still running on June 1st 1956.

ALBERTINE BY MOONLIGHT
by D. G. Bellini

MADAME LEONIE URWIG	HATTIE JACQUES
DR ADALBERT GALLERY	PHILIP HOLLES
ANTIOCHE	JON ROLLASON
TIMOLEON	ANTHONY BATEMAN
GABRIELLE	.. PAT SANDYS
MAC	.. EMRYS JONES
ALBERTINE	MARCIA ASHTON
ORIANE	HELEN CHRISTIE
COUNT MOGADOR	DESMOND WALTER-ELLIS
PALAMEDE	.. BILL FRASER
ALAIN OF MONTCORNET	GORDON WHITING
BALTHAZAR	HENRY LONGHURST
CHESS PLAYERS MICHAEL BILTON, MACKENZIE ROBERTSON	
CHAUFFEUR	GEOFFREY PALMER
CLERK OF THE COURT	HENRY HUTTEROTH

Presented by JAMES P. SHERWOOD
Directed by JOAN KEMP-WELCH

ANNIVERSARY WALTZ
by Jerome Chodorov and Joseph Fields

MILLIE	PAULINE HENRIQUES
PETER WALTERS	ANTHONY VALENTINE
ALICE WALTERS	BARBARA KELLY
DEBBIE WALTERS	MAXINE ASLANOFF
BUD WALTERS	BERNARD BRADEN
CHRIS STEELMAN	LARRY CROSS
JANICE REVERE	KAY CALLARD
HARRY	JOHN STERLAND
SAM	MAURICE DURANT
MR GANS	NICHOLAS JOY
MRS GANS	ALETHA ORR
HANDYMAN	ROSS PENDLETON

Presented by H. M. TENNENT LTD
by arrangement with JOSEPH M. HYMAN *and* BERNARD HART
Directed by JOSEPH FIELDS   *Decoration by* FREDERICK FOX

BRAZILIANA
Ballet-Musical from Rio de Janeiro

With NELSON FERRAZ
AGOSTINHA REIS, OLIVIA MARINHO, MARIA LUIZA, DINA
ANTUNES, NAIR EUGENIA, ELZA AMBROSIO, LEDA MARIA,
MARIA BAHIANA, BERNI BAIA, JOSE PRATES, JONAS MOURA,
DOMINGOS CAMPOS, HAROLDO COSTA, JOAO MELLO, MATEUS,
WALDEMAR BASTOS, ROBERTO PEREIRA, ARY DE SILVA
Presented by CONTINENTAL OPERA AND BALLET ENTERTAINMENTS LTD
Régisseur: HAROLDO COSTA
Choreography by GILBERTO BREA, JOSE PRATES
Musical Direction by JOSE PRATES   *Decoration by* DIRCEU NERY

147

Lyric, Hammersmith   *September 8 - February 4*
Apollo   *February 23 - March 17*

THE BUCCANEER
A Musical Play by Sandy Wilson

A MEMBER OF PARLIAMENT	ANTHONY VICCARS
MRS BARRACLOUGH	BETTY WARREN
MABEL GRAY	SALLY BAZELY
MR DONKIN	BERNARD CLIFTON
WALTER MAXIMUS	RONALD RADD
PETER CURTIS	JOHN FAASSEN
1ST WAITRESS	BILLIE LOVE
2ND WAITRESS	JULLIA SMITH
MONTGOMERY	KENNETH WILLIAMS
MRS WINTERTON	THELMA RUBY
MARILYN	PAMELA TEARLE
CAROLINE	JILL DOWNS
LAURA	SANDRA MARSH
MARK	ANTHONY BRYANT
JEREMY	GEOFFREY UNDERWOOD
FELICITY	JULLIA SMITH
POLICEMAN	ANTHONY VICCARS
NANNY	BILLIE LOVE

Presented by TENNENT PRODUCTIONS LTD
Directed by WILLIAM CHAPPELL   *Decoration by* PETER SNOW

Haymarket   *April 11 -*

THE CHALK GARDEN
by Enid Bagnold

MISS MADRIGAL	PEGGY ASHCROFT
MAITLAND	GEORGE ROSE
2ND APPLICANT	RUTH LODGE
3RD APPLICANT	JANET BURNELL
LAUREL	JUDITH STOTT
MRS ST MAUGHAM	EDITH EVANS
NURSE	MAVIS WALKER
OLIVIA	RACHEL GURNEY
THE JUDGE	FELIX AYLMER

Presented by TENNENT PRODUCTIONS LTD
in association with IRENE MAYER SELZNICK
Directed by JOHN GIELGUD
Decoration by REECE PEMBERTON *and* SOPHIE HARRIS

Globe   *December 22 - March 17*

CHARLEY'S AUNT
by Brandon Thomas

JACK CHESNEY	GERALD HARPER
BRASSETT	A. J. BROWN
CHARLEY WYKEHAM	RICHARD WARING
LORD FANCOURT BABBERLEY	FRANKIE HOWERD

AMY SPETTIGUE	JOY RODGERS
KITTY VERDUN	WENDY WILLIAMS
COLONEL SIR FRANCIS CHESNEY ..	CHARLES CULLUM
STEPHEN SPETTIGUE	WENSLEY PITHEY
DONNA LUCIA D'ALVADOREZ	MARJORIE STEWART
ELA DELAHAY	JANE DOWNS

Presented by H. M. TENNENT LTD
Directed by WILLIAM CHAPPELL   *Decoration by* MOTLEY

Palace   *December 21 - March 3*

CINDERELLA
Written by Emile Littler
Music and Lyrics by Hastings Mann and Jack Strachey

FATHER TIME	PETER EVANS
FAIRY GODMOTHER	SYLVIA NORMAN
DANDINI	PAULA MARSHALL
LIZZIE *and* DIZZIE	DESMOND *and* MARKS
BARON HARDUP..	SAM WOODCOCK
PRINCE CHARMING	JEAN TELFER
BUTTONS..	DAVID NIXON
CINDERELLA	ERICA YORKE
FLIP	BILLY NELSON
FLAP	CHUCK O'NEIL
FLOP	BILLY MORRIS
PRINCIPAL DANCER	LINDA MCMULLIN

Presented and Produced by EMILE LITTLER
Decoration by DORIS ZINKEISEN
Choreography by MICHAEL CHARNLEY *and* BARBARA AITKEN

Palace   *October 24 - November 12*

CLASSICAL THEATRE OF CHINA
Artistic Director: Chao Feng

Presented by PETER DAUBENY PRESENTATIONS LTD
by arrangement with LEON HEPNER
and on behalf of THE BRITAIN-CHINA FRIENDSHIP ASSOCIATION

Piccadilly   *April 23 - 28*

COMMEMORATION BALL
by Stanley Parker

WORKMEN	ROBIN WENTWORTH, NEVILLE PEARSON
WOODWARD	VINCENT HOLMAN
PETER CUNNINGHAM	PHILIP CARR
THE HON. TEDDY BERESFORD ..	NICHOLAS STEVENSON
SUSAN FLOUZET	ELVI HALE
JULIAN FABER	NORMAN WOOLAND
ANGELA DAY	ANN SUMMERS
LORD BASTERFIELD	MICHAEL SHEPLEY
MADAME CAROLINE de CHARENTON ..	ISABEL JEANS
LADY PAULINE MEREDITH	VIVIENNE DRUMMOND

149

NINETTE	Virginia Vernon
FIRST YOUNG MAN	.. Toby Perkins
SECOND YOUNG MAN	Brian Tipping Codd
THE DEAN of the COLLEGE	Nicholas Meredith
GUESTS .. .. .. Hazel Bainbridge, Francis Lyndall,	
Robin Wentworth, Neville Pearson	

Presented by Players Ventures Ltd
A Players' Theatre *Production*
Directed by Jack Williams *Decoration by* Reginald Woolley

Garrick **September 6 - October 29**

THE COUNT OF CLERAMBARD
by Marcel Aymé, translated by Norman Denny

VICOMTE OCTAVE de CLERAMBARD ..	Alec McCowen
COMTESSE LOUISE de CLERAMBARD ..	Valerie Taylor
MADAME de LERE	.. Helen Haye
COMTE HECTOR de CLERAMBARD ..	Clive Brook
PRIEST	.. Peter Sallis
A MONK	Michael Partridge
POPPY	Mai Zetterling
MADAME GALUCHON	Blanche Fothergill
EVELYNE..	Nicola Delman
ETEINNETTE	Leni Freed
BRIGITTE	Sylvia Childs
MAITRE GALUCHON	Wensley Pithey
FIRST DRAGOON	Alan White
SECOND DRAGOON	Anthony Burley
DOCTOR	Norman Welsh

Presented by Jack de Leon
by arrangement with Jack Buchanan *and* John Forbes-Sempill
Directed by Murray Macdonald
Decoration by Hutchinson Scott

**St Martin's (transferred from
the New Watergate)** **March 1 - May 26**
Duchess **May 28 -**

CRANKS
A Revue written and devised by John Cranko
Music by John Addison

With Hugh Bryant, Anthony Newley, Annie Ross, Gilbert Vernon

Presented by K.G.G. Productions Ltd
by arrangement with Bright Enterprises Ltd
Decoration by John Piper

150

Royal Court   *In repertory April 9 -*

THE CRUCIBLE
by Arthur Miller

BETTY PARRIS	MARCIA MANOLESCEU
REVEREND SAMUEL PARRIS	.. JOHN WELSH
TITUBA	.. CONNIS SMITH
ABIGAIL WILLIAMS	.. MARY URE
SUSANNA WALLCOTT	HELENA HUGHES
MRS ANN PUTNAM	RACHEL KEMPSON
THOMAS PUTNAM	NIGEL DAVENPORT
MERCY LEWIS	JOSEE RICHARD
MARY WARREN	JOAN PLOWRIGHT
JOHN PROCTOR	MICHAEL GWYNN
REBECCA NURSE	AGNES LAUCHLAN
REVEREND JOHN HALE	KENNETH HAIGH
ELIZABETH PROCTOR	ROSALIE CRUTCHLEY
FRANCIS NURSE	STEPHEN DARTNELL
EZEKIEL CHEEVER	CHRISTOPHER FETTES
JOHN WILLARD	GEORGE SELWAY
HOPKINS	.. ALAN BATES
DEPUTY-GOVERNOR DANFORTH ..	GEORGE DEVINE
JUDGE HAYTHORNE	ROBERT STEPHENS
SARAH GOOD	BARBARA GRIMES

Presented by THE ENGLISH STAGE COMPANY
Directed by GEORGE DEVINE, *assisted by* TONY RICHARDSON

Duke of York's   *September 13 - 24*

LA DAME AUX CAMELIAS
by Alexandre Dumas *fils*

NANINE	.. MADELEINE CLERVANNE
VARVILLE	MARCEL JOURNET
NICHETTE	SIMONE MATIL
MARGUERITE GAUTIER	EDWIGE FEUILLERE
VALENTIN	JEAN BRECK
OLYMPE	JACQUELINE MARBAUX
SAINT GAUDENS	MAURICE VARNY
PRUDENCE	CHARLOTTE CLASIS
GASTON	MAURICE BRAY
ARMAND DUVAL	JACQUES DACQMINE
GIRAY	PIERRE LE COQ
GUSTAVE	MICHEL MAURETTE
MONSIEUR DUVAL	JACQUES BERLIOZ
UN COMMISSIONAIRE	YVES MARTIN
LE DOCTEUR	ANDRE LAURENT
ESTHER	CATHERINE BRIEUX
ANAIS	PIERRETTE TISON
ARTHUR	YVES SERGENT
UN VALET DE PIED	FRANÇOIS DUCAR

Presented by PETER DAUBENY PRESENTATIONS LTD
by arrangement with LEON HEPNER, FERNANDO LUMBROSO *and* NADINE FAREL

Directed by EDWIGE FEUILLERE   *Decoration by* BERNARD EVEIN

151

Westminster   *August 24 - February 4*

DEAD ON NINE
by Jack Popplewell

TOM HAMMOND..	..	..	..	MAURICE KAUFMANN
ROBERT LEIGH ..	..	..	..	GRIFFITH JONES
MARION DALE ..	..	..	..	JEAN LODGE
ESMERALDA LEIGH	..	..	..	HY HAZELL
RICHARD FARROW	..	..	..	ANDREW CRUICKSHANK
GLADYS ..	..	..	..	GABRIELLE HAMILTON
LESLIE BOOTH ..	..	..	..	ANTHONY SNELL

Presented by JAMES P. SHERWOOD
Directed by GEOFFREY WARDWELL *Decoration by* GEOFFREY GHIN

Aldwych   *February 15 - March 17*

DOCTOR JO
by Joan Morgan

CLARE BERESFORD	..	..	..	BARBARA COUPER
MRS FOTHERGILL	..	..	..	HAZEL BAINBRIDGE
DR MARLOWE ..	..	..	..	CLAUDE JONES
JIM BERESFORD ..	..	..	..	CLIVE PARRITT
DR ALAN BERESFORD ..	..	..	..	HUGH WILLIAMS
JOANNA MARLOWE ..	..	..	..	SONIA DRESDEL
ROBERTS	..	..	..	JOHN WYNYARD
MRS BARNES ..	..	..	..	JUDITH CRAIG

Presented by JACK WALLER
Directed by JACK WILLIAMS *Decoration by* MICHAEL EVE

Royal Court   *In repertory May 15 - 30*

DON JUAN and THE DEATH OF SATAN
by Ronald Duncan

DON JUAN

ALFREDO ..	..	..	..	NIGEL DAVENPORT
DON JUAN TENORIO ..	..	..	..	KEITH MICHELL
CAPTAIN AVELLENEDA ..	..	..	..	CHRISTOPHER FETTES
CAPTAIN CARLOS	..	..	..	GEORGE SELWAY
CATALION ..	..	..	..	STEPHEN DARTNELL
DON LUIS MEIJA	..	..	..	ROBERT STEPHENS
DON GONZALO ..	..	..	..	.. JOHN WELSH
A GUITARIST ..	..	..	..	GEOFFREY SISLEY
DONA ISABELLA	..	..	..	JOSEE RICHARD
ANTONIO	..	..	..	JOHN OSBORNE
DONA ANA ..	..	..	..	ROSALIE CRUTCHLEY
THE ABBESS ..	..	..	..	AGNES LAUCHLAN
BRIGIDA ..	..	..	..	BARBARA GRIMES
SCULPTOR ..	..	..	..	NIGEL DAVENPORT

THE DEATH OF SATAN

DON JUAN TENORIO	..	..	..	KEITH MICHELL
CATALION ..	..	..	..	STEPHEN DARTNELL
SATAN	..	..	..	MICHAEL GWYNN
BERNARD SHAW	..	..	..	.. JOHN WELSH
OSCAR WILDE ..	..	..	..	CHRISTOPHER FETTES

152

LORD BYRON	..	..	..	..	ROBERT STEPHENS
A BISHOP	..	..	..	..	GEORGE SELWAY
LIONEL	..	..	..	..	.. JOHN OSBORNE
EVELYN	..	..	..	..	RACHEL KEMPSON
ANTHONY LISSENDEN	..	..	..	..	NIGEL DAVENPORT
MARCIA LISSENDEN	..	..	..	..	ROSALIE CRUTCHLEY
A RECEPTIONIST	..	..	..	..	JOAN PLOWRIGHT

Presented by THE ENGLISH STAGE COMPANY
Directed by GEORGE DEVINE
Decoration by JOHN MINTON *and* RICHARD NEGRI

Comedy   *January 26 -*

FRESH AIRS

**A Revue devised by Laurier Lister, with Lyrics by Michael Flanders
and Music by Donald Swann**

With MAX ADRIAN, MOYRA FRASER, ROSE HILL,
BERNARD HUNTER, PATRICIA LANCASTER, JULIAN ORCHARD,
HERMIONE HARVEY, GRAHAM MCCORMACK, ROBERT GARD,
ANN PIDGEON, MICHAEL YOUNG, DIANA MURDOCH

Presented by LAURIER LISTER PRODUCTIONS LTD
Directed by LAURIER LISTER *and* MAX ADRIAN
Decoration by MALCOLM BURGESS

New   *May 23 -*

GIGI
by Colette and Anita Loos

GIGI	..	..	..	..	.. LESLIE CARON
MME ALVAREZ	..	..	..	..	.. ENA BURRILL
ANDREE	..	..	..	..	KATHLEEN MICHAEL
GASTON LACHAILLE (TONTON)	..			..	.. TONY BRITTON
VICTOR	..	..	..	..	.. ESME PERCY
ALICIA de ST EPHLAM	..	..	..	..	ESTELLE WINWOOD
SIDONIE	..	..	..	..	.. JESSIE EVANS

Presented by DONALD ALBERY
Directed by PETER HALL   *Decoration by* DISLEY JONES

Piccadilly   *December 15 - April 14*

A GIRL CALLED JO
**A Musical Adaptation of Louisa M. Alcott's 'Little Women' and 'Good Wives'
Book and Lyrics by Peter Myers, Alec Grahame and David Climie
Music by John Pritchett**

MR MARCH	..	..	..	..	KENNETH EDWARDS
MRS MARCH	..	..	..	..	NOEL DYSON
MEG	..	..	..	..	MARION GRIMALDI

JO	..	..	..	..	..	JOAN HEAL
AMY	..	..	..	..	..	VIRGINIA VERNON
BETH	..	..	..	..	..	DIANE TODD
AUNT MARCH	..	..	..	..	HAZEL HUGHES
HANNAH	..	..	..	..	GWEN NELSON
GENERAL LAWRENCE	..	..	..	JAMES RAGLAN
LAURIE	..	..	..	..	DENIS QUILLEY
JOHN BROOKE	..	..	..	..	EDWARD WOODWARD
DR VANCE	..	..	..	..	EDOUARD ASHLEY
TIPSY GUEST	..	..	..	..	DONALD BARCLAY
MRS KIRKE	..	..	..	..	BESSIE LOVE
BOBBY	..	..	..	..	GEORGE HOWELL
SALLY	..	..	..	..	MARGARET SAWYER
PROFESSOR BHAER	..	..	..	PETER DYNELEY

Presented by LINNIT AND DUNFEE LTD
Directed by DENIS CAREY   Musical Direction by MARK LUBBOCK
Decoration by HUTCHINSON SCOTT

Lyric, Hammersmith   *April 4 - 21*

THE GOOD SAILOR
A dramatisation of the novel 'Billy Budd' by Herman Melville
by Louis O. Coxe and Robert Chapman

JENKINS	..	..	..	..	BERNARD BRESSLAW
THE DANSKER	..	..	..	..	NORMAN MACOWAN
JACKSON	..	..	..	..	CHARLES REA
CLAGGART	..	..	..	..	LEO MCKERN
BUTLER	..	..	..	..	LAWRENCE JAMES
TALBOT	..	..	..	..	EDWARD JUDD
KINCAID	..	..	..	..	ANTHONY SAGAR
MESSBOY	..	..	..	..	ANTHONY ADAMS
O'DANIEL	..	..	..	..	SEAN CONNERY
PAYNE	..	..	..	..	CLIFTON JONES
SQUEAK	..	..	..	..	RONALD FRASER
BILLY BUDD	..	..	..	..	PHILIP BOND
GARDINER	..	..	..	..	CHRISTOPHER TAYLOR
SURGEON	..	..	..	..	JOHN ATKINSON
EDWARD FAIRFAX VERE	..	..	ANDRE MORELL
JOHN RATCLIFFE	..	..	..	AUBREY DEXTER
PHILIP MICHAEL SEYMOUR	..	..	KYNASTON REEVES
BORDMAN WYATT	..	..	..	DAVID YATES
REA	..	..	..	..	DINSDALE LANDEN
DUNCAN	..	..	..	..	KEITH GRIEVE
HALLAM	..	..	..	..	NICHOLAS BRADY
STOLL	..	..	..	..	PAUL WILLIAMSON
DRUMMER BOY	..	..	..	ANTHONY FORD
OTHER SAILORS	..	..	..HENRY CADDOW, HENRY COMOR,
				CLIVE ROSLIN

Presented by MARK MARVIN PRODUCTIONS LTD
in association with ANTHONY BRADY FARRELL *and* GABRIEL KATZKA
Directed by FRITH BANBURY   Decoration by REECE PEMBERTON

THE GOOD SOLDIER SCHWEIK
adapted from the novel of Jaroslav Hasek, by Ewan MacColl

JOSEPH SCHWEIK .. .. .. MAXWELL SHAW

1. *Civilian Life*

MRS MULLER	AVIS BUNNAGE
PALIVEK	BRIAN MURPHY
BRETSCHNEIDER	ROBERT GRANT
AN EXAMINER	PETER SMALLWOOD
A CLERK	BRIAN MURPHY
A TEACHER	PETER SMALLWOOD
A PRINTER	GERARD DYNEVOR
A CHAIRMAN	ROBERT JONES
A CARD-PLAYER	BARRY CLAYTON
A BURGLAR	CLIVE BARKER
A JAILER	GLYNN EDWARDS
TWO PSYCHIATRISTS ..	HOWARD GOORNEY, ROBERT GRANT

2. *Army Life*

DR BAUTZE	GERRY RAFFLES
DR GRUNSTEIN	HOWARD GOORNEY
SOLDIERS	BRIAN MURPHY, BARRY CLAYTON, ROBERT JONES, GERARD DYNEVOR, ROBERT GRANT
BARONESS VON BOTZENHEIM	AVIS BUNNAGE
LISE	BARBARA BROWN
PASTOR KATZ	GERRY RAFFLES
LIEUTENANT LUKASH	PETER SMALLWOOD
MME KATI WENDLER	AVIS BUNNAGE
BLAHNIK	ROBERT JONES
1ST BARMAID	OLIVE MCFARLAND
AN ARTILLERYMAN	BRIAN MURPHY
BALOUN	GLYNN EDWARDS
2ND BARMAID	BARBARA BROWN
AN OFFICER-CADET	GERARD DYNEVOR
A MILITARY POLICE CORPORAL ..	GERRY RAFFLES
3RD BARMAID	AVIS BUNNAGE
A MAIDSERVANT	OLIVE MCFARLAND
A COLONEL	BARRY CLAYTON

3. *The Journey to the Front*

A BALD-HEADED GENTLEMAN ..	.. ROBERT GRANT
A TRAIN GUARD	BRIAN MURPHY
A POLICE SERGEANT	HOWARD GOORNEY
A POLICE CONSTABLE	GERARD DYNEVOR
LIEUTENANT DUBB	ROBERT JONES
SERGEANT-MAJOR NASAKLE	HOWARD GOORNEY

Presented by THEATRE WORKSHOP
controlled by PIONEER THEATRES LTD

Directed by JOAN LITTLEWOOD

With a cartoon décor executed by GEOFF MILLER
from drawings by ERN BROOKS

155

HAMLET
Prince of Denmark
by William Shakespeare

BERNARDO	GARETH JONES
FRANCISCO	MICHAEL ALLINSON
MARCELLUS	JOHN TURNER
HORATIO..	MICHAEL DAVID
GHOST of HAMLET'S FATHER	JOHN PHILLIPS
HAMLET	PAUL SCOFIELD
CLAUDIUS	ALEC CLUNES
GERTRUDE	DIANA WYNYARD
POLONIUS	ERNEST THESIGER
LAERTES	RICHARD JOHNSON
OPHELIA ..	MARY URE
VOLTIMAND	PETER WHITBREAD
CORNELIUS	ANTHONY SERVICE
ROSENCRANTZ ..	GERALD FLOOD
GUILDENSTERN	DAVID DE KEYSER
REYNALDO	NORMAN SCACE
FIRST PLAYER	HARRY H. CORBETT
SECOND PLAYER	AUBREY WOODS
THIRD PLAYER	ANTHONY SERVICE
FOURTH PLAYER	NORMAN BIRD
FIFTH PLAYER	GARETH JONES
SIXTH PLAYER	JOHN TURNER
FORTINBRAS	RICHARD PASCO
A CAPTAIN	MICHAEL ALLINSON
A MESSENGER	ANTHONY SERVICE
AN ATTENDANT	NORMAN SCACE
A SAILOR	CHURTON FAIRMAN
FIRST GRAVEDIGGER	HARRY H. CORBETT
SECOND GRAVEDIGGER..	AUBREY WOODS
A PRIEST	NORMAN BIRD
OSRIC	TIMOTHY FINDLEY
A GENTLEMAN	ROBERT ROBINSON

Presented by TENNENT PRODUCTIONS LTD
Directed by PETER BROOK
Decoration by GEORGES WAKHEVITCH

HOME AND AWAY
by Heather McIntyre

ANNIE KNOWLES	SHEILA EVES
ELSIE KNOWLES	IRENE HANDL
MARY KNOWLES	BARBARA CHRISTIE
JOHNNY KNOWLES	DEREK BLOMFIELD
GEORGE KNOWLES	EDWARD CHAPMAN
MARGIE GROVES	DANDY NICHOLS
TED GROVES	STUART SAUNDERS
SYD JARVIS	JAMES VIVIAN
LEWIS	DERMOT PALMER
JEAN	MARGARET ST BARBE-WEST

TOM	..	..	..	..	Joe Gibbons
MRS JARVIS	..	..	..	..	Diana Beaumont
ALBERT WEST	..	..	..	..	Verne Morgan

Presented by STANLEY WILLIS-CROFT
in association with GEORGE MAYNARD PRODUCTIONS LTD
by arrangement with JACK BUCHANAN and JOHN FORBES-SEMPILL
Directed by MARTIN LANDAU
Decoration by GEORGE TOYNBEE-CLARKE

Winter Garden   May 2 -

HOTEL PARADISO
by Georges Feydeau and Maurice Desvallières
English translation by Peter Glenville

BONIFACE	..	..	..	..	Alec Guinness
ANGELICA	..	..	..	..	Martita Hunt
MARCELLE	..	..	..	..	.. Irene Worth
COT	..	..	..	..	Frank Pettingell
MAXIME	..	..	..	..	Kenneth Williams
VICTOIRE	..	..	..	..	Billie Whitelaw
MARTIN	..	..	..	..	Douglas Byng
PORTERS	..	Cyril Wheeler, John Grant, Michael Malnick,			
		Leslie Kyle, Thomas Elliott			
VIOLETTE	..	..	..	..	.. Jale Davaz
MARGUERITE	..	..	..	..	.. Ann Warren
PAQUERETTE	..	..	..	..	Alanna Boyce
PERVENCHE	..	..	..	..	Virginia Holt
ANNIELLO	..	..	..	..	Ronald Radd
GEORGES	..	..	..	..	Michael Bates
A LADY	..	..	..	..	Phyllis Montefiore
A DUKE	..	..	..	..	Douglas Stewart
TABU	..	..	..	..	Michael Malnick
POLICE INSPECTOR BOUCHARD	..	..	..	John Salew

Presented by H.M. TENNENT LTD and PETER GLENVILLE
Directed by PETER GLENVILLE   Decoration by OSBERT LANCASTER

Duke of York's   May 9 -
THE HOUSE BY THE LAKE
by Hugh Mills

COLONEL FORBES	..	..	..	.. Frank Royde
STELLA	..	..	..	..	.. Jenny Laird
JANET	..	..	..	..	Flora Robson
BRENDA	..	..	..	..	Doreen Morton
MAURICE	..	..	..	.. Andrew Cruickshank
COLIN	..	..	..	..	.. Paul Lee
IRIS	..	..	..	..	Sylvia Coleridge
MR HOWARD	..	..	..	.. Alan MacNaughtan
NURSE THOMSON	..	..	..	Annette Kerr

Presented by PETER DAUBENY PRESENTATIONS LTD
Directed by JOHN FERNALD

157

JULIUS CAESAR
by William Shakespeare

FLAVIUS	JOHN WOODVINE
MARULLUS	CHARLES GRAY
A CITIZEN	CLIFFORD WILLIAMS
JULIUS CAESAR	GERALD CROSS
CASCA	JACK GWILLIM
CALPURNIA	ROSEMARY HARRIS
MARK ANTONY	JOHN NEVILLE
A SOOTHSAYER	JOB STEWART
BRUTUS	PAUL ROGERS
CASSIUS	RICHARD WORDSWORTH
CICERO	DENIS HOLMES
CINNA	DUDLEY JONES
LUCIUS STRATO	DAVID SAIRE
DECIUS BRUTUS	JOHN WOOD
METELLUS CIMBER	HAROLD KASKET
TREBONIUS	JAMES VILLIERS
PORTIA	WENDY HILLER
LIGARIUS	EDWARD HARVEY
SERVANT to CAESAR	TOM KNEEBONE
PUBLIUS	RONALD ALLEN
ARTEMIDORUS	DEREK FRANCIS
POPILIUS LENA	BRYAN PRINGLE
SERVANT to ANTONY	KEITH TAYLOR
SERVANT to OCTAVIUS CAESAR ..	JOHN GREENWOOD
CINNA the POET	AUBREY MORRIS
OCTAVIUS CAESAR	JOHN FRASER
LEPIDUS	DUDLEY JONES
LUCILIUS	DEREK FRANCIS
PINDARUS	CLIFFORD WILLIAMS
MESSALA..	ANTHONY WHITE
TITINIUS	DENIS HOLMES
MESSENGER to Antony and Octavius ..	DERRY NESBITT
CLITUS	JOB STEWART
DARDANIUS	AUBREY MORRIS
VOLUMNIUS	RONALD ALLEN

Presented by OLD VIC TRUST LTD
in association with THE ARTS COUNCIL
Directed by MICHAEL BENTHALL   *Decoration by* AUDREY CRUDDAS

KING HENRY V
by William Shakespeare

CHORUS	JOHN NEVILLE
KING HENRY the FIFTH	RICHARD BURTON
DUKE of EXETER	JACK GWILLIM
EARL of WESTMORELAND	DENIS HOLMES
ARCHBISHOP of CANTERBURY	HAROLD KASKET
BISHOP of ELY	JOHN WOODVINE
RAMBURES	JAMES VILLIERS
BARDOLPH	AUBREY MORRIS
NYM	JOB STEWART
PISTOL	RICHARD WORDSWORTH

MISTRESS QUICKLY	..	..	..	RACHEL ROBERTS
BOY	..	..	..	JOHN GREENWOOD
DUKE of BEDFORD	..	..	..	PETER NEEDHAM
LORD SCROOP	..	..	..	DEREK FRANCIS
EARL of CAMBRIDGE	..	..	..	EDWARD HARVEY
SIR THOMAS GREY	..	..	..	BRYAN PRINGLE
CHARLES the SIXTH	..	..	..	GERALD CROSS
LEWIS	..	..	..	JOHN WOOD
THE CONSTABLE of FRANCE	..	..	CHARLES GRAY
MONTJOY	..	..	..	ANTHONY WHITE
FLUELLEN	..	..	..	DUDLEY JONES
GOWER	..	..	..	DEREK FRANCIS
JAMY	..	..	..	JOHN FRASER
MACMORRIS	..	..	..	JOHN WOODVINE
GOVERNOR of HARFLEUR	..	..	BRYAN PRINGLE
KATHERINE	..	..	..	ZENA WALKER
ALICE	..	..	..	RACHEL ROBERTS
DUKE of ORLEANS	..	..	..	HAROLD KASKET
DUKE of GLOUCESTER	..	..	KEITH TAYLOR
SIR THOMAS ERPINGHAM	..	..	EDWARD HARVEY
COURT	..	..	..	TOM KNEEBONE
BATES	..	..	..	JOHN FRASER
WILLIAMS	..	..	..	CLIFFORD WILLIAMS
DUKE of SALISBURY	..	..	..	RONALD ALLEN
DUKE of YORK	..	..	..	BRYAN PRINGLE
ISABEL	..	..	..	MARGARET COURTENAY

Presented by OLD VIC TRUST LTD
in association with THE ARTS COUNCIL

Directed by MICHAEL BENTHALL   *Decoration by* AUDREY CRUDDAS

Palace   *In repertory July 26 - September 10*

KING LEAR
by William Shakespeare

THE EARL of KENT	..	..	..	ANTHONY NICHOLLS
THE EARL of GLOUCESTER	..	..	GEORGE DEVINE
EDMUND..	..	..	..	HAROLD LANG
LEAR	..	..	..	JOHN GIELGUD
GONERIL	..	..	..	HELEN CHERRY
THE DUKE of ALBANY	..	..	..	RAYMOND WESTWELL
REGAN	..	..	..	MOIRA LISTER
THE DUKE of CORNWALL	..	..	ANTHONY IRELAND
CORDELIA	..	..	..	CLAIRE BLOOM
THE DUKE of BURGUNDY	..	..	PAUL HARDWICK
THE KING of FRANCE	..	..	..	JEREMY BURNHAM
EDGAR	..	..	..	RICHARD EASTON
OSWALD	..	..	..	JOHN GARLEY
KNIGHT	..	..	..	POWYS THOMAS
FOOL	..	..	..	DAVID O'BRIEN
CURAN	..	..	..	DAVID MARLOWE
SERVANTS to CORNWALL	..	KEN WYNNE, DAVID CONVILLE, MICHAEL MALNICK
AN OLD MAN	..	..	..	PAUL HARDWICK
A DOCTOR	..	..	..	PETER RETEY
A SOLDIER in CORDELIA'S ARMY	..	MICHAEL SPICE
A CAPTAIN in EDMUND'S ARMY	..	MICHAEL MALNICK
A HERALD	..	..	..	BEVERLEY CROSS

159

Presented by THE SHAKESPEARE MEMORIAL THEATRE
by arrangement with EMILE LITTLER
Directed by GEORGE DEVINE
Decoration by ISAMU NOGUCHI   *Music by* ROBERTO GERHARD

Globe
March 22 -

A LIKELY TALE
by Gerald Savory

OSWALD PETERSHAM	..	..	..	ROBERT MORLEY
LOLA PETERSHAM	..	..	..	VIOLET FAREBROTHER
MIRABELLE PETERSHAM	..	..	..	MARGARET RUTHERFORD
URSULA BUDGEON	..	..	..	JUDY PARFITT
GREGORY LUPTON	..	..	..	RICHARD PEARSON
JONAH PETERSHAM	..	..	..	ROBERT MORLEY

Presented by H. M. TENNENT LTD
and ROBERT MORLEY PRODUCTIONS LTD
Directed by PETER ASHMORE

Royal Court
In repertory May 8 -

LOOK BACK IN ANGER
by John Osborne

JIMMY PORTER	..	..	..	KENNETH HAIGH
CLIFF LEWIS	..	..	..	ALAN BATES
ALISON PORTER	..	..	..	MARY URE
HELENA CHARLES	..	..	..	HELENA HUGHES
COLONEL REDFERN	..	..	..	JOHN WELSH

Presented by THE ENGLISH STAGE COMPANY
Directed by TONY RICHARDSON

Lyric, Hammersmith
June 1 -

LOVE AFFAIR
by Dulcie Gray

JULIA FAYNE	..	..	..	..	JULIE SOMERS
MARION FIELD	..	..	..	..	DULCIE GRAY
PHILIP GRANT	..	..	..	..	MICHAEL DENISON
MRS CHILLINGWORTH	..	..	..	..	DOROTHY TURNER
SPENCER BENTON	..	..	..	..	JAMES GROUT
ROSEMARY de VILLIERS	..	..	..	..	MARY LAW
MACNAB	..	..	..	..	MERVYN BLAKE
MONSIEUR HERO	..	..	..	..	BRIAN OULTON
RUPERT BLISS	..	..	..	..	IAN HOLM

Presented by DEREK SALBERG
by arrangement with TENNENT PRODUCTIONS LTD
on behalf of ALEXANDRA THEATRE, BIRMINGHAM
Directed by MICHAEL DENISON

Apollo   *September 14 - November 5*
Duke of York's   *November 14 - March 10*

LUCKY STRIKE
by Michael Brett

SUSIE	MARJORIE FORSYTH
KEITH SALESBY	HARVEY HALLSMITH
MRS SALESBY	AMBROSINE PHILLPOTTS
CATHERINE STEVENS	JANE DOWNS
HUGH WALLIS	PETER ROSSER
JOE HURST	DOUGLAS IVES
BILL GILES	MICHAEL BARBER
CHARLIE MAGGS .. .. .,	ARTHUR LOVEGROVE
SIR WILLIAM GARRICK, C.B.E.	JOHN BOXER
GEORGE PONTING	GEOFFREY TYRRELL
TOM SPRAGGE	WILLIAM FRANKLYN

Presented by DONALD ALBERY *for* DONMAR PRODUCTIONS LTD
Directed by JACK MINSTER   *Decoration by* FANNY TAYLOR

Fortune   *December 24 - January 21*

THE MARVELLOUS STORY OF PUSS IN BOOTS
adapted from the story by Charles Perrault, by Nicholas Stuart Gray

COBB	PATRICK TROUGHTON
DANDY	PHILIP THOMAS
THE PRINCESS ISOBEL	JOY PARKER
JONETTE	JILL DIXON
LAVENA	ROSEMARY WALLACE
GERARD	RICHARD GALE
PUSS	Nicholas STUART GRAY
THE OGRE	ALAN JUDD
THE CHANCELLOR	MICHAEL BATES
GENERAL DIGGORY	ANDREW FAULDS
THE KING	DAVID KING-WOOD

Presented by LONDON CHILDREN'S THEATRE
Directed by NICHOLAS STUART GRAY
Decoration by REGINALD WOOLLEY *and* JOAN JEFFERSON FARJEON

Hippodrome   *November 4 - April 28*

MEET ME ON THE CORNER

With MAX BYGRAVES,
KATHARINE FEATHER, GUY FIELDING, LATONA, GRAHAM AND
CHADEL, CHANNING POLLOCK, LOUIE RAMSAY, JOAN WINTERS

Presented by VAL PARNELL   *Directed by* CHARLES HENRY
Produced by VAL PARNELL   *Decoration by* R. ST JOHN ROPER

Old Vic　　　　　*In repertory September 27 - December 19*

THE MERRY WIVES OF WINDSOR
by William Shakespeare

SHALLOW	GERALD CROSS
SLENDER	JOB STEWART
SIR HUGH EVANS	DUDLEY JONES
PAGE	JACK GWILLIM
SIR JOHN FALSTAFF	PAUL ROGERS
BARDOLPH	DENIS HOLMES
PISTOL	JOHN WOOD
NYM	DEREK FRANCIS
ANNE PAGE	ZENA WALKER
MISTRESS FORD	MARGARET RAWLINGS
MISTRESS PAGE	WENDY HILLER
SIMPLE	KEITH TAYLOR
HOST of the Garter Inn	HAROLD KASKET
MISTRESS QUICKLY	RACHEL ROBERTS
RUGBY	JOHN WOODVINE
DOCTOR CAIUS	AUBREY MORRIS
FENTON	JOHN FRASER
FORD	RICHARD WORDSWORTH
ROBIN	BUNNY MAY
JOHN	ANTHONY WHITE
ROBERT	DERRY NESBITT

Presented by OLD VIC TRUST LTD
in association with THE ARTS COUNCIL
Directed by DOUGLAS SEALE　　*Decoration by* PAUL SHELVING

Lyric, Hammersmith　　　　　*February 8 - March 24*

MISALLIANCE
by Bernard Shaw

JOHNNY TARLETON	BERNARD FOX
BENTLEY SUMMERHAYS	PETER BARKWORTH
HYPATIA TARLETON	ANN WALFORD
MRS TARLETON	URSULA JEANS
LORD SUMMERHAYS	ALAN WEBB
JOHN TARLETON	ROGER LIVESEY
JOEY PERCIVAL	JOHN WESTBROOK
LINA SZCZEPANOWSKA	MIRIAM KARLIN
A MAN	DONALD PLEASENCE

Presented by TENNENT PRODUCTIONS LTD
Directed by LIONEL HARRIS
Decoration by HUTCHINSON SCOTT

Comedy　　　　　*December 14 - January 14*
Westminster　　　　　*February 7 - May 12*

MORNING'S AT SEVEN
by Paul Osborn

THEODORE SWANSON	FREDERICK LEISTER
CORA SWANSON	MONA WASHBOURNE
AARONETTA GIBBS	MARGARET VINES

IDA BOLTON	..	..	..	..	MARDA VANNE
CARL BOLTON	..	..	..	..	FREDERICK PIPER
HOMER BOLTON	..	..	..	..	PETER JONES
MYRTLE BROWN	..	..	..	..	TUCKER MCGUIRE
ESTHER CRAMPTON	..	..	..	..	NAN MONRO
DAVID CRAMPTON	..	..	..	..	CHARLES HESLOP

Presented by ANNA DEERE WIMAN *in association with* E. P. CLIFT
Directed by JACK MINSTER *Decoration by* PAUL MAYO

Duchess   September 1 - March 3

MR KETTLE AND MRS MOON
by J. B. Priestley

MRS TWIGG	..	..	..	..	PHYLLIS MORRIS
GEORGE KETTLE	..	..	..	..	CLIVE MORTON
MONICA TWIGG	..	..	..	..	WENDY CRAIG
ALDERMAN HARDACRE	..	..	..	..	JULIAN SOMERS
SUPERINTENDENT STREET	..	..	..	RICHARD WARNER
DELIA MOON	..	..	..	..	FRANCIS ROWE
HENRY MOON	..	..	..	..	RAYMOND FRANCIS
CLINTON	..	..	..	..	BECKETT BOULD
DR GRENOCK	..	..	..	..	JOHN MOFFATT

Presented by TOM ARNOLD *Directed by* TONY RICHARDSON

Globe   August 17 - December 17

MRS WILLIE
by Alan Melville

WILLIE	..	..	..	..	..	CYRIL RAYMOND
PAUL	..	..	..	..	..	TERENCE ALEXANDER
WAITER	..	..	..	..	..	JAMES SHARKEY
ILENA	..	..	..	..	..	YVONNE ARNAUD
NELLIE	..	..	..	..	..	MOLLY FRANCIS
MRS GREGSON	..	..	..	..	MARIAN SPENCER
JANE	..	..	..	..	..	ANN WALFORD
LORD ALLERDALE	..	..	..	..	WILLIAM MERVYN
VITULESCU	..	..	..	..	CARL JAFFE
NURSE OTWAY	..	..	..	..	DAPHNE HEARD
MR BUTLER	..	..	..	..	MICHAEL NIGHTINGALE

Presented by H. M. TENNENT LTD
Directed by WALLACE DOUGLAS *Decoration by* MICHAEL WEIGHT

Palace   In repertory July 21 - September 17

MUCH ADO ABOUT NOTHING
by William Shakespeare

LEONATO	..	..	..	..	ANTHONY NICHOLLS
MESSENGER	..	..	..	..	JEREMY BURNHAM
BEATRICE	..	..	..	..	PEGGY ASHCROFT
HERO	..	..	..	..	JUDITH STOTT
DON PEDRO	..	..	..	..	ANTHONY IRELAND

BENEDICK	.. ..	.. John Gielgud
DON JOHN	.. ..	Raymond Westwell
CLAUDIO..	.. ..	Richard Easton
CONRADE	.. ..	Michael Malnick
BORACHIO	.. ..	.. Harold Lang
ANTONIO	.. ..	Powys Thomas
MARGARET	.. ..	Moira Lister
URSULA ..	.. ..	Helen Cherry
PAGE to BENEDICK	.. .. ..	Timothy Harley
BALTHAZAR	.. ..	Beverley Cross
DOGBERRY	.. ..	George Devine
VERGES ..	.. .. ..	David O'Brien
WATCHMEN	.. ..	John Garley, David Marlowe, Peter Retey, Nicholas Brady
FRIAR FRANCIS	.. .. ..	Paul Hardwick
A SEXTON	.. ..	.. Ken Wynne

Presented by The Shakespeare Memorial Theatre
by arrangement with Emile Littler
Directed by John Gielgud *Decoration by* Mariano Andreu
Music by Leslie Bridgewater

Royal Court　　　　　　*In repertory April 2 - May 19*

THE MULBERRY BUSH
by Angus Wilson

ANN PADLEY ..	.. .. ..	Helena Hughes
PETER LORD ..	.. .. ..	Kenneth Haigh
CORA FELLOWES	.. ..	Rachel Kempson
ROSE PADLEY ..	.. ..	Gwen Ffrangcon-Davies
JAMES PADLEY	.. .. ..	.. John Welsh
KURT LANDECK	.. ..	Christopher Fettes
CRADDOCK ..	.. ..	Stephen Dartnell
SIMON FELLOWES	.. ..	.. Alan Bates
GERALDINE LOUGHTON-MOORE	..	Agnes Lauchlan
CAPTAIN WALLCOTT	.. ..	Nigel Davenport

Presented by The English Stage Company
Directed by George Devine *Decoration by* Motley

Haymarket　　　　　　*July 27 - September 3*

NINA
by André Roussin translated by Arthur Macrae

GEORGES de FORVILLE CHAMBERY	..	Michael Hordern
ADOLPHE TESSIER	.. .. ..	James Hayter
NINA TESSIER ..	.. .. ..	Coral Browne
AGENT de POLICE	.. .. ..	Lockwood West
RENE DUVIVIER	.. .. ..	Raymond Young

Presented by Tennent Productions Ltd
Directed by Rex Harrison *Decoration by* Arthur Barbosa

ONE BRIGHT DAY
by Sigmund Miller

GEORGE LAWRENCE	..	..	.. DEREK FARR
LOUISE GORDON	..	..	GILLIAN OWEN
STANLEY ARCHER	..	..	MICHAEL SCOTT
FREDERICK NEWBERRY	..	..	REGINALD LONG
JULIAN PRESCOTT	..	..	.. CLIVE BROOK
GINNY ..	..	..	MARGOT BOYD
TOM McGOWAN ..	..	..	HAMLYN BENSON
SHEILA PRESCOTT	..	..	.. MARY HINTON
MARGOT PRESCOTT	..	..	RENEE ASHERSON
ARTHUR MITCHELL	..	..	NAUNTON WAYNE
PAUL LABARCA	..	..	.. TONY CHURCH
JOHN HAGERTY ..	..	..	JOBY BLANSHARD
DOCTOR FERGUSON	..	..	MILTON ROSMER
THEODORE CAHILL	..	..	.. GERALD CASE
PAUL RUST ('RUSTY')	..	..	NICOLAS TANNAR

Presented by PETER SAUNDERS

Directed by WALLACE DOUGLAS   *Decoration by* MICHAEL WEIGHT

OTHELLO
The Moor of Venice
by William Shakespeare

RODERIGO	..	..	RICHARD WORDSWORTH
IAGO ..	..	..	.. JOHN NEVILLE
			alternating with RICHARD BURTON
BRABANTIO	..	..	.. JACK GWILLIM
OTHELLO	..	..	RICHARD BURTON
			alternating with JOHN NEVILLE
MICHAEL CASSIO	..	..	ANTHONY WHITE
DUKE OF VENICE	..	..	DEREK FRANCIS
GRATIANO	..	..	EDWARD HARVEY
LODOVICO	..	..	CHARLES GRAY
OFFICER ..	..	..	DERRY NESBITT
TWO MESSENGERS	..	KEITH TAYLOR, CLIFFORD WILLIAMS	
DESDEMONA	..	..	ROSEMARY HARRIS
MONTANO	..	..	.. DENIS HOLMES
THREE GENTLEMEN	RONALD ALLEN, JOHN WOODVINE, JOHN WOOD		
A MESSENGER	..	..	PETER NEEDHAM
EMILIA ..	..	..	WENDY HILLER
A HERALD	..	..	BRYAN PRINGLE
BIANCA ..	..	..	RACHEL ROBERTS

Presented by OLD VIC TRUST LTD
in association with THE ARTS COUNCIL

Directed by MICHAEL BENTHALL   *Decoration by* LOUDON SAINTHILL

THE PAJAMA GAME
Book by George Abbott and Richard Bissell
Music and Lyrics by Richard Adler and Jerry Ross

HINES	.. ..	MAX WALL
PREZ	.. ..	FRANK LAWLESS
JOE	.. ..	ROBERT CRANE
HASLER	.. ..	FELIX FELTON
SID SOROKIN	.. ..	EDMUND HOCKRIDGE
GLADYS	.. ..	ELIZABETH SEAL
MABEL	.. ..	JOAN EMNEY
1ST HELPER	.. ..	FRANKLYN FOX
2ND HELPER	.. ..	IVOR MEGGIDO
CHARLIE	.. ..	STANLEY BEADLE
BABE WILLIAMS	.. ..	JOY NICHOLS
MAE	.. ..	JESSIE ROBINS
BRENDA	.. ..	OLGA LOWE
POOPSIE	.. ..	SUSAN IRVIN
SALESMAN	.. ..	ARTHUR LOWE
POP	.. ..	CHARLES ROLFE

Presented by WILLIAMSON MUSIC LTD. *and* PRINCE LITTLER
by arrangement with FREDERICK BRISSON,
ROBERT E. GRIFFITH *and* HAROLD S. PRINCE
Directed by GEORGE ABBOTT *and* JEROME ROBBINS
Decoration by LEMUEL AYERS   *Choreography by* BOB FOSSE

PETER PAN
by J. M. Barrie

PETER PAN	.. ..	PEGGY CUMMINS
MR DARLING	.. ..	FRANK THRING
MRS DARLING	.. ..	ROSEMARY SCOTT
WENDY MOIRA ANGELA DARLING	..	ROBERTA WOOLLEY
JOHN NAPOLEON DARLING	..	NICKY EDMETT
MICHAEL NICHOLAS DARLING	.. ..	JOHN HALL
NANA	.. ..	KENNETH ROBINSON
LIZA	.. ..	ELAINE MILLER
TINKER BELL	.. ..	JANE WREN
TOOTLES	.. ..	CAVAN KENDALL
NIBS	.. ..	ADRIAN HAGGARD
SLIGHTLY	.. ..	WILLIAM INGRAM
CURLY	.. ..	PAUL BIRRELL
FIRST TWIN	.. ..	ALAN GLASS
SECOND TWIN	.. ..	PETER STEVENS
JAMES HOOK	.. ..	FRANK THRING
SMEE	.. ..	RUSSELL THORNDIKE
GENTLEMAN STARKEY	.. .. ..	NORMAN ROSSINGTON
COOKSON	.. ..	GILBERT BAILEY
CECCO	.. ..	JOSEPH CHELTON
MULLINS	.. ..	JAMES GILL
JUKES	.. ..	DAVID ASHMAN
NOODLER	.. ..	LIONEL GADSDEN
SKYLIGHTS	.. ..	LIONEL WHEELER

CABIN BOY	..	..	..	..	KENNETH ROBINSON
BLACK PIRATE	..	..	..	..	.. AYTON MEDAS
GREAT BIG LITTLE PANTHER	..		..	DAVID ASHMAN
TIGER LILY	..	..	..	..	.. SALLY HOME
MERMAID	..	..	..	..	LILIAN GRASSON
BABY MERMAID	..	..	..	..	ELAINE MILLER
BADGER	..	..	..	..	.. JOHN DAW
CROCODILE	..	..	..	..	.. JOHN ORMOND

Presented by the DANIEL MAYER COMPANY
Directed by JOHN FERNALD *Decoration by* FANNY TAYLOR

Theatre Royal, Drury Lane *January 25 -*

PLAIN AND FANCY

Book by Joseph Stein and Will Glickman

Lyrics by Arnold B. Horwitt, and Music by Albert Hague

RUTH WINTERS ..	..	..	..	SHIRL CONWAY
DAN KING ..	..	..	..	RICHARD DERR
A MAN ..	..	..	..	TERENCE COOPER
ANOTHER MAN ..	..	..	..	IVOR EMMANUEL
KATIE YODER ..	..	..	..	GRACE O'CONNOR
PAPA YODER ..	..	..	..	MALCOLM KEEN
ISAAC MILLER ..	..	..	..	BERNARD SPEAR
EMMA MILLER ..	..	..	..	VIRGINIA SOMERS
EZRA REBER ..	..	..	..	REED DE ROUEN
HILDA MILLER ..	..	..	..	.. JOAN HOVIS
PETER REBER ..	..	..	..	JACK DRUMMOND
RACHEL ..	..	..	..	.. RITA VARIAN
SAMUEL ZOOK ..	..	..	..	HARRY NAUGHTON
JACOB YODER ..	..	..	..	MICHAEL DARBYSHIRE
SAMUEL LAPP ..	..	..	..	.. JOSEPH SEALY
ABNER ZOOK ..	..	..	..	TERENCE COOPER
IKE PILERSHEIM ..	..	..	..	.. BARRIE IRWIN
MOSES ZOOK ..	..	..	..	FRANK RAYNOR
ABNER ZOOK ..	..	..	..	ROBERT ALGAR
BESSIE ..	..	..	..	LEANDER FEDDEN
SARAH ..	..	..	..	RENEE FELLOWES
ESTHER ..	..	..	..	BARBARA LEWIS
REBECCA..	..	..	..	.. OLIVE LUCIUS
MARY ..	..	..	..	PATRICIA MORTIMER
STATE TROOPER	..	..	..	IVOR EMMANUEL

Presented by PRINCE LITTLER *and* CHAPPELL AND COMPANY LTD
Directed by MORTON DA COSTA *Decoration by* RAOUL PENE DUBOIS

Garrick *November 3 -*

LA PLUME DE MA TANTE
A French Revue

Music by Gerard Calvi, English Lyrics by Ross Parker

With JACQUES LEGRAS, ROBERT DHERY, COLETTE BROSSET,
CHRISTIAN DUVALEIX, PIERRE OLAF, NICOLE PARENT,
LAURENCE SOUPAULT, FRANK DAUBRAY, ROGER CACCIA,
PAMELA AUSTIN

Presented by JACK HYLTON *by arrangement with* JACK BUCHANAN
and JOHN FORBES-SEMPILL

Choreography by COLETTE BROSSET *Staged by* ALEC SHANKS

THE POWER AND THE GLORY
by Graham Greene
adapted for the stage by Denis Cannan and Pierre Bost

TENCH	BRIAN WILDE
THE CHIEF of POLICE	ROGER DELGADO
DIAZ	ROBERT ROBINSON
A PRIEST	PAUL SCOFIELD
A LIEUTENANT of POLICE	HARRY H. CORBETT
A BOY	MEURIG WYN-JONES
MARIA	PATIENCE COLLIER
BRIGITTA	ANN COOKE
FRANCISCO	ALEX SCOTT
MIGUEL	OSCAR QUITAK
A POLICEMAN	CHURTON FAIRMAN
MESTIZO	ROBERT MARSDEN
THE GOVERNOR'S COUSIN	WILLOUGHBY GODDARD
A DRUNKEN PRISONER	JOHN TURNER
LOPEZ	GERALD FLOOD
A SPINSTER	HENZIE RAEBURN
THE WARDER	NORMAN SCACE
A FARMER'S WIFE	BERYL ANDREWS
ALVAREZ	JOHN TURNER
VITTORIO	MAURICE BANNISTER
A SCHOOLMASTER	DAVID DE KEYSER
OBREGON	GARETH JONES
OBREGON'S WIFE	VERONICA WELLS
RAMON	BARRY MARTIN
LOLA	ANN MAURESO
AN INDIAN	DAVID SPENSER
A PEASANT WOMAN	CATHERINE WILLMER
A VILLAGER	WILLIAM ROBERTSON
AN OLD VILLAGER	NORMAN BIRD
A YOUNG WOMAN	CARMEN VICKERS
A STRANGER	OSCAR QUITAK

Presented by TENNENT PRODUCTIONS LTD

Directed by PETER BROOK   *Decoration by* GEORGES WAKHEVITCH

Duke of York's   *September 28 - November 12*

THE PUNCH REVUE
A Revue with Book by Ronald Duncan
devised by Vida Hope

with Words and Music by
Geoffrey Parsons, Berkeley Fase, Louis McNeice, B. A. Young,
Alex Atkinson, John Betjeman, Benjamin Britten, Larry Adler,
Donald Swann, W. H. Auden, J. B. Boothroyd, Vida Hope,
T. S. Eliot, Alan Rawsthorne, Geoffrey Wright, George
Schwartz, William Plomer, Paul Dehn, Herbert Farjeon and
David Higham

With BINNIE HALE, PAUL DANEMAN, ALFIE BASS, DENIS
MARTIN, JOYCE BLAIR, MALCOLM GODDARD, WENDY
MCCLURE, SHEILA KENNEDY, JUNE LAVERICK, ANNETTE
GIBSON, ROSALINE HADDON, JAMES BROWNE, ANDREW
DOWNIE, JOHN PALMER, MICHAEL MURRAY

Presented by OSCAR LEWENSTEIN *and* WOLF MANKOWITZ
in association with 'Punch'
Directed by VIDA HOPE   *Musical Direction by* GEOFFREY WRIGHT
Decoration by JOAN *and* DAVID DE BETHEL

Haymarket   *October 26 - January 14*

THE QUEEN AND THE REBELS
by Ugo Betti
translated by Henry Reed

THE PORTER	JOHN KIDD
ENGINEER	JOHN GILL
THE TRAVELLER	LEO MCKERN
RAIM	DUNCAN LAMONT
ARGIA	IRENE WORTH
BIANTE	ALAN TILVERN
MAUPA	BRIAN WALLACE
ELISABETTA	GWENDOLINE WATFORD
PEASANT WOMAN	MARY LLEWELLIN
A PEASANT	PATRICK MAGEE
A YOUNG PEASANT	ANGELA LLOYD

Presented by HENRY SHEREK
Directed by FRANK HAUSER   *Decoration by* AUDREY CRUDDAS

St Martin's   *May 31 -*

THE RAINMAKER
by N. Richard Nash

H. C. CURRY	WILFRID LAWSON
NOAH CURRY	GORDON TANNER
JIM CURRY	NEIL MCCALLUM
LIZZIE CURRY	GERALDINE PAGE
FILE	MICHAEL GOODLIFFE
SHERIFF THOMAS	LAUNCE MARASCHAL
BILL STARBUCK	SAM WANAMAKER

Presented by E. P. CLIFT
in association with SAM WANAMAKER PRODUCTIONS LTD
Directed by JACK MINSTER *and* SAM WANAMAKER

Lyric   *February 14 - April 21*
Lyric, Hammersmith   *April 30 - May 26*

RING FOR CATTY
by Patrick Cargill and Jack Beale

NURSE CATTY	MARY MACKENZIE
LEONARD WHITE	PATRICK MCGOOHAN
JOHN RHODES	WILLIAM HARTNELL
BILL JONES	ANTHONY PARKER
DONALD GRAY	TERENCE ALEXANDER
CHRIS WALKER	ANDREW RAY

MATRON	..	..	..	..	WYNNE CLARK
MRS RHODES	..	..	..	..	BETTY BASKCOMB
MADGE WILLIAMS	..	..	..	JOAN DRUMMOND
WARD SISTER	..	..	..	..	KATHERINE PARR
MRS WHITE	..	..	..	..	LYDIA FORD

Presented by MICHAEL CODRON
Directed by HENRY KENDALL
Decoration by JOAN *and* DAVID DE BETHEL

Saville   *February 23 -*

THE RIVALS
by Richard Brinsley Sheridan

FAG	..	..	..	..	PETER SALLIS
THOMAS	..	..	..	..	MICHAEL KENT
LUCY	..	..	..	..	PETRA DAVIES
MISS LYDIA LANGUISH	..	KAY HAMMOND *and* GWEN CHERRELL
MISS JULIA MELVILLE	..	..	..	PEGGY SIMPSON
MRS MALAPROP	..	..	..	ATHENE SEYLER
SIR ANTHONY ABSOLUTE	..	..	JOHN CLEMENTS
CAPTAIN ABSOLUTE	..	..	..	LAURENCE HARVEY
MR FAULKLAND	..	..	..	PAUL DANEMAN
BOB ACRES	..	..	..	MICHAEL MEDWIN
SIR LUCIUS O'TRIGGER	..	..	..	WILLIAM MERVYN
DAVID	..	..	..	..	BRIAN HAYES

Presented by JOHN CLEMENTS   *Directed by* WILLIAM CHAPPELL
Decoration by PETER RICE   *Music by* LESLIE BRIDGEWATER

Piccadilly   *September 15 - November 12*

ROMANCE IN CANDLELIGHT
A Play with Songs
Book by Eric Maschwitz, Music and Lyrics by Sam Coslow

GASTON	..	..	..	..	JACQUES PILS
THE MARQUIS de la CHASSE	..	..	ROGER DANN
FRANÇOIS	..	..	..	RICHARD CURNOCK
MICHÈLE	..	..	..	MARGARET BURTON
MARGARET	..	..	..	SALLY ANN HOWES
CAROLINE	..	..	..	PATRICIA BURKE
SIR PERCY	..	..	..	CHARLES CLAY
ANDRE	..	..	..	JAY DENYER
SINGERS	..	TREVOR GRIFFITHS, WENDY HARCOURT-BROWN,
		MAUREEN McGREGOR, ROY PATTISON

Presented by EMILE LITTLER
Directed by RICHARD BIRD   *Decoration by* DORIS ZINKEISEN

170

Piccadilly   *May 17 -*

ROMANOFF AND JULIET
by Peter Ustinov

FIRST SOLDIER ..	JOE GIBBONS
SECOND SOLDIER	DAVID LODGE
THE GENERAL ..	PETER USTINOV
HOOPER MOULSWORTH..	JOHN PHILLIPS
VADIM ROMANOFF	FREDERICK VALK
IGOR ROMANOFF	MICHAEL DAVID
JULIET ..	KATY VAIL
THE SPY	DAVID HURST
BEULAH MOULSWORTH..	JACQUELINE LACEY
EVDOKIA ROMANOFF	MARIANNE DEEMING
JUNIOR CAPTAIN MARFA ZLOTOCHIENKI	DELPHI LAWRENCE
FREDDIE VANDERSTUTT	WILLIAM GREENE
THE ARCHBISHOP ..	EDWARD ATIENZA

Presented by LINNIT AND DUNFEE LTD
Directed by DENIS CAREY

Duchess   *August 2 - 20*

SEE THE STARS
A comedy revue of mimicry and satire
With ARTHUR BLAKE
Directed by IRVING COHEN

Saville   *July 7 - December 17*

THE SHADOW OF DOUBT
by Norman King

ARTHUR ..	JOHN CLEMENTS
LAURA ..	JANE BAXTER
GLADYS ..	EILEEN WAY
HUGHIE ..	PETER COLLINGWOOD
FRANK ..	PATRICK BARR
MANNING	RAYMOND HUNTLEY
CANTRUP	HENRY HEWITT
LIZ ..	ANNE LEON

Presented by JOHN CLEMENTS PLAYS LTD
Directed by ALLAN DAVIS *Decoration by* LAURENCE IRVING

St Martin's   *February 2 - February 4*

SHE SMILED AT ME
A New Musical Play, based on T. W. Robertson's 'Caste'
Music and Lyrics by Allon Bacon

HON. GEORGE D'ALROY	PETER BYRNE
CAPTAIN HAWTREE	ROBIN BAILEY
ECCLES ..	LESLIE DWYER
ESTHER ECCLES ..	JEAN KENT

POLLY ECCLES	..	..	..	..	MERCY HAYSTEAD
SAM GERRIDGE		..	..	..	HUGH PADDICK
POLICEMAN	..	..	..	..	.. ROBIN FORD
POSTMAN	..	..	..	..	.. BRIAN TAIT
ADA ..	..	..	..	..	DOREEN LOCKE
MAUDE ..	..	..	..	..	DAPHNE PERETZ
DIXON ..	..	..	..	..	.. ROBIN FORD
THE MARQUISE de ST MAUR		..	..	..	LINDA GRAY

Presented by MELVILLE GILLAM

Directed by JACK WILLIAMS   *Decoration by* ROBERT WEAVER

Duchess   *May 1 - 12*

THE SILVER WHISTLE
by Robert McEnroe

MR BEEBE	..	..	..	..	ERNEST THESIGER
MRS HANMER ..	..	..	..	.. OLGA LINDO
MISS HOADLEY ..	..	..	..	JOYCE BARBOUR
MISS TRIPP	..	..	..	JENNIFER WRIGHT
THE REVEREND WATSON		..	..	.. ROBIN BAILEY
MRS SAMPLER ..	..	..	..	MARY MERRALL
MRS GROSS	..	..	..	.. UNA VENNING
MR CHERRY ..	..	..	..	BARTLETT MULLINS
OLIVER ERWENTER	..	..	..	PETER CUSHING
OMAR ..	..	..	..	.. *by himself*
EMMETT ..	..	..	..	.. ALFIE BASS
THE BISHOP	..	..	..	PETER STEPHENS
MISS GUNN	..	..	..	CHRISTINE BOCCA
MR BEACH	..	..	..	PETER VAUGHAN
MR SMEDLEY ..	..	..	..	RICHARD FOAT
POLICE CONSTABLE	..	..	..	STUART ALLEN

Presented by MARK MARVIN PRODUCTIONS LTD
in association with ANTHONY BRADY FARRELL *and* GABRIEL KATZKA
Directed by MARTIN LANDAU

St Martin's   *October 12 - January 28*

SMALL HOTEL
by Rex Frost

SHEILA PRYOR ..	..	..	..	PAM MARMONT
MRS GAMMON ..	..	..	..	GLADYS HENSON
EFFIE RIGLER ..	..	..	..	ELEANORE BRYAN
ALAN PRYOR ..	..	..	..	.. SYDNEY KING
MRS SAMSON-BOX	..	..	..	MARJORIE FIELDING
ALBERT ..	..	..	..	GORDON HARKER
ROLAND ..	..	..	..	MORAY WATSON
ROSEMARY	..	..	..	ROSEMARIE DUNHAM
THE FOREIGNER	..	..	..	STANLEY ZEVIC
MR FINCH	..	..	..	ANTHONY SHARP
CAROLINE MALLETT ..	..	..	..	DIANA KING

Presented by LINNIT AND DUNFEE LTD
Directed by MURRAY MACDONALD

172

Lyric   *April 25 -*

SOUTH SEA BUBBLE
by Noel Coward

JOHN BLAIR KENNEDY	ARTHUR MACRAE
CAPTAIN CHRISTOPHER MORTLOCK ..	PETER BARKWORTH
SIR GEORGE SHOTTER	.. IAN HUNTER
LADY ALEXANDRA SHOTTER	.. VIVIEN LEIGH
PUNALO ALANI	.. ALAN WEBB
SANYAMO	WILLIAM PEACOCK
EDWARD HONEY	.. JOHN MOORE
CUCKOO HONEY	.. JOYCE CAREY
ADMIRAL TURLING	NICHOLAS GRIMSHAW
MRS TURLING	DAPHNE NEWTON
ROBERT FROME	ERIC PHILLIPS
HALI ALANI	RONALD LEWIS

Presented by H. M. TENNENT LTD
in association with LAURENCE OLIVIER
Directed by WILLIAM CHAPPELL   *Decoration by* PETER SNOW

Piccadilly   *November 15 - December 10*
Haymarket   *January 24 - April 7*

THE STRONG ARE LONELY
by Fritz Hochwalder, translated by Eva le Gallienne

ALFONSO FERNANDEZ	DONALD WOLFIT
FATHER ROCHUS LIEBERMAN	WILL LEIGHTON
FATHER LADISLAUS OROS	.. DAVID OXLEY
CANDIA	JOSEPH CHELTON
NAGUACU	GEORGE EUGENIOU
JOSE BUSTILLOS .. .. ROBERT ALGAR *and later* ERNEST HARE
ANDRE CORNELIS	DEREK OLDHAM
FATHER WILLIAM CLARKE	PETER VAUGHAN
DON PEDRO de MIURA	ROBERT HARRIS
CAPTAIN ARAGO	RONALD HARWOOD
CAPTAIN VILLANO	GEORGE SELWAY
LORENZO QUERINI	ERNEST MILTON
CARLOS GERVANZONI .. PETER BENNETT *and later* LLEWELLYN REES
GARCIA QUESEDA	JOSEPH CHELTON
ALVARO CATALDE	.. ALAN WILSON
SERGEANT OF THE GUARD	PETER NOEL COOK
FATHER REINEGG	DOUGLAS QUAYLE
FATHER TORRES .. TONY FORD *and later* JOHN GRAHAM
ACATU	DOUGLAS QUAYLE
BARRIGUA	HORACE SEQUEIRA
INDIANS .. .. .. ALAN WILSON, DANIEL MOYNIHAN
RIVI .. .. .. DOUGLAS PHAIR *and later* JOHN GRAHAM

Presented by ADVANCE PLAYERS' ASSOCIATION LTD
Directed by MARGARET WEBSTER

Adelphi   *December 14 -*

SUCH IS LIFE
A New Laughter Revue
With AL READ
JACK TRIPP   SHIRLEY BASSEY
Presented by JACK HYLTON
Directed by ALEC SHANKS *and* JOAN DAVIS

SUMMER SONG
Book by Eric Maschwitz and Hy Kraft
Lyrics by Eric Maschwitz
with the music of Anton Dvorak

TOMASHEK	DEREK SYDNEY
DVORAK	LAURENCE NAISMITH
PORTER	THOMAS BAPTISTE
PEPIK	DAVID HANNAFORD
KAROLKA	SALLY ANN HOWES
FATHER JAN	TREVOR GRIFFITHS
UNCLE MAREK	MARK DALY
MRS MASLO	WINIFRED BRAEMAR
ABE	EDRIC CONNOR
BLODEK	DAVID GEARY
MILLI	BONITA PRIMROSE
MARENKA	PEGGY VERNON
ANDULA	ROMA HODSON
RUZENA	MAUREEN McGREGOR
DOROTA	ALISON McGUIRE
GILMORE	FRANK TILTON
MA FLANNAGAN	MARJORIE RHODES
SHAUN	DAVID HUGHES
FEENEY	MICHAEL GOLDEN
MASLO	JOHN ADAMS
JOE	VAN ATKINS
JAKE	DEREK SYDNEY
BARSTOW	JOSS CLEWES
FIRST REPORTER	RAYMOND LLOYD
SECOND REPORTER	JOSS CLEWES
STEWARD	CLEM HOLT
SAILOR	ROY PATTISON

Presented by GEORGE AND ALFRED BLACK
by arrangement with JACK HYLTON
Directed by CHARLES HICKMAN

SUMMERTIME
by Ugo Betti
English version by Henry Reed

FRANCESCA	GERALDINE McEWAN
AUNT CLEOFE	GWEN FFRANGCON-DAVIES
MARIA	BARBARA NEW
AUNT OFELIA	ESMA CANNON
ADELAIDE	MAUREEN QUINNEY
ALBERTO	DIRK BOGARDE
	and later NIGEL STOCK
THE POSTMAN	TONY CHURCH
NOEMI	VIVIENNE DRUMMOND
THE DOCTOR	MICHAEL GWYNN
CONSALVO	MARK DIGNAM
THE FARMER	RONALD BARKER

Presented by TOBY ROWLAND LTD
Directed by PETER HALL   *Decoration by* JAMES BAILEY

THE SUN OF YORK
by O. and I. Wigram

FATHER URSWICK	DIARMUID KELLY
PRIEST	PAUL CRAIG
BROTHER DOMINIC MANCINI	RICHARD CAZIMIR
MORTON, BISHOP of ELY	VALENTINE DYALL
JANE SHORE	GABRIELLE BRUNE
ELIZABETH WOODVILLE	SHEILA MORIARTY
PRINCE EDWARD	VERNON MORRIS
PAGE	DAVID MORTON
ANTHONY WOODVILLE	JOHN GORDON
LORD RICHARD GREY	DAVID BRIERLEY
HOST	MURRAY HAYNE
RICHARD, DUKE of GLOUCESTER	LESLIE FRENCH
DUKE of BUCKINGHAM	DAVID RITCH
LORD HASTINGS	DEREK BLOMFIELD
ANNE NEVILLE	JULIA HARLAND
DUCHESS of YORK	WINIFRED EVANS
SERVITOR	KENN KENNEDY
BISHOP of BATH AND WELLS	ANTHONY WOODRUFF
SIR ROBERT BRACKENBURY	JOHN GORDON
SIR WILLIAM CATESBY	RICHARD CAREY
PRINCE RICHARD	HUW EVANS
GUARD	ANTHONY WOODRUFF
PRIEST	MURRAY HAYNE
DOCTOR	DIARMUID KELLY
NUN	SALLY ASTRID
YOKEL	DAVID BRIERLEY
SOLDIER	ERNST TAHDEL

Presented by ALFRED FARRELL
by arrangement with LONDON THEATRE GUILD LTD
Directed by LESLIE FRENCH

SUSPECT
by Edward Percy and Reginald Denham

MRS SMITH	FLORA ROBSON
GOUDIE	BETTY HENDERSON
DR RENDLE	PETER WILLIAMS
JANET RENDLE	ELAINE USHER
ROBERT SMITH	BRIAN NISSEN
REV. ALBERT COMBERMERE	ARTHUR HOWARD
LADY CONST	ROSEMARY SCOTT
SIR HUGO CONST	JOHN WELSH

Presented by E. P. CLIFT *and* ANNA DEERE WIMAN
Directed by FLORA ROBSON

Duchess   *March 8 - April 14*

TABITHA

A Mystery Comedy by Arnold Ridley and Mary Cathcart Borer

MARTIN BRENTWOOD	JACK WATLING
JANET BOWERING	JANET BARROW
MARY TRELLINGTON	.. ANNE LEON
MR FAWCETT	MORRIS SWEDEN
RUTH PRENDERGAST	MARJORIE FIELDING
ELEANOR TRELLINGTON	.. GILLIAN LIND
LAVINIA GOLDSWORTHY	CHRISTINE SILVER
DET. INSPECTOR BRUTON	PHILIP STAINTON
DR BROWNLIE	FRANKLYN SCOTT

Presented by JOHN WILDBERG *and* HAROLD FRENCH
Directed by HAROLD FRENCH

Palace   *April 16 - May 5*

THEATRE NATIONAL POPULAIRE
in
LE TRIOMPHE DE L'AMOUR
by Marivaux

DON JUAN
by Moèrlie

MARIE TUDOR
by Hugo

Les Comédiennes:
ZANIE CAMPAN, MARIA CASARES, MONIQUE CHAUMETTE,
CATHERINE LE COUEY, CHRISTIANE MINAZZOLI

Les Comédiens:
LUCIEN ARNAUD, MARC CHEVALIER, COUSSONNEAU, JEAN-
PIERRE DARRAS, GEORGES LYCAN, ROGER MOLLIEN, JEAN-
PAUL MOULINOT, PHILIPPE NOIRET, GEORGES RIQUIER,
GUY SAINT JEAN, ANDRE SCHLESSER, DANIEL SORANO, JEAN
TOPART, JEAN VILAR, GEORGES WILSON, JEAN WINCKLER

Directeur: JEAN VILAR
Presented by PETER DAUBENY PRESENTATIONS LTD
by arrangement with LEON HEPNER

Royal Court   *February 9 - March 20*
Aldwych   *March 21 -*

THE THREEPENNY OPERA
by Bertolt Brecht, Music by Kurt Weill
English adaptation by Marc Blitzstein

STREET SINGER	EWAN MACCOLL
STREET URCHIN	.. UNA VICTOR
FILCH	VICTOR BARING

Whores: BETTY	.. .. ..	.. ALIKI HANSEN
MOLLY ..	.. .. ..	PATRICIA BLACK
DOLLY ..	.. .. ..	SYLVIA LANGOVA
COAXER ..	.. .. ..	RENEE GODDARD
Mack's Gang: READYMONEY MATT	..	GEORGE MURCELL
CROOKFINGER JAKE	..	WARREN MITCHELL
BOB THE SLASHER	..	GEORGE TOVEY
WALT DREARY	.. ..	CHARLES HILL
MR J. J. PEACHUM	.. .. ..	ERIC POHLMANN
MRS PEACHUM	.. .. ..	.. LISA LEE
POLLY PEACHUM	.. .. ..	DAPHNE ANDERSON
TIGER BROWN ..	.. .. ..	GEORGE A. COOPER
SMITH ..	.. ..	CHARLES STANLEY
JENNY ..	.. ..	MARIA REMUSAT
LUCY ..	.. ..	GEORGIA BROWN
REVEREND KIMBALL	.. .. ..	ROLAND RANDEL
FIRST CONSTABLE	.. .. ..	MICHAEL MURRAY
SECOND CONSTABLE	.. .. ..	JOHN CORBETT
MACHEATH (MACK THE KNIFE)	.. ..	BILL OWEN

Presented by OSCAR LEWENSTEIN, WOLF MANKOWITZ
and HELEN ARNOLD
Directed by SAM WANAMAKER
Musical Direction by BERTHOLD GOLDSCHMIDT
Decoration by CASPAR NEHER

Old Vic   *In repertory April 3 -*

TROILUS AND CRESSIDA
by William Shakespeare

Trojans

PRIAM ..	.. ..	JOB STEWART
HECTOR ..	.. .. ..	.. JACK GWILLIM
TROILUS ..	.. ..	.. JOHN NEVILLE
PARIS ..	.. .. ..	RONALD ALLEN
DEIPHOBUS	.. .. ..	JOHN WOODVINE
HELENUS ..	.. .. ..	.. JOHN WOOD
AENEAS	.. ..	.. DENIS HOLMES
ANTENOR	.. .. ..	JAMES VILLIERS
PANDARUS	.. .. ..	.. PAUL ROGERS
HELEN ..	.. .. ..	WENDY HILLER
ANDROMACHE ..	.. ..	.. MARGARET COURTENAY
CASSANDRA	.. .. ..	RACHEL ROBERTS
CRESSIDA	.. .. ..	ROSEMARY HARRIS

Greeks

AGAMEMNON	.. .. ..	DEREK FRANCIS
MENELAUS	.. .. ..	EDWARD HARVEY
ULYSSES	.. .. ..	.. RICHARD WORDSWORTH
NESTOR	.. .. ..	.. DUDLEY JONES
AJAX ..	.. .. ..	LAURENCE HARDY
ACHILLES	.. .. ..	CHARLES GRAY
PATROCLUS	.. .. ..	JEREMY BRETT
DIOMEDES	.. .. ..	ANTHONY WHITE
THERSITES	.. .. ..	CLIFFORD WILLIAMS
CALCHAS	.. .. ..	GERALD CROSS

Presented by OLD VIC TRUST LTD
in association with THE ARTS COUNCIL
Directed by TYRONE GUTHRIE   *Decoration by* FREDERICK CROOKE

177   M

TWENTY MINUTES SOUTH
Devised and Composed by Peter Greenwell
Book and Lyrics by Maurice Browning

POSTMAN	GRAHAM McCORMACK
SYBIL BATES	TOTTI TRUMAN TAYLOR
ETHEL BANISTER	NATALIE KENT
PAPER BOY	BRIAN TIPPING CODD
FRED	BRIAN BLADES
HARRY	DOUGLAS SQUIRES
BERT	JACK MANUEL
KITTY HEMMING	DAPHNE ANDERSON
GEORGE BANISTER	MICHAEL KENT
JANE BANISTER	JOAN BAILEY
SUSAN BANISTER	LOUIE RAMSAY
HENRY BATES	MICHAEL DARBYSHIRE
ROGER BATES	ROBIN HUNTER
BOB WILLIAMS	DONALD SCOTT
MISS FLYNN	JOSEPHINE GORDON
MISS MASON	VALERIE SWINNARD
MISS MARTIN	MAVIS TRAILL
MR CASEY	BRIAN TIPPING CODD
MR GRAY	KENNETH LUCKMAN
OFFICE BOY	GRAHAM McCORMACK
ARTHUR HARRIS	JOHN LE MESURIER
MR THOMPSON	PHILIP LEWTAS
MRS THOMPSON	JANE MARTIN
MRS BROWNLOW	BETTY FELSTEAD

Presented by PLAYERS VENTURES LTD.

Directed by HATTIE JACQUES   *Decoration by* REGINALD WOOLLEY

WAITING FOR GODOT
by Samuel Beckett

ESTRAGON	PETER WOODTHORPE
VLADIMIR	PAUL DANEMAN *and later* HUGH BURDEN, RICHARD DARE *and* WILLIAM SQUIRE
LUCKY	TIMOTHY BATESON
POZZO	PETER BULL
BOY	MICHAEL WALKER

Presented by THE ARTS THEATRE COMMITTEE

Directed by PETER HALL   *Decoration by* PETER SNOW

THE WALTZ OF THE TOREADORS
by Jean Anouilh
translated by Lucienne Hill

GENERAL ST PE	HUGH GRIFFITH
HIS WIFE	BEATRIX LEHMANN
GASTON	TRADER FAULKNER

ESTELLA ..	..	..	..	..	.. ANNE BISHOP
SIDONIA	..	..	..	..	HILDA BRAID
DOCTOR BONFANT	..	..	..	..	WALTER HUDD
MLLE de STE-EUVERTE	..	..	..		BRENDA BRUCE
EUGENIE	..	..	..	..	GABRIELLE DAYE
MME DUPONT-FREDAINE	..	..		..	JOY ANDREWS
FATHER AMBROSE	..	..	..		.. LAURIE MAIN
PAMELA ..	..	..	..	..	JULIET DUNCOMBE

Presented by DONALD ALBERY *and* CAMPBELL WILLIAMS
Directed by PETER HALL

Winter Garden   **August 31 - March 24**

THE WATER GIPSIES
Book and Lyrics by A. P. Herbert
Music by Vivian Ellis

ALBERT BELL	..	..	..	..	.. JERRY VERNO
MRS HIGGINS	..	..	..	..	.. DORIS HARE
MRS FOX	..	..	..	..	PRUDENCE HYMAN
MR FOX ..	..	..	..	..	.. IAN FRAZER
MR PONDER	..	..	..	..	BOBBY WEBBER
MR PEWTER	..	..	..	..	WILLIAM CLOTHIER
MRS PEWTER	..	..	..	..	PHYLLIS BRIDGWATER
DAISY FIG	..	..	..	..	VIVIENNE MARTIN
MRS FIG ..	..	..	..	..	.. JOYCE ENDEAN
MR FIG ..	..	..	..	..	ALAN MARTELL
SAILOR ..	..	..	..	..	JOHN DEIGHTON
SOLDIER ..	..	..	..	..	JOHN DELANEY
POTMAN ..	..	..	..	..	.. TOM SWIFT
JANE BELL	..	..	..	..	PAMELA CHARLES
MR BRYAN	..	..	..	..	.. PETER GRAVES
ERNEST HIGGINS	..	..	..		WALLAS EATON
MERVYN SWALLOW	..	..	..		MICHAEL ANTHONY
FAY MEADOWS ..	..	..	..		GEORGINA COOKSON
GRETA CLARE ..	..	..	..		HAZEL JENNINGS
MICHAEL DEW ..	..	..	..		.. DAVID REES
LILY BELL	..	..	..	..	.. DORA BRYAN
MR MOUNTAIN ..	..	..	..		.. JAMES PERRY
FRED GREEN	..	..	..	..	.. LAURIE PAYNE
MISS MARY AUSTIN	..	..	..		MOLLY GREENWOOD
MISS KATIE AUSTIN	..	..	..		PATRICIA MARTIN
BUNNY MOSS ..	..	..	..		.. ROY GODFREY
MR GREEN	..	..	..	..	ERNEST BUTCHER
MRS GREEN	..	..	..	..	MARGO CUNNINGHAM
MR OLIVER	..	..	..	..	MICHAEL ANTHONY
MR WALKER	..	..	..	..	GEORGE JAMES
RUTH WALKER ..	..	..	..		PRUDENCE HYMAN
NORMAN..	..	..	..	..	NORMAN HACKFORTH
WAITER	..	..	..	..	.. IAN FRAZER
BETTY ..	..	..	..	..	.. JUNE CLARE
GLADYS ..	..	..	..	..	MAUREEN SHELLEY
MAISIE	..	..	..	..	MARIE LIVANN
AILEEN ..	..	..	..	..	.. JOAN PETHERS
NITTY ..	..	..	..	..	GRIFFITH LEWIS
ROMEO ..	..	..	..	..	.. JAMES PERRY
SHEPHERDESS ..	..	..	..		.. JOYCE ENDEAN
FLOOR WAITER ..	..	..	..		RICHARD RYAN

Presented by PETER SAUNDERS
Directed by CHARLES HICKMAN   *Decoration by* BERKELEY SUTCLIFFE

Aldwych
October 11 - February 11

THE WHOLE TRUTH
by Philip Mackie

DEENIE ..	..	..	..	..	.. ELLEN BLUETH
LEWIS PAULTON		..	..	..	ERNEST CLARK
BRENDA PAULTON		..	..	..	SARAH LAWSON
CARLISS ..	..	..	..	..	LESLIE PHILLIPS
A VISITOR	..	..	..	..	.. FAITH BROOK
BRIGGS ..	..	..	..	..	JOHN RUSSELL
BRETT ..	..	..	..	..	.. ARNOLD BELL
PETTY ..	..	..	..	..	ROBERT BRUCE

Presented by HENRY SHEREK
Directed by LESLIE LINDER *Decoration by* MICHAEL EVE

Saville
December 21 - February 18

THE WILD DUCK
by Henrik Ibsen
adapted by Max Faber

PETERSEN	..	..	..	GRAHAM STUART
JENSEN ..	..	..	..	.. JOHN BENNETT
MAID ..	..	..	..	JACQUELINE FORSTER
OLD EKDAL	..	..	..	GEORGE RELPH
MRS BERTHA SORBY	..	..		PEGGY LIVESEY
CHAMBERLAIN KASPERSEN	..	..		AIDAN TURNER
CHAMBERLAIN BALLE ..	..	..		MICHAEL HITCHMAN
CHAMBERLAIN FLOR	..	..		.. ALEX SCOTT
GREGERS WERLE	..	..		MICHAEL GOUGH
HJALMAR EKDAL	..	..		EMLYN WILLIAMS
HAAKON WERLE	..	..		CHARLES CARSON
1st GUEST	..	..	..	BARRY BARTON
2nd GUEST	..	..	..	HARRY BOWERS
GRAABERG	..	..	..	ROBERT BEAUMONT
GINA EKDAL	..	..	..	ANGELA BADDELEY
HEDVIG	..	..	..	DOROTHY TUTIN
DR RELLING	..	..	..	LAURENCE HARDY
MOLVIK ..	..	..	..	ROBERT BEAUMONT

Presented by JOHN CLEMENTS
Directed by MURRAY MACDONALD *Decoration by* LAURENCE IRVING

Hippodrome
May 3 - 26

WILD GROWS THE HEATHER
Adapted from 'The Little Minister' by J. M. Barrie, by Hugh Ross Williamson
Lyrics by William Henry, Music by Robert Lindon

ROB DOW	..	..	..	.. PAUL CURRAN
JOE CRUIKSHANK	..	..	..	PETER SINCLAIR
SNECKY HOBART	..	..	..	GERALD LAWSON
THOMAS WHAMOND	..	..	..	RICHARD GOLDING
ANDREW MEALMAKER ..	..	..		.. DAVID KEIR
MICAH DOW	..	..	..	SYDNEY DEVINE

REV. GAVIN DISHART .. .. .. BILL O'CONNOR
BABBIE .. .. VALERIE MILLER
NANNY WEBSTER .. .. .. MADELEINE CHRISTIE
THE EARL OF RINTOUL .. .. GERALD WELCH
CAPTAIN HALLIWELL .. .. .. PATRICK NEWELL
SERGEANT DAVIDSON .. .. .. PETER DIMUANTES
JEAN .. .. EIRA HEATH
MRS MACLEARY .. .. .. HILARY PATERSON
FELICE .. .. ANNETTE GREEN

Presented by JACK WALLER
Directed by RALPH READER

Duke of York's   July 14 - August 27

WILD THYME
Book and Lyrics by Philip Guard
Music by Donald Swann

GEOFF MORRIS .. .. DENIS QUILLEY
ANN .. .. JANE WENHAM
MR ARNOLD .. .. FRANK DUNCAN
YVETTE LEROUX .. .. BETTY PAUL
SEYMOUR VERITY .. .. .. COLIN GORDON
WILLY JAY .. .. PAUL MANNING
MAVIS JAY .. .. STELLA CHAPMAN
CYRIL JAY .. .. DAVID GODFREY
ERNIE WALKER .. .. .. JULIAN ORCHARD
SALLY WALKER .. .. SHIRLEY HALL
JANICE WALKER .. .. .. PATRICIA ROWSELL
DENZIL .. .. FRANK DUNCAN
MAY .. .. RUTH PORCHER
HARRY .. .. ARCHIE HARRADINE
JOAN .. .. GWEN NELSON
MONSIEUR AUBERGINE .. .. FRANK DUNCAN

Presented by LAURIER LISTER
Directed by WENDY TOYE   Decoration by RONALD SEARLE

Old Vic   In repertory November 1 - January 27

THE WINTER'S TALE
by William Shakespeare

SINGER .. .. GILLIAN NEASON
POLIXENES .. .. CHARLES GRAY
LEONTES .. .. PAUL ROGERS
HERMIONE .. .. WENDY HILLER
MAMILLIUS .. .. BUNNY MAY
CAMILLO.. .. .. DENIS HOLMES
EMILIA .. .. MARGARET COURTENAY
ANOTHER LADY .. .. .. ANNETTE CROSBIE
ROGERO .. .. DEREK FRANCIS
ANTIGONUS .. .. GERALD CROSS
PAULINA .. .. MARGARET RAWLINGS
STEWARD .. .. HAROLD KASKET
GAOLER .. .. DERRY NESBITT

181

DOCTOR	..	..	..	..	EDWARD HARVEY
OFFICER ..	..	..	..	..	RONALD ALLEN
MARINER	..	..	..	..	BRYAN PRINGLE
BEAR ..	..	..	..	..	JAMES VILLIERS
OLD SHEPHERD		..	..	..	DUDLEY JONES
CLOWN ..	..	..	..	..	AUBREY MORRIS
CLEOMENES	..	..	..	..	JOHN WOODVINE
DION ..	..	..	..	..	ANTHONY WHITE
TIME ..	..	..	..	..	.. JOB STEWART
FLORIZEL	..	..	..	..	JOHN FRASER
PERDITA	..	..	..	..	.. ZENA WALKER
AUTOLYCUS	..	..	..	..	.. JOHN NEVILLE
DORCAS ..	..	..	..	..	ROSEMARY HARRIS
MOPSA ..	..	..	..	..	RACHEL ROBERTS

Presented by OLD VIC TRUST LTD *in association with* THE ARTS COUNCIL

Directed by MICHAEL BENTHALL   *Decoration by* PETER RICE

182

SUMMARIES OF

PRINCIPAL REPERTORY PRODUCTIONS

and plays at

THE EDINBURGH FESTIVAL 1955

and

THE BRITISH DRAMA LEAGUE

COMMUNITY DRAMA FESTIVAL 1956

Casts are given where the play has been reviewed,
and for all the productions of
The Shakespeare Memorial Theatre.

THE ARTS THEATRE CLUB
Season July 1 1955 - June 1 1956

WAITING FOR GODOT *by* SAMUEL BECKETT August 3–September 3
Directed by PETER HALL (transferred to the Criterion)

THE BURNT FLOWER-BED *by* UGO BETTI September 9–October 15
Directed by PETER HALL

KOMUSO *by* ROBERT NICHOLS November 8–December 11 *Directed by* GUY
VERNEY

LISTEN TO THE WIND *by* ANGELA AINLEY JEANS, *Music by* VIVIAN ELLIS
December 16–January 21 *Directed by* PETER HALL

DARKLING CHILD *by* W. S. MERWIN January 27–February 19 *Directed*
by FRITH BANBURY

THE WALTZ OF THE TOREADORS *by* JEAN ANOUILH February 24–
March 25 *Directed by* PETER HALL (transferred to the Criterion)

THE COMEDY OF ERRORS *by* WILLIAM SHAKESPEARE, *adapted by* LIONEL
HARRIS *and* ROBERT MCNAB March 28–May 13 *Directed by* LIONEL HARRIS
Music by JULIAN SLADE

ANGNA ENTERS *in Dance Mime* May 15–27

OFF THE MAINLAND *by* ROBERT SHAW May 30–July 1 *Directed by*
ANDRE VAN GYSEGHEM

Presented by THE LONDON ARTS THEATRE COMMITTEE LTD

Decoration by PAUL MAYO

THE BIRMINGHAM REPERTORY THEATRE
Season July 1 1955 - June 1 1956

THE LONG SUNSET *by* R. C. SHERRIFF August 30–September 24 *Directed by* BERNARD HEPTON

THE INDIFFERENT SHEPHERD *by* PETER USTINOV September 27–October 22 *Directed by* BERNARD HEPTON

BEAUTY IN THE WOOD *by* JULES SUPERVIELLE, *adapted by* LUCIENNE HILL October 25–November 19 *Directed by* DOUGLAS SEALE

CASTE *by* T. W. ROBERTSON November 22–December 17 *Directed by* DOUGLAS SEALE

THE MARVELLOUS STORY OF PUSS IN BOOTS *by* NICHOLAS STUART GRAY December 21–February 18 *Directed by* DOUGLAS SEALE

THE CLANDESTINE MARRIAGE *by* GEORGE COLMAN *and* DAVID GARRICK February 21–March 17 *Directed by* DOUGLAS SEALE

ANATOL *by* ARTHUR SCHNITZLER, *in a new adaptation by* FAY *and* MICHAEL KANIN March 20–April 14 *Directed by* BERNARD HEPTON

JULIUS CAESAR *by* WILLIAM SHAKESPEARE April 17–May 12 *Directed by* BERNARD HEPTON

ANNE BOLEYN *by* PETER ALBERY May 15–June 9 *Directed by* DOUGLAS SEALE

CAESAR AND CLEOPATRA *by* BERNARD SHAW June 12–July 7 *Directed by* DOUGLAS SEALE (also later at the Paris Festival, Théâtre Sarah Bernhardt; at the Festival Theatre, Malvern; and at the Old Vic, London)

Presented by THE BIRMINGHAM REPERTORY COMPANY *in association with* THE ARTS COUNCIL *Governing Director* SIR BARRY JACKSON

Principal Players: DOREEN ARIS, CHARMIAN EYRE, JILL FORREST, NANCIE JACKSON, GLADYS PARR, JACQUELINE WILSON, GEOFFREY BAYLDON, ROBERT CHETWYN, ALBERT FINNEY, COLIN GEORGE, BERNARD HEPTON, RONALD HINES, ERIC JONES, KENNETH MACKINTOSH, REDMOND PHILLIPS, MICHAEL ROBBINS, ALAN ROWE, GEOFFREY TAYLOR

186

THE BRISTOL OLD VIC COMPANY
Season July 1 1955 - June 1 1956

THE MATCHMAKER *by* THORNTON WILDER September 5-24 *Produced by* JOHN MOODY

THE MULBERRY BUSH *by* ANGUS WILSON September 27–October 15 *Produced by* ANDRE VAN GYSEGHEM

ONDINE *by* JEAN GIRAUDOUX, *adapted by* MAURICE VALENCY October 18– November 5 *Produced by* JOHN MOODY

UNCLE VANYA *by* ANTON CHEKHOV, *translated by* CONSTANCE GARNETT November 8–26 *Produced by* JOHN MOODY

VOLPONE or THE FOX *by* BEN JONSON November 29–December 17 *Produced by* JOHN HARRISON

DICK WHITTINGTON *specially written for the Bristol Old Vic by* V. C. CLINTON BADDELEY, *Music by* GAVIN GORDON December 22–February 11 *Produced by* OWEN REED

KING LEAR *by* WILLIAM SHAKESPEARE February 14–March 3 *Produced by* JOHN MOODY

DON JUAN or THE LOVE OF GEOMETRY *by* MAX FRISCH, *adapted by* PETER PHILP, *translated by* NELL MOODY March 6-24 *Produced by* JOHN MOODY

THE SKIN OF OUR TEETH *by* THORNTON WILDER March 27–April 14 *Produced by* ROYSTON MORLEY

THE EMPTY CHAIR *by* PETER USTINOV April 17–May 5 *Produced by* JOHN MOODY

THE RIVALS *by* RICHARD BRINSLEY SHERIDAN May 8-26 *Produced by* JOHN MOODY

THE CASTLE OF DECEPTION *by* PETER PHILP May 29–June 16 *Produced by* WARREN JENKINS

Presented by THE BRISTOL OLD VIC COMPANY

Director JOHN MOODY

Decoration by
PATRICK ROBERTSON, NICHOLAS GEORGIADIS, DISLEY JONES

Principal Players: MOIRA SHEARER, ERIC PORTER, JOHN HUMPHRY, ALAN DOBIE, GRAHAM CROWDEN, DEREK GODFREY, JOHN CAIRNEY, EDWARD HARDWICKE, PHYLLIDA LAW, PETER O'TOOLE

THE EDINBURGH GATEWAY COMPANY
Season July 1 1955 - June 1 1956

CONSPIRATORS *by* ROBERT KEMP World Première August 20–September 10 Edinburgh Festival Production *Directed by* COLIN CHANDLER

BENEATH THE WEE RED LUMS *by* T. M. WATSON September 12–24 *Directed by* LENNOX MILNE

WAITING FOR GILLIAN *by* RONALD MILLAR September 26–October 8 *Directed by* LENNOX MILNE

THE MERCHANT OF VENICE *by* WILLIAM SHAKESPEARE October 10–22 *Directed by* LENNOX MILNE

OUR MAGGY
by D. Heddle, World Première October 24 - November 5

CLARA PLAISTOW	PAMELA BAIN
GEOFFREY TALBOT	MICHAEL ELDER
MRS PENNETHORNE	MARILLYN GRAY
MRS ROSS	NELL BALLANTYNE
MAGGY	MARY HELEN DONALD
HUMPHREY PUMPHERSTON	TOM FLEMING
DAPHNE BROCK	ANNE EATON
MARY HOCKRIDGE	ALISON DALGLEISH
DAN GRIFFITHS	JOHN MACKENZIE
DAME LAURA SWANAGE	MAUD RISDON
KARL FLEISCHMANN	NORMAN FRASER
HARRY JARVIS	LIAM HOOD

Directed by LENNOX MILNE

HEATHER ON FIRE *by* MORAY MCLAREN November 7–19 *Directed by* JAMES GIBSON

BENEATH THE WEE RED LUMS *by* T. M. WATSON November 21–26 *Directed by* LENNOX MILNE

BACHELORS ARE BOLD *by* T. M. WATSON November 28–December 10 *Directed by* LENNOX MILNE

THE BOY DAVID *by* J. M. BARRIE December 12–24 *Directed by* LENNOX MILNE

SUSIE TANGLES THE STRINGS *by* GRAHAM MOFFAT December 26–January 21 *Directed by* JAMES GIBSON

COME TO THE FAIR
by R. J. B. Sellar, World Première January 23 - February 4

THE REVEREND ARTHUR DOUGLAS	GEORGE DAVIES
LOUISE	NELL BALLANTYNE
NELLIE	MEG REID
JEAN	MARY HELEN DONALD
BIDDY	MARILLYN GRAY
JOHN LOGAN	LAIDLAW DALLING

MURPHY	..	..	..	NORMAN FRASER
A PHOTOGRAPHER	..	..	..	BRIAN MAHONEY
MIRA ..	..	..	..	.. JEAN MARTIN
MISS BROWN ..	..	..	..	.. ANNE EATON
BARRY BENEDICT	..	..	..	JAMES ROUGHEAD

Directed by LENNOX MILNE

GHOSTS AND OLD GOLD *by* REID KENNEDY February 6–18 *Directed by* BRIAN CAREY

A NEST OF SINGING BIRDS *by* ROBERT KEMP February 20–March 3 *Directed by* JAMES GIBSON *and* ROBERT KEMP

HAME *by* A. D. MACKIE March 5–17 *Directed by* JAMES GIBSON

JUNO AND THE PAYCOCK *by* SEAN O'CASEY March 19–24 *Directed by* JAMES GIBSON

Presented by THE EDINBURGH GATEWAY COMPANY LTD

Decoration by PETER NORRIS

Principal Players: LENNOX MILNE, TOM FLEMING, GEORGE DAVIES, MARILLYN GRAY, MARY HELEN DONALD, NORMAN FRASER, JAMES GIBSON, NELL BALLANTYNE

Guest Artistes: WILSON BARRETT, JEAN MARTIN, JAMES ROUGHEAD, IAN MACNAUGHTON, MICHAEL ELDER, LAIDLAW DALLING, JOHN YOUNG, DAVID STEUART, JUNE SHIELDS, BRYDEN MURDOCH, BRIAN CAREY, MAUD RISDON

THE CITIZENS' THEATRE, GLASGOW
Season July 1 1955 - June 1 1956

THE WAYWARD SAINT *by* PAUL VINCENT CARROLL September 20–October 1

WITNESS FOR THE PROSECUTION *by* AGATHA CHRISTIE October 3–15

WHAT EVERY WOMAN KNOWS *by* J. M. BARRIE October 17–29

POINT OF DEPARTURE *by* JEAN ANOUILH October 31–November 12

THE HONOURS OF DRUMLIE *by* JAMES SCOTLAND November 14–26

THE GENTLE GUNMAN *by* ROGER MACDOUGALL November 28–December 10

WHIGMALEERIES (Pantomime) December 15–January 28

OUR MAGGY *by* D. HEDDLE January 30–February 11

JULIUS CAESAR *by* WILLIAM SHAKESPEARE February 14–25

MISERY ME *by* DENIS CANNAN February 27–March 10

THE MATCHMAKER *by* THORNTON WILDER March 12–24

BENEATH THE WEE RED LUMS *by* T. M. WATSON March 26–April 7

THE APPLE CART *by* BERNARD SHAW April 9–21

THE ORIGINAL JOHN MACKAY
by Alastair M. Dunnett, April 23 - May 5

ANGUS FERGUSON	GEORGE DAVIES
ERNIE FRASER	FULTON MACKAY
KIRSTY MACKAY	MOLLY URQUHART
HARRY HACKABY	WALTER CARR
MRS HACKABY	AILEEN O'GORMAN
MALKY	JOHN GRIEVE
LEONARD BEECHER	DONALD LAYNE-SMITH
HON. ANNE LORIMER	NORA LAIDLAW
JOHN MACKAY	ANDREW KEIR
MR BODDAM	HARRY WALKER
HECTOR	JOHN CARLIN
MRS CRAIGIE	JOAN SCOTT
SURVEYORS	ROBERT BENSON, MARY CAUGHIE

Presented by THE CITIZENS' THEATRE LTD

Direction by RICHARD MATHEWS, *except for* OUR MAGGY
which was directed by LEA ASHTON

Decoration by NEVIL DICKIN, *except for* OUR MAGGY
which was decorated by JAMES ROBB

Principal Players: ELIZABETH ASHLEY, MADELINE CHRISTIE, VALERIE MILLER, MOLLY URQUHART, PAUL CURRAN, RICHARD GALE, ALAN JUDD, ANDREW KEIR, DONALD LAYNE-SMITH

KING'S THEATRE, GLASGOW
April 23 - 28

LET WIVES TAK TENT
Adapted from Molière's 'L'Ecole des Femmes', by Robert Kemp

ALAN	..	..	..	..	ALEX MCAVOY
ALISON	..	..	..	..	NELL BALLANTYNE
AGNES	..	..	..	..	.. PAMELA BAIN
WALTER	..	..	..	..	LAIDLAW DALLING
MR OLIPHANT	..	..	..	..	DUNCAN MACRAE
MR GILCHRIST		..	..	..	.. JAMES GIBSON
A LAWYER	..	..	..	..	.. ROBERT BAIRD
MR REEKIE	..	..	..	..	IAIN CUTHBERTSON
MR MONTGOMERY		..	..	..	.. JOHN YOUNG

Presented during the HENRY SHEREK SEASON
of plays at the KING'S THEATRE

Directed by FREDDIE CARPENTER

GOLDERS GREEN HIPPODROME
April 16 - 21

STARLIGHT
by Michael Clayton Hutton

BETH	..	..	..	..	DANDY NICHOLS
PAUL STRATTON		..	..	..	DAVID AYLMER
JANE	..	..	..	..	.. JILL BENNETT
HENRY CHARLTON		..	..	..	ANTHONY IRELAND
LYDIA SHERIDAN		..	..	..	.. FAY COMPTON
LARRY STRANGE		..	..	..	PATRICK CARGILL

Presented by JOHN FORBES-SEMPILL

Directed by JOHN COUNSELL

THE SHAKESPEARE MEMORIAL THEATRE
Stratford-upon-Avon
Season July 1 1955 - June 1 1956

THE MERRY WIVES OF WINDSOR
by William Shakespeare
In repertory July 12 - November 24

JUSTICE SHALLOW	EDWARD ATIENZA
ABRAHAM SLENDER	GEOFFREY BAYLDON
SIR HUGH EVANS	WILLIAM DEVLIN
MASTER PAGE	RALPH MICHAEL
MISTRESS PAGE	ANGELA BADDELEY
ANNE	JILL DIXON
WILLIAM	PHILIP THOMAS
MASTER FORD	KEITH MICHELL
MISTRESS FORD	JOYCE REDMAN
SIR JOHN FALSTAFF	ANTHONY QUAYLE
BARDOLPH	ROBERT HUNTER
PISTOL	JAMES GROUT
NYM	MERVYN BLAKE
ROBIN	JOHN ROGERS
THE HOST OF THE GARTER INN	PATRICK WYMARK
DOCTOR CAIUS	MICHAEL DENISON
MISTRESS QUICKLY	ROSALIND ATKINSON
FENTON	TRADER FAULKNER
SIMPLE	GEOFFREY SASSE
RUGBY	JOHN SOUTHWORTH
JOHN	REX ROBINSON
ROBERT	ALAN HAYWOOD

Directed by GLEN BYAM SHAW *Decoration by* MOTLEY

Music by LESLIE BRIDGEWATER

TITUS ANDRONICUS
by William Shakespeare
In repertory August 16 – November 25

SATURNINUS	FRANK THRING
BASSIANUS	RALPH MICHAEL
MARCUS ANDRONICUS	ALAN WEBB
A ROMAN CAPTAIN	JAMES GROUT
TITUS ANDRONICUS	LAURENCE OLIVIER
LUCIUS	MICHAEL DENISON
QUINTUS	LEON EAGLES
MARTIUS	JOHN MACGREGOR
MUTIUS	IAN HOLM
TAMORA	MAXINE AUDLEY
ALARBUS	ROBERT ARNOLD
CHIRON	KEVIN MILES
DEMETRIUS	LEE MONTAGUE
AARON	ANTHONY QUAYLE
LAVINIA	VIVIEN LEIGH
AEMILIUS	GEOFFREY BAYLDON

A MESSENGER	RON HADDRICK
YOUNG LUCIUS	PHILIP THOMAS
A NURSE	ROSALIND ATKINSON
A CLOWN	EDWARD ATIENZA
FIRST GOTH	MERVYN BLAKE
SECOND GOTH	.. DAVID KING
THIRD GOTH	TRADER FAULKNER
PUBLIUS	GABRIEL WOOLF
A ROMAN	.. HUGH CROSS

Directed by PETER BROOK

Decoration and Music by PETER BROOK
with MICHAEL NORTHEN, DESMOND HEELEY
and WILLIAM BLEZARD

HAMLET
by William Shakespeare
Entered in repertory April 10

BERNARDO	.. PAUL VIEYRA
FRANCISCO	ROBERT ARNOLD
HORATIO	ANTHONY NICHOLLS
MARCELLUS	RON HADDRICK
THE GHOST	MARK DIGNAM
CLAUDIUS	HARRY ANDREWS
GERTRUDE	DIANA CHURCHILL
CORNELIUS	.. PETER CELLIER
VOLTIMAND	DAVID WILLIAM
LAERTES	ANDREW FAULDS
POLONIUS	GEORGE HOWE
HAMLET	.. ALAN BADEL
OPHELIA	DILYS HAMLETT
REYNALDO	PATRICK WYMARK
ROSENCRANTZ	.. JOHN GARLEY
GUILDENSTERN	.. EMRYS JAMES
THE FIRST PLAYER	.. CLIVE REVILL
PLAYER KING	JOHN MACGREGOR
PLAYER QUEEN	.. JUNE BROWN
DRUMMER	GILBERT COBBETT
FORTINBRAS	.. BASIL HOSKINS
A CAPTAIN	.. PETER CELLIER
LADIES	VIRGINIA MASKELL, STEPHANIE BIDMEAD
ATTENDANTS	ALAN HAYWOOD, JOHN SOUTHWORTH
A SAILOR	PETER PALMER
A GRAVEDIGGER	PATRICK WYMARK
A CARPENTER	JOHN MACGREGOR
A PRIEST	GEORGE LITTLE
OSRIC	DAVID WILLIAM
A LORD	.. LEON EAGLES

Directed by MICHAEL LANGHAM

Decoration by MICHAEL NORTHEN *and* DESMOND HEELEY

Music by ALEXANDER GIBSON

193

THE MERCHANT OF VENICE
by William Shakespeare
Entered in repertory April 17

ANTONIO	Anthony Nicholls
SALERIO	.. Emrys James
SOLANIO	Robert Arnold
BASSANIO	Basil Hoskins
LORENZO	David William
GRATIANO	Andrew Faulds
PORTIA	Margaret Johnston
NERISSA	Prunella Scales
PAGE	Christopher Warby
BALTHASAR	George Little
SHYLOCK	Emlyn Williams
THE PRINCE OF MOROCCO	Mark Dignam
LAUNCELOT GOBBO	.. John Garley
OLD GOBBO	George Howe
LEONARDO	John Southworth
JESSICA	Jeannette Sterke
THE PRINCE OF ARRAGON	.. Clive Revill
STEPHANO	.. Paul Vieyra
SERVANT..	Alan Haywood
TUBAL	Ron Haddrick
SINGER	Rex Robinson
THE DUKE OF VENICE	George Howe
CLERK	.. Leon Eagles

Directed by Margaret Webster *Decoration by* Alan Tagg
Music by Leslie Bridgewater

OTHELLO
by William Shakespeare
Entered in repertory May 29

RODERIGO	.. John Garley
IAGO	Emlyn Williams
BRABANTIO	Anthony Nicholls
OTHELLO	Harry Andrews
CASSIO	.. Basil Hoskins
THE DUKE OF VENICE	Mark Dignam
LODOVICO	Andrew Faulds
SENATORS	David William, George Little
DUKE'S OFFICERS	John MacGregor, Ronald Wallace
FIRST MESSENGER	.. Leon Eagles
SECOND MESSENGER	Michael Tate
DESDEMONA	Margaret Johnston
GRATIANO	Toby Robertson
MONTANO	Ron Haddrick
OFFICERS AT CYPRUS	Peter Cellier, Rex Robinson, Robert Arnold
EMILIA	Diana Churchill
HERALD	.. Peter Palmer
TRUMPETER	Stanley Wheeler
CLOWN	Patrick Wymark
FIRST MUSICIAN	John Southworth
BIANCA	Jeannette Sterke

Directed by Glen Byam Shaw *Decoration by* Motley
Music by Antony Hopkins

194

THE BRITISH DRAMA LEAGUE
Community Drama Festival
National Final 1956

Scala   *June 16*

BRECKNOCK LITTLE THEATRE (Wales) in
PROFILE
by T. C. Thomas

INSPECTOR LEWIS	..	..	..	CLIFF PALLISTER
P.C. HARDING	..	..	..	GEOFFREY HARDING
MRS WILLIS	..	..	..	OLIVE ELLIOTT ROWLANDS
MISS FEDDON	..	..	..	MARIE GOGGINS
THE MAN	..	..	..	NIGEL SMITH
P.C. MORGAN	..	..	..	TREVOR ROWLANDS

Directed by T. C. THOMAS

BANGOR DRAMA CLUB (Northern Ireland) in
THE ROPE
by Eugene O'Neill

ABRAHAM BENTLEY	..	..	..	GEORGE O'PREY
ANNIE	..	..	..	NATALIE MURPHY
PAT SWEENEY	..	..	..	HOWARD STEWART
MARY	..	..	..	PATRICIA CROWE
LUKE BENTLEY	..	..	..	COLIN BLAKELY

Directed by GEORGE CROWE

THE DRAMATISTS, STOKE-ON-TRENT (England) in
THE BESPOKE OVERCOAT
by Wolf Mankowitz

MORRY	..	..	..	..	HAROLD HORTON
FENDER	..	..	..	..	JOHN GRAHAM BROSTER
RANTING	..	..	..	..	PETER JONES
A CLERK	..	..	..	..	DOUGLAS PEARCE

THE GREENOCK PLAYERS (Scotland) in
THE REVE'S TALE
A Scot's version of the tale by Chaucer, by Colin MacLean

DOUGAL SIM	..	..	..	..	J. L. DOW
HIS WIFE	..	..	..	..	RAY LINN CRAIG
JEAN	..	..	..	..	AGNES MacNEILL
ALAN	..	..	..	..	IAN McCAIG
JOHN	..	..	..	..	CHRIS CATHCART

Directed by COLIN BROWN

THE EDINBURGH FESTIVAL 1955
August 21 - September 11

JULIUS CAESAR *by* WILLIAM SHAKESPEARE Royal Lyceum Theatre First performance August 22 *Presented by* The Old Vic Trust. *Directed by* MICHAEL BENTHALL

LA DAME AUX CAMELIAS *by* ALEXANDRE DUMAS *fils* Royal Lyceum Theatre First performance September 5 *Presented by* The Edinburgh Festival Society *Directed by* EDWIGE FEUILLERE

A LIFE IN THE SUN *by* THORNTON WILDER Assembly Hall First performance August 22 *Presented by* The Edinburgh Festival Society *in association with* Tennent Productions Ltd; commissioned for the apron stage of the Assembly Hall *Directed by* TYRONE GUTHRIE

Index

198

Reid, Alexander, 22, 24, 87
Reluctant Debutante, The, 107, 125
Reve's Tale, The, 105
Richard III, 41-6
Richardson, Sir Ralph, 44, 130
Richardson, Tony, 123
Ridley, Arnold, 78
Ridley, M. R., 48, 81
Rivals, The, 109, 111
Roberts, Rachel, 50
Robson, Flora, 97-9
Rogers, Paul, 66-7
Romanoff and Juliet, 3, 115-8
Romeo and Juliet, 43
Rope, The, 105
Rose, George, 120
Rowe, Frances, 28
Royal Court Theatre, 4, 61, 70-1, 99, 121
Ruby, Thelma, 16, 29

Saint Joan, 111
St Martin's Theatre, 16
Salad Days, 30
Saville Theatre, 3, 109
Scala Theatre, 102-5
Scofield, Paul, 76-7, 96-7
Scottish Community Drama Association, 106
Sellar, R. J. B., 22, 25-6, 87
Separate Tables, 7, 131
Seyler, Athene, 111
Shadow of Doubt, The, 109-11
Shakespeare, William, 1, 5, 33, 36, 42-9, 58, 63-5, 69, 74-6, 80-2, 89, 114, 121
Shakespeare Memorial Theatre, Stratford-upon-Avon, 1-3, 36, 74-6, 80, 83, 192-4
Shaw, George Bernard, 6, 11-4, 56-61, 66, 71, 99, 100, 115, 136, 139
Sherek, Henry, 3, 87, 118, 140
Sheridan, R. B., 109, 111
Silver, Christine, 78
Sleeping Prince, The, 131
Spider's Web, The, 31
Starlight, 78-9
Stewart, Job, 50
Strong are Lonely, The, 38-41
Summer Song, 15
Summertime, 34, 36
Swann, Donald, 54
Synge, J. M., 114

Tabitha, 78

Tagg, Alan, 82
Tamburlaine, 2
Tennent Productions, 3, 28
Theatre Royal, Windsor, 78
Theatre Workshop, 9, 139
Thomas, T. C., 104
Thompson, Jimmy, 16
Thorndike, Dame Sybil, 80, 131, 133
Threepenny Opera, The, 8, 61-2
Titus Andronicus, 1, 63
Troilus and Cressida, 1-2, 63-7
Tutin, Dorothy, 108, 110

Ure, Mary, 77
Ustinov, Peter, 3, 56, 115-8, 136

Valk, Frederick, 117-8
Van Druten, John, 113
Vilar, Jean, 2
Vines, Margaret, 53

Waiting for Godot, 8, 14, 18-22
Walpole, Hugh, 78
Waltz of the Toreadors, The, 4, 15, 68-70, 93
Wanamaker, Sam, 17
Wareing, Alfred, 30
Warren, Betty, 29
Washbourne, Mona, 53
Water Gipsies, The, 15
Watford, Gwendoline, 38
Webb, Alan, 59
Webster, Margaret, 82
Weill, Kurt, 61-2
Welles, Orson, 1, 43
Welsh, John, 74
Westminster Theatre, 52
White, Wilfrid Hyde, 128
Whole Truth, The, 30-4
Wild Duck, The, 34, 109-11, 139
Wilder, Thornton, 34-6
Williams, Clifford, 67
Williams, Emlyn, 83-4, 111, 138
Williams, Kenneth, 29
Williams, Tennessee, 10, 14, 87-91
Wilson, Angus, 9, 70-2, 74, 121
Wilson, Sandy, 28-30
Winwood, Estelle, 108
Winter Garden Theatre, 15, 92, 94
Witness for the Prosecution, 141
Wolfit, Donald, 41
Woodthorpe, Peter, 21
Wordsworth, Richard, 50, 66
World's Wonder, The, 22, 24
Worth, Irene, 34, 36-8, 93-4